Question
and Answer
Encyclopedia

Canada

p

Question
and Answer
Encyclopedia

Canada

This is a Parragon Publishing book
First published in 2003

Parragon Publishing
Queen Street House
4 Queen Street
Bath BA1 1HE, UK

Copyright © Parragon 2003

ISBN 1-40541-728-5

Printed in China

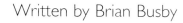

Written by Brian Busby

Illustrated by
SGA Illustration and Design Agency

Project Manager: Vicci Parr
Designer: Fiona Grant
Photo Researcher: Charlotte Lippmann
Consultant: Constance Brissenden

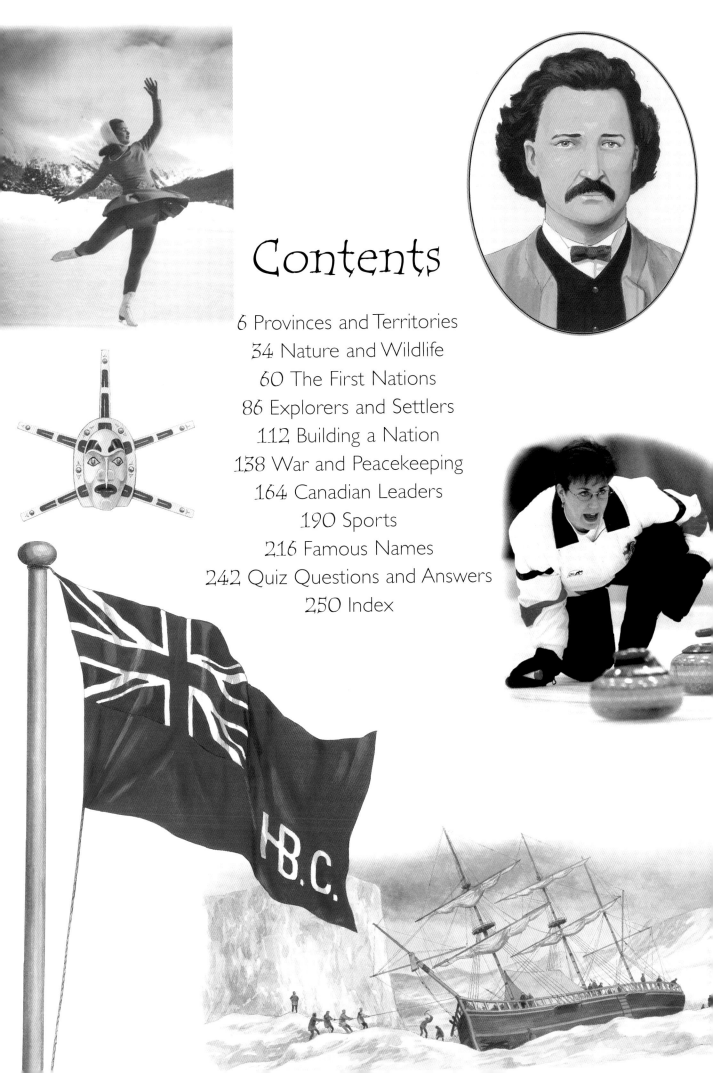

Contents

Provinces
and Territories

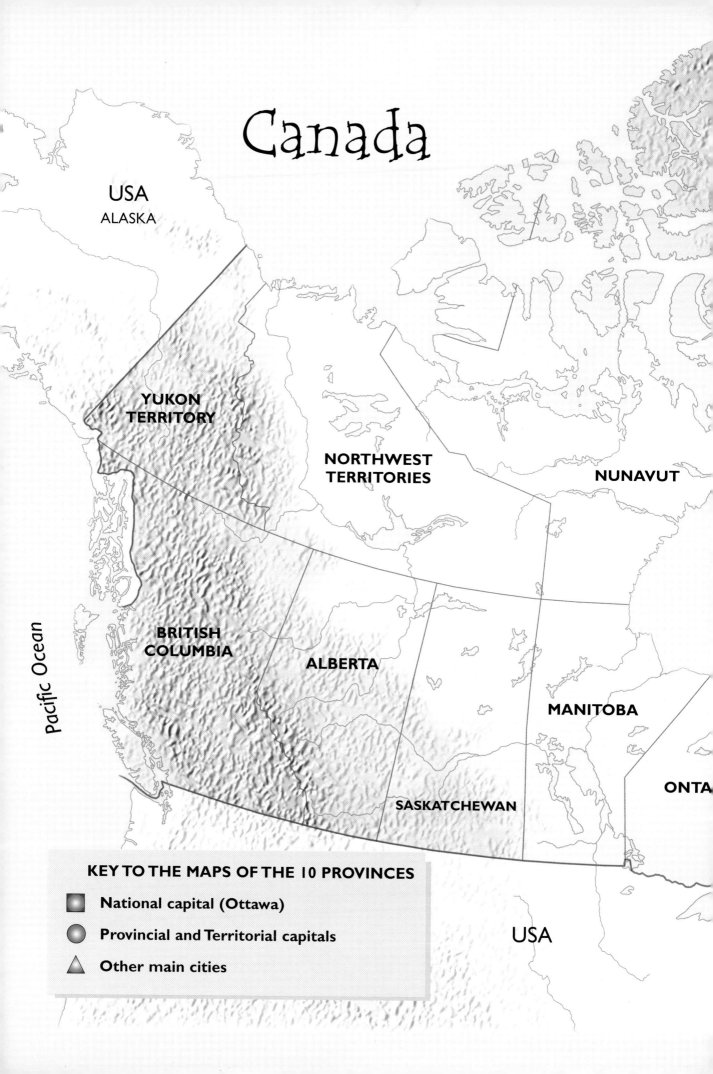

Canada

USA
ALASKA

Pacific Ocean

YUKON TERRITORY

NORTHWEST TERRITORIES

NUNAVUT

BRITISH COLUMBIA

ALBERTA

MANITOBA

ONTA

SASKATCHEWAN

USA

KEY TO THE MAPS OF THE 10 PROVINCES

National capital (Ottawa)

Provincial and Territorial capitals

Other main cities

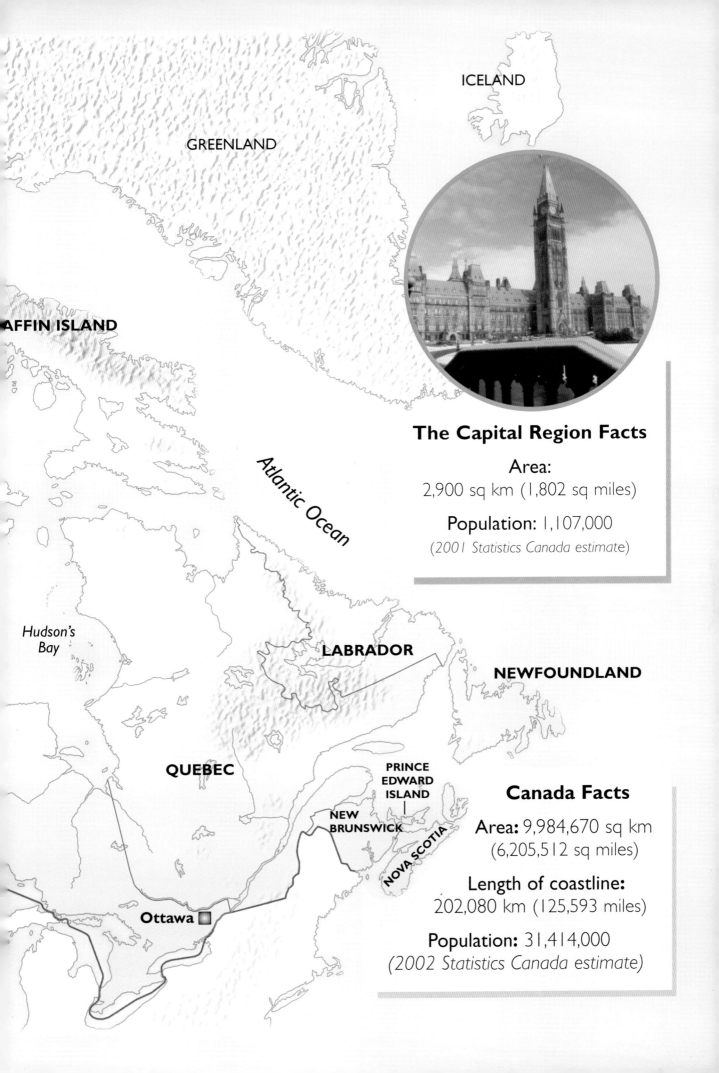

ICELAND

GREENLAND

AFFIN ISLAND

Atlantic Ocean

The Capital Region Facts

Area:
2,900 sq km (1,802 sq miles)

Population: 1,107,000
(2001 Statistics Canada estimate)

Hudson's
Bay

LABRADOR

NEWFOUNDLAND

QUEBEC

PRINCE
EDWARD
ISLAND

NEW
BRUNSWICK

NOVA SCOTIA

Canada Facts

Area: 9,984,670 sq km
(6,205,512 sq miles)

Length of coastline:
202,080 km (125,593 miles)

Population: 31,414,000
(2002 Statistics Canada estimate)

Ottawa

A map of Rupert's Land

What does Canada's motto "A Mari usque ad Mare" mean?

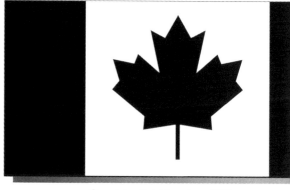

Canada's official flag since 1965.

THE COUNTRY'S MOTTO IS LATIN FOR "FROM SEA TO SEA." ALTHOUGH ITS use dates back to the late 19th century, the motto wasn't adopted officially until 1921.

What misunderstanding gave Canada its name?

When nearing the Native village of Stadacona in 1535, French explorer Jacques Cartier heard the Huron-Iroquois word *kanata*, meaning "village" or "settlement." Cartier misunderstood the word, believing it to indicate the territory controlled by Donnacona, the village leader. Canada was adopted by the French to cover the area of New France covered by the St Lawrence Valley.

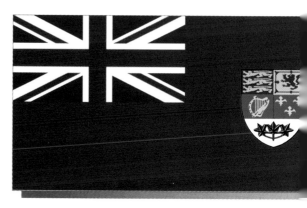

The Red Ensign was Canada's unofficial flag from the time of Confederation until 1965.

Where was Rupert's Land?

In 1670, King Charles II of England granted a huge area of land comprising the entire Hudson's Bay drainage system to the Hudson's Bay Company. The territory, named after the king's cousin, Prince Rupert, included land found in present-day Quebec, Ontario, Manitoba, Saskatchewan, Alberta, Nunavut, and the Northwest Territories. In what is the world's largest land transaction, the Canadian government purchased Rupert's Land for £300,000 in 1869.

How long is the Trans-Canada Highway?

The longest paved road in the world, the Trans-Canada Highway is 7,821 kilometres (4,860 miles) in length. Completed in 1962, it runs from St John's, Newfoundland and Labrador through all ten provinces to Victoria, British Columbia.

Which provinces have different names in English and French?

Half of Canada's ten provinces are known by different names in French: Newfoundland and Labrador (Terre-Neuve et Labrador), Nova Scotia (Nouvelle-Écosse), Prince Edward Island (Île-du-Prince Edward), New Brunswick (Nouveau-Brunswick), and British Columbia (Columbie-Britannique).

Who started the Flag Debate?

In 1964, Prime Minister Lester B Pearson argued in Parliament that Canada should have its own flag. Although variations on the Red Ensign had been flown since the time of Confederation, to that point Canada had never had an official flag. During six months of debate, Canadians from across the country submitted hundreds of designs for consideration. The new flag was officially unfurled on February 15, 1965.

Which mammal appeared on the world's first pictorial postage stamp?

IN 1851, THE PROVINCE OF CANADA ISSUED A THREE-PENCE POSTAGE STAMP designed around the image of a beaver. Designed by Sir Sanford Fleming, the three-pence stamp is considered the first to feature an image.

Sir Sanford Fleming was a distinguished civil engineer, inventor, scientist, explorer, and designer of the first pictorial postage stamp.

Which provinces are bilingual?

Although French and English are the official languages of Canada, the only province to declare itself officially bilingual is New Brunswick. Nearly 35 percent of the province claim French as their mother tongue.

Why did Newfoundland change its name?

In 2001, THE PROVINCE OF NEWFOUNDLAND BECAME THE PROVINCE OF

Newfoundland and Labrador to better reflect its geography and people. Although roughly two and a half times the size of the Island of Newfoundland, Labrador is home to less than six percent of the province's population.

Which Native Canadian tribe is now extinct?

The Beothuks were a small tribe that lived on the south and northeast coasts of the Island of Newfoundland. Their death as a people is usually blamed on European settlers and disease. The last known Beothuk, a woman named Shawnandithit, died of consumption in 1829.

What is the difference between the Atlantic Provinces and the Maritime Provinces?

Nova Scotia, Prince Edward Island, New Brunswick, and Newfoundland and Labrador comprise the Atlantic Provinces. With the exception of Newfoundland and Labrador, these provinces are also considered the Maritime Provinces.

The flag of Labrador.

This flag of Newfoundland and Labrador represents the entire province.

Which famous painter designed a flag?

Thirty years after joining the rest of Canada, the official flag of Newfoundland and Labrador remained the Union Jack. In 1979, a commission was formed to select a new flag. A year later, one of the six designs submitted by St John's painter Christopher Pratt was selected as the new provincial flag.

Labrador Sea

QUEBEC

NEWFOUNDLAND AND LABRADOR

Happy Valley–Goose Bay

St John'

Gulf of St Lawrence

Where can you visit a Viking village?

L'Anse aux Meadows, located on the northern tip of Newfoundland's Great Northern Peninsula, is the site of the only authentic Viking settlement found in North America. Discovered in 1960 by Helge and Anne Stine Ingstad, it is believed that the village was inhabited from approximately AD 990 to 1050.

Who was Joe the Barrelman?

In the late 1930s, Joseph Smallwood, future Premier of Newfoundland, hosted a radio show as Joe the Barrelman. Broadcast daily, the show dealt with Newfoundland traditions and history.

How was Trinity Bay, Newfoundland connected to Valentia, Ireland?

In 1858, the two towns were linked by the successful laying of the world's first transatlantic cable. The first message telegraphed across the Atlantic Ocean was: "Europe and America are united by telegraphy. Glory to God in the Highest, on earth peace, goodwill toward men."

A view of Cabot Tower on Signal Hill in St John's.

Who received a signal at Signal Hill?

On December 12, 1901, Italian inventor Guglielmo Marconi received the world's first radio transmission at Signal Hill. The message, a letter "S" sent in Morse code from Cornwall, England, proved his theory that electrical signals could be sent without wires.

Where is the heaviest object ever moved?

In 1997, the gravity base structure of the Hibernia Oil Platform was moved from St John's to its resting place 315 kilometres (195 miles) southeast in the Atlantic Ocean. Made almost entirely of concrete, the structure weighed over 600,000 tonnes. The completed platform weighs 1,200,000 tonnes, is 224 metres (739 feet) tall, and is designed to withstand the impact of a 6,000,000-tonne iceberg.

What does Nova Scotia mean?

The flag of Nova Scotia.

NOVA SCOTIA IS LATIN FOR "NEW SCOTLAND." THE NAME OF THE province can be traced back to 1621 when King James I of England granted Sir William Alexander the land.

NEW BRUNSWICK

Cape Breton Island

NOVA SCOTIA

Halifax

Which Premier became a Prime Minister?
Sir John Thompson is the only person to have been both a Premier of a province and a Prime Minister of Canada. He became Premier of Nova Scotia in 1882 after the resignation of Simon Holmes. Ten years later, as a federal Member of Parliament, he became Prime Minister when his predecessor, Sir John Abbott, resigned.

Who was the first person to sail alone around the world?
Nova Scotian Joshua Slocum made the journey on his boat *The Spray*. He wrote about his voyage, which lasted from 1895 until 1898, in his classic book *Sailing Alone Around the World*. Slocum, who couldn't swim, disappeared while at sea in 1909.

Which is Canada's oldest university?
The University of King's College, which was founded in Windsor, Nova Scotia in 1789, is the oldest university in the Commonwealth found outside the British Isles. King's College is now located in Halifax as part of Dalhousie University.

Who was the Cape Breton Giant?
At 7 feet 9 inches, Cape Breton's Angus McAskill was known as both the tallest man in the world and the world's strongest man. He was born in Scotland in 1825 and emigrated to Nova Scotia with his family as a young boy.

What was the Halifax Explosion?

During the First World War, on December 6, 1917, a Belgian relief vessel collided with a French munition ship in Halifax Harbour setting off a fire that would create the largest man-made explosion prior to Hiroshima. Nearly 3 square kilometres (1.8 square miles) of the city were destroyed by the blast, the subsequent tidal wave, and fire. Over 10,600 of 50,000 citizens of Halifax were killed or injured in the tragedy.

Which other provinces were once part of Nova Scotia?

Prince Edward Island became a separate colony in 1799. In 1848, New Brunswick and Cape Breton were also partitioned. Cape Breton rejoined Nova Scotia 36 years later.

What was Canada's first newspaper?

The first newspaper published in what would become Canada was *The Halifax Gazette*. It made its debut on March 23, 1752 and ceased publication 13 years later. The oldest newspaper still in existence is Montreal's *The Gazette*, which was established in 1778.

Which Nova Scotia ship is featured on the dime?

THE BLUENOSE WAS A SCHOONER DESIGNED FOR FISHING AND RACING. LAUNCHED in Lunenburg, Nova Scotia in 1921, in the nearly two decades it was in competition, the ship lost only one race. *The Bluenose* has been featured on the dime since 1937.

The Bluenose is Canada's most famous ship. It was wrecked off the coast of Haiti in 1946.

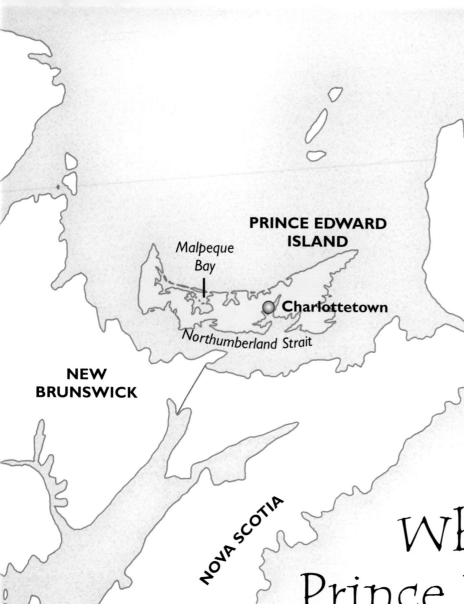

Which Island-born poet served as Poet Laureate of the United States?
Mark Strand was born in Summerside, Prince Edward Island in 1934, but was raised and educated in the United States. Among his many books is *Blizzard of One*, which won the 1999 Pulitzer Prize for Poetry.

What do the four trees on the provincial flag represent?
The mature oak tree represents England, while the three saplings symbolize Kings, Queens, and Princes, the three counties of Prince Edward Island. The relationship is reflected in the province's motto: *Parva sub ingenti*, Latin for "The small under the protection of the great."

Who was Prince Edward?

THE ISLAND, CALLED ABEGWEIT ("CRADLED IN THE WAVES") BY the Mi'kmaq, and Île St-Jean by the French, was renamed after the son of King George III of England. In 1799, at the time the honour was bestowed, Prince Edward was stationed with the British Army in Halifax. The Dominion of Canada's first monarch, Queen Victoria, was the daughter of Prince Edward.

Who were the first Islanders?
The first people to inhabit Prince Edward Island were the Mi'kmaq. It is believed that they may have migrated across a low plain now covered by the Northumberland Strait.

Why is the province's soil red?
The redness of Prince Edward Island's soil is due to the high iron-oxide content, otherwise called rust. Known as Charlottetown soil, it is the most predominant on the island, and has been designated as the provincial soil.

The flag of Prince Edward Island.

Who lived at Green Gables?
Built in the mid-19th century, Green Gables (pictured to the left) was the home of David Macneill and Lucy Woolner Macneill, cousins of Lucy Maud Montgomery's grandfather. Their farm inspired the setting of *Anne of Green Gables*. Located in Prince Edward Island National Park, the house attracts hundreds of thousands of visitors each year.

What is "The Island Hymn"?
The hymn is a patriotic piece of music written by Lucy Maud Montgomery. It was composed in 1908, the same year Montgomery's best known work, *Anne of Green Gables*, was published.

What was the Charlottetown Conference?

HELD IN 1864, THE CHARLOTTETOWN CONFERENCE WAS THE FIRST TO discuss a union of the colonies of British North America. Initially, the conference was organized as another step in a possible union of Prince Edward Island, Nova Scotia, and New Brunswick. Although the conference earned the province the title "the cradle of Confederation," Prince Edward Island didn't enter the Dominion until 1873.

Whose town is Charlottetown?
The city, originally known as Charlotte Town, was named in honour of Queen Charlotte, wife of King George III of England. It became the capital of the island in 1799, only one year after the work began on building the settlement. With a population of fewer than 33,000, Charlottetown is the country's smallest provincial capital.

Charlottetown as it appeared not long after its establishment in 1768.

Where is "old" Brunswick?

NEW BRUNSWICK IS NAMED AFTER THE DUCHY OF BRUNSWICK-LUNENBURG in Germany. In 1784, at the time of the colony's creation, the duchy was ruled by King George III of England. Other names suggested for the province were New Ireland and Pittsylvania, for then-British Prime Minister William Pitt.

Which New Brunswick cities are larger than its capital?
With populations of 125,000 and 60,000 respectively, the cities of Saint John and Moncton are both larger than Fredericton, the provincial capital. Fredericton's population of 47,000 makes it the smallest provincial capital after Charlottetown.

The flag of New Brunswick.

Which prominent Quebec separatist leader was born in New Brunswick?
René Lévesque, the founder of the Parti Québécois, former Premier of Quebec, and leader of the *Oui* side in the 1980 Quebec referendum, was born in Campbellton, New Brunswick. In August 1922, Lévesque's parents travelled from their New Carlisle, Quebec home to a New Brunswick hospital for the birth.

Who won France's top literary award?
New Brunswick author Antonine Maillet received the Prix Goncourt for her novel *Pélagie-la-Charrette*. She was the first person outside France to win the award. The book was translated into English as *Pélagie*.

What is the name of the ship on the provincial flag?
The galley depicted on New Brunswick's flag doesn't depict a particular ship, but is meant to represent shipping and shipbuilding, two of the provinces principal economic activities leading up to the 20th century.

QUEBEC

NEW BRUNSWICK

Fredericton

Saint John

NOVA SCOTIA

Bay of Fundy

USA

Who is considered the Father of Canadian Poetry?
The poetry of New Brunswicker Sir Charles G D Roberts served to inspire many other Canadian poets, including his cousin Bliss Carman. Today, Roberts is best remembered for his modern animal stories, a genre he and fellow Canadian Ernest Thompson Seton are credited with inventing.

Confederation Bridge took three and a half years and one billion Canadian dollars to build.

Where is Canada's longest bridge?

AT JUST UNDER 13 KILOMETRES (8 MILES) IN LENGTH, THE CONFEDERATION Bridge is the country's longest. The bridge opened in 1997, joining Cape Jourimain, New Brunswick with Borden-Carleton, Prince Edward Island. It is the world's longest bridge over ice-covered waters.

The flag of Quebec.

Who named Quebec?

QUEBEC IS DERIVED FROM AN ALGONQUIAN WORD

meaning "where the river narrows." The word was first used by the French only in naming the site of the future city of Quebec. The territory of New France that lay along the St Lawrence Valley was referred to by the French as Canada. It was the British who first called the area Quebec, renaming the land in 1763.

Ungava Bay

NEWFOUNDLAND AND LABRADOR

Hudson's Bay

QUEBEC

St Lawrence River

ONTARIO

NEW BRUNSWICK

Quebec ○

Montreal △

USA

USA

What ran between La Prairie and Saint-Jean-sur-Richelieu?
Completed in 1836, Canada's first railway line linked La Prairie, outside Montreal, with Saint-Jean-sur-Richelieu on the Richelieu River. The 23-kilometre (14-mile) railway, built by the Champlain and St Lawrence Railway, was designed to transport freight between the St Lawrence and Richelieu rivers.

Which city features a cross-shaped skyscraper?
One of Canada's most famous buildings, the cruciform Place Ville Marie, is located in downtown Montreal. The 42-storey building was completed in 1962 and contains more rental space than New York's Empire State Building.

The flag of the City of Montreal.

Who was *La Corriveau*?
In 1763 Marie-Josephte Corriveau admitted to the bloody murder of her husband. She was hanged outside the Plains of Abraham and her body was displayed in an iron cage. Marie-Josephte Corriveau soon entered into legend as *La Corriveau*, with many additional horrific crimes being added to her past.

Just one of the many dams comprising the massive James Bay hydroelectric project.

Which construction project is in its fourth decade?

Work on the James Bay project, the largest hydroelectric development in North America, began in 1971. When completed, nine rivers will have been diverted and dammed, and an area the size of Belgium will have been flooded. The cost of the entire project is expected to be close to 80 billion Canadian dollars.

Which peoples are represented on the flag of Montreal?

Its flag features a fleur-de-lys, rose, shamrock, and thistle, representing respectively the French, the English, the Irish, and the Scots. The flag is based on the city's coat of arms, which dates back to the early 19th century.

Which revolution was quiet?

Between 1960 and 1966 Quebec underwent a period of change known as the Quiet Revolution. During these years the province increased spending on social programs and nationalized its private electricity companies. The slogan of the day was *"Maîtres chez nous!"* ("Masters in our own house!").

Who were the Quebec Bulldogs?

With roots going back to 1886, the Bulldogs were one of Canada's earliest hockey teams. In 1917, they became one of the original four teams in the National Hockey League. However, financial troubles prevented the franchise from play during the first two seasons. They finally fielded a team in 1919, but managed only one season before moving to Hamilton, where they became the Tigers.

Who was the world's strongest man?

Louis Cyr, born in St Cyprien de Napierville, Quebec in 1863, was one of the foremost professional strongmen of the 19th century. In 1895, he performed what is considered his greatest feat, lifting 1,971 kilograms (4,337 pounds) on his back. Over a century later, Cyr's lift is still considered a world record.

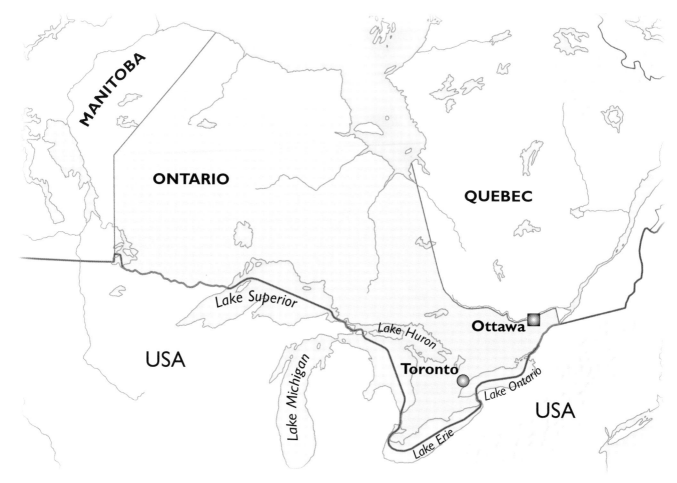

What does Ontario mean?

ONTARIO IS DERIVED FROM AN IROQUOIAN WORD MEANING

"beautiful water." Although Europeans first used the word in naming Lake Ontario only, the use spread. However, it wasn't until Confederation on July 1, 1867 that the name was applied to what was then Canada's western-most province.

Toronto, on Lake Ontario, is Canada's largest city.

Which political party held power in Ontario for 42 years?
Under the leadership of George Alexander Drew the Ontario Conservative Party won the 1943 provincial election. The party remained in power until 1985, when they were defeated by the Liberals.

The flag of Ontario.

Which princess was born in Ottawa?

In 1943, Princess Margriet was born to Princess Juliana and Prince Bernhardt of the Dutch royal family. Ottawa provided refuge for the couple during the German occupation of the Netherlands. The city's annual tulip festival began as a result of a gift from Juliana, who served as Queen of the Netherlands from 1948 until 1980.

Which Nobel Prize winner once worked as a journalist in Toronto?

American author Ernest Hemingway twice worked for *The Toronto Daily Star* (now known as *The Toronto Star*). It was during his second stint with the newspaper, in 1923, that he met Morley Callaghan. Hemingway encouraged Callaghan, then a law student, to pursue a career in letters.

Why is the CN Tower so tall?

THE WORLD'S TALLEST FREESTANDING STRUCTURE WAS BUILT TO SOLVE problems with television transmission and other communication signals in the Toronto area. Completed in 1976, at over half a kilometre (just under half a mile) in height the tower is nearly twice the height of Toronto's tallest building and continues to dominate the city skyline.

Which Canadian and American cities are linked by a tunnel?

Opened in 1930, the Detroit-Windsor Auto Tunnel, linking Detroit, Michigan and Windsor, Ontario, is the only international automobile tunnel in the world. The 1929 Ambassador Bridge, the world's longest international suspension bridge, also joins the two cities.

Where can you find Canada's five tallest skyscrapers?

Canada's five tallest buildings are all found in Toronto. At 290 metres (957 feet), First Canadian Place is the tallest, but is barely half the height of the CN Tower. All five of the buildings were constructed between 1967 and 1990.

Where is Berlin, Ontario?

The city of Kitchener began as Berlin, a community founded by German-speaking settlers. During the First World War, Berlin changed its name in honour of Field Marshall Lord Horatio H Kitchener.

What does Manitoba mean?

ALTHOUGH THE ORIGIN OF THE PROVINCE'S NAME IS UNCERTAIN, it is thought to come from either the Cree word *manitowapow* or the Ojibway *Manitou bou*. Both mean "the place where the spirit speaks."

Where did Europeans first sight Manitoba?
It is likely that in 1612 Sir Thomas Button became the first European to see the shores of Manitoba. The explorer was on an expedition to determine the fate of Henry Hudson and to search out the Northwest Passage. Manitoba is unique among Canadian provinces in that its northern territory was explored and settled before the south.

Why was Manitoba known as the "postage stamp province"?
In 1870, when it became Canada's fifth province, Manitoba was much smaller than it is today. Consisting of only 36,000 square kilometres (22,374 square miles), its size and square shape earned it the nickname. Although the borders were expanded in 1881, it wasn't until 1912 that Manitoba achieved its current size.

Where is the Polar Bear Capital of the World?
Churchill, Manitoba, on Hudson's Bay, has earned the title as the only settlement in the world where polar bears can be observed in the wild.

The flag of Manitoba.

Who was Flin Flon?
The city of Flin Flon was named after Professor Josiah Flintabbatey Flonatin, the fictional hero of *The Sunless City*. Published in 1905, the novel concerns the discovery of a subterranean city that is rich in gold.

Which Manitoban was a bestseller in French and English?
A native of Saint Boniface, Manitoba, Gabrielle Roy was the first Canadian author to achieve considerable critical and commercial success in both official languages. Her first novel, *Bonheur d'occasion* – translated as *The Tin Flute* – was an international bestseller.

Where is Canada's most famous intersection?

The corner of Winnipeg's Portage Avenue and Main Street holds an important place in the history of western Canada. The intersection was once the meeting point of two major fur-trading trails, one following the Assiniboine River to the west, the other leading to Hudson's Bay and the north. Portage and Main has been a major point of commercial activity since the earliest days of Western Canada.

Is Golden Boy gold?

THE STATUE OF THE RUNNING BOY PERCHED ATOP THE MANITOBA

Legislature is gilded in 24-carat gold. The 4-metre-tall (13 feet) figure statue was hoisted into place when the legislature was built in 1919. Between 2001 and 2002 the statue underwent a full restoration.

Golden Boy is a famous Manitoban symbol, and was actually sculpted and cast in Paris, France.

What Cree word gave Saskatchewan its name?

Kisiskatchewanisipi, meaning "swift-flowing river," was first used to describe the Saskatchewan River. The word was adapted and adopted in naming the District of Saskatchewan, one of the territories that merged to create the province in 1905.

The flag of Saskatchewan.

Which Saskatchewan city is the Sunshine Capital of Canada?

Estevan in the southeast part of the province is Canada's sunniest city. It averages 2,540 hours of sunshine annually.

Which future Prime Minister lost his first five elections?

Between 1925 and 1939, John Diefenbaker twice ran unsuccessfully for Parliament, twice failed in bids for a seat in the Saskatchewan legislature, and lost a campaign to become Mayor of Prince Albert, Saskatchewan. In 1940, he finally achieved elected office, winning a seat in the federal Parliament. Seventeen years later he became Canada's thirteenth Prime Minister.

Where is Pile o' Bones?

Pile o' Bones, a translation of *wascana*, a Cree word meaning the place where bison bones were stacked, was the original name for Regina. In 1882, the future capital of Saskatchewan was renamed in honour of Queen Victoria. The new name was suggested by her daughter, Princess Louise Caroline Alberta, the wife of the Governor General of Canada at that time. Regina is often referred to as the Queen City.

NORTHWEST TERRITORIES

ALBERTA

MANITOBA

SASKATCHEWAN

△ Saskatoon

Cypress Hills

○ Regina

USA

What are "Prairie giants"?

Easily the most distinctive and visible of prairie structures, grain elevators have been described as "Prairie giants" and "castles of the new world." Used in cleaning, weighing, and storage, the grain elevator derives its name from a belt and bucket mechanism that lifts grain to chutes located at the top of the structure. The first elevators were built of timber in the late 19th century; sheet metal and concrete have since been used in their construction.

Grain elevators are the dominant structures of the Prairie landscape.

Where can one visit the world's largest urban park?
Covering 931 hectares (2,300 acres), Regina's Wascana Centre is the largest urban park in the world. Over twice the size of Vancouver's Stanley Park and three times the size of New York's Central Park, Wascana Centre encloses the Saskatchewan Legislature and surrounds man-made Wascana Lake.

What was the Regina Manifesto?
The manifesto was a founding document of the Co-operative Commonwealth Federation, precursor to the New Democratic Party. Adopted in 1933, during the height of the Great Depression, the Regina Manifesto called for unemployment insurance, health insurance, workers' compensation, and many other social programs that were later adopted by successive federal governments.

Where do Mounties train?
All basic training of RCMP recruits takes place at Depot Division in Regina. The six-month course covers a variety of subjects, including driving, shooting, and criminal law. Regina once served as home of the force, but the headquarters were moved to Ottawa in the early 20th century.

Which city is named after a berry?
The name of Saskatoon, the province's largest city, has its origins in *mis-sask-quah-too-min*, the Cree word for the serviceberry, an edible red berry that grows in the area of the South Saskatchewan River.

Why is Alberta known as the "Princess Province"?

ALBERTA WAS NAMED AFTER PRINCESS LOUISE CAROLINE ALBERTA, THE fourth daughter of Queen Victoria. The province was created from the District of Alberta and parts of the districts of Athabasca, Assiniboia, and Saskatchewan in 1905.

The flag of Alberta.

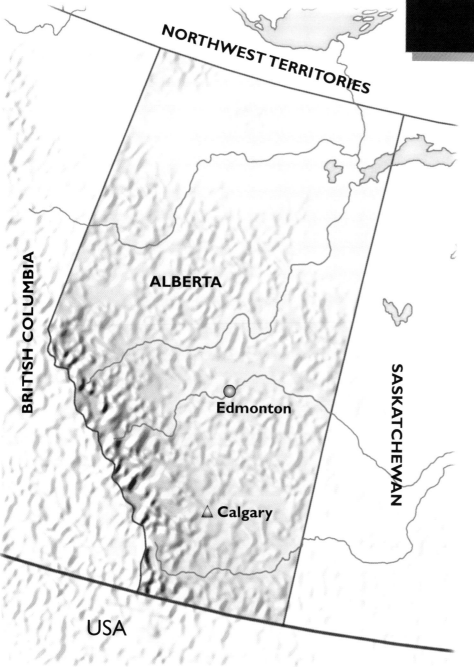

NORTHWEST TERRITORIES

BRITISH COLUMBIA

ALBERTA

SASKATCHEWAN

○ Edmonton

△ Calgary

USA

Who were the United Farmers of Alberta?

Formed in 1909, the UFA was established to promote rural economic, social, and political issues. They were elected as the provincial government in 1921 and remained in office for 14 years. After losing the election of 1935, the UFA withdrew from direct political action. It has since evolved into the United Farmers of Alberta Co-operative Limited.

What is Oil City?

First known as Original Discovery No 1, Oil City is the location of western Canada's first oil-producing well. Members of the Kutenai tribe first discovered the resource on the site. The first well was drilled by a Dominion surveyor in 1878.

What was Canada's first national park?

Established in 1885, Alberta's Banff National Park ranks as Canada's first. The 6,641-square-kilometre park (4,127 square miles) is also the most popular, attracting close to five million visitors annually.

Which lands are bad?

The Badlands are an arid area of gullies, ridges, and columns in southern Alberta. Although not a desert, it is one of the most arid parts of the country. While the original settlers dubbed the lands "bad" for farming, they were later found to be rich in coal and fossils. Many of the country's most significant dinosaur finds have taken place in the Badlands.

The unique features of the fossil-rich Alberta Badlands.

Where is the Gateway to the North?

By FAR THE MOST NORTHERN OF CANADA'S MAJOR CITIES, Edmonton is sometimes called the Gateway to the North. Established as a Hudson's Bay Company fort in 1795, Alberta's capital is located near the geographical centre of the province.

Who was "Bible Bill"?

William Aberhart, Premier of Alberta from 1935 until his death in 1943, first achieved public recognition as a radio evangelist. His *Back to the Bible* radio program attracted an audience of 300,000 listeners.

Which parties have held power in Alberta?

Alberta's political history is unusual in that there have been only three changes of government in its nearly one hundred-year history. Four parties have governed Alberta: the Liberals (1905–1921), the United Farmers of Alberta (1921–1935), the Social Credit Party (1935–1971), and the Progressive Conservatives (1971–present).

Edmonton is the capital of Alberta.

Why is this province "British" Columbia?

PRIOR TO THE ESTABLISHMENT OF THE COLONY IN 1858, THE MAINLAND of British Columbia was most often referred to as New Caledonia. The name *British* Columbia was chosen to emphasize the new colony's status as a territory of Great Britain. For decades, the American government had laid claim to the southern portion of the colony.

The flag of British Columbia.

Which two colonies merged to form British Columbia?
The original territory of British Columbia covered only the mainland. Vancouver Island was a separate, older colony of Great Britain. It wasn't until 1866 that the two colonies merged.

What may or may not be living in Okanagan Lake?
One of British Columbia's largest lakes, Okanagan Lake is said to be inhabited by a sea serpent named Ogopogo. Known by the Salish as "snake in the lake," and the Chinook as "wicked one" or "great beast in the lake," the mysterious creature is depicted in ancient petroglyphs. Its name comes from the 1926 "Ogopogo Song," a favourite of English music halls.

How did British Columbia get two capital cities?
When the colonies of Vancouver Island and British Columbia became one, there was much disagreement as to which city should serve as the seat of government. Islanders preferred their old capital Victoria, while mainlanders argued for New Westminster, their former capital. For several years the cities alternated, but Victoria eventually became the permanent capital of the colony and future province.

Which famous British Columbian was born in British Guiana?
Sir James Douglas, the "Father of British Columbia," founded Fort Camosun – now Victoria – in 1843. He served as the first governor of the colony of Vancouver Island. He was born in British Guiana in 1803.

Who was Bill Smith?

A newspaper editor and politician, Smith is better known under his unusual name Amor de Cosmos. As de Cosmos he worked hard for British Columbia to join Confederation and later served as Premier. He said he changed his name to reflect his greatest loves: "order, beauty, the world, the universe."

How did Vancouver become Terminal City?

British Columbia's largest city earned its nickname as the terminus of the transcontinental railway. William Van Horne, a chief financier of the railway, chose the site in 1886. It was Van Horne who insisted that the new city be named after English explorer George Vancouver.

YUKON TERRITORY

NORTHWEST TERRITORIES

ALASKA

BRITISH COLUMBIA

Rocky Mountains

ALBERTA

Vancouver Island

Vancouver

Victoria

USA

What is the largest mountain range in Canada?

THE ROCKY MOUNTAINS HOLD THE DISTINCTION OF BEING NOT ONLY CANADA'S LARGEST MOUNTAIN range, but also the largest in the western hemisphere. It runs nearly the entire length of British Columbia and forms part of the province's border with Alberta.

The Rocky Mountains are Canada's largest mountain range (also pictured opposite).

Which territory is the largest?

WITH A TOTAL AREA OF 1,830,000 SQUARE KILOMETRES

(1,137,352 square miles), Nunavut is not only the largest territory, but is larger than any province. It covers approximately 18 percent of the country.

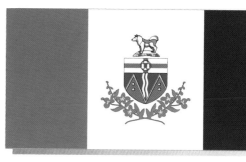

The flag of the Northwest Territories.

USA
ALASKA
Banks Island
Victoria Island
Baffin Island
Dawson
YUKON TERRITORY
NORTHWEST TERRITORIES
NUNAVUT
Iqaluit
Whitehorse
Yellowknife
BRITISH COLUMBIA
SASKATCHEWAN
QUEBEC
ALBERTA
MANITOBA
ONTARIO

Where did Yellowknife get its name?
The capital of the Northwest Territories takes its name from the copper deposits that were used by the Athapaskan tribe to make tools.

The flag of Nunavut.

What figures are featured on the Nunavut flag?
The flag is dominated by an inukshuk, a stone monument used as a landmark and in hunting caribou. An Inuit word, inukshuk means "man-like." The flag also features the North Star, the traditional guide to navigation.

The flag of the Yukon Territory.

What showered down on the Northwest Territories in 1978?

A Soviet spy satellite, *Cosmos 954*, re-entered the Earth's atmosphere scattering debris over a 46,000-square-kilometre area (28,589 square miles) of the Northwest Territories and what is now Nunavut. The clean-up operation, which sought to collect nuclear contaminated debris, took over a year.

What is the coldest place in Canada?

At minus 19.9° Celsius, Eureka, on Ellesmere Island in Nunavut, has the coldest average annual temperature in Canada. The lowest temperature ever recorded in Canada, minus 62.8° Celsius, was recorded at Snag, Yukon on February 3, 1947.

Dawson was the most populous city in Canada's north during the Klondike Gold Rush

Which territory had Dawson as its capital?

WHEN THE YUKON TERRITORY WAS ESTABLISHED IN 1898, DURING THE Klondike Gold Rush, Dawson was chosen as its capital. At its height, the city had 25,000 citizens, but the population decreased dramatically after the rush was over. In 1953, the capital was moved to the more populous city of Whitehorse.

Who was the first woman to lead a national party?

In 1989, Audrey McLaughlin, a Yukon Member of Parliament, was elected leader of the federal New Democratic Party, becoming the first woman to lead a major national political party in North America. McLaughlin lead the party until 1995, when another woman, Alexa McDonough, succeeded her.

What is Canada's smallest capital city?

Iqaluit, the capital of Nunavut, has a population of approximately 4,400 – less than one person for every thousand found in the metropolitan region of Toronto, Ontario's capital.

Nature and Wildlife

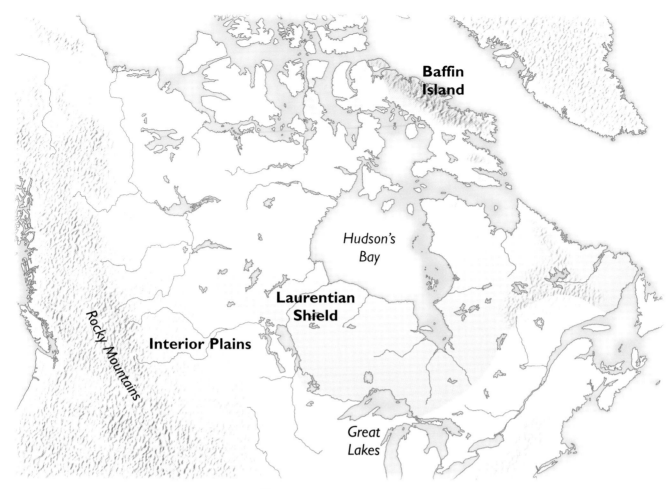

Baffin
Island

Hudson's
Bay

Laurentian
Shield

Rocky Mountains

Interior Plains

Great
Lakes

What is
the Laurentian Shield?

KNOWN ALSO AS THE CANADIAN SHIELD AND THE
PRECAMBRIAN SHIELD, THE LAURENTIAN SHIELD
is a vast area of hard rock extending from Hudson's Bay. Covering over
40 percent of Canada, the shield can reach a thickness of over three
kilometres (1.8 miles), and contains most of the country's metallic minerals.

Which is Canada's largest island?

Baffin Island in the Arctic Ocean is Canada's largest island. At 507,451 square kilometres
(315,382 square miles), it is over twice the size of the next largest island,
Victoria Island (217,290 square kilometres/135,046 square miles). Although sparsely
populated, Baffin Island is home to Iqaluit, Canada's most northern capital city.

What are the most northern, southern, eastern, and western points in Canada?

Canada's most northern point is Cape Columbia on Ellesmere Island in Nunavut.
Cape Columbia is 4,627 kilometres (2,875 miles) north of the country's most southern point,
the uninhabited Middle Island in Lake Erie. The most eastern Canadian land is found at
Cape Spear in Newfoundland and Labrador, which is 5,187 kilometres (3,223 miles) away
from the most western point, Mount St Elias in the Yukon.

Which provinces do not border on the United States?

Prince Edward Island, Nova Scotia, and Newfoundland and Labrador are the only provinces
that do not share a land border with the United States.

What is the highest point in Canada?

AT AN ELEVATION OF 5,959 METRES (19,664 FEET), THE COUNTRY'S highest point is the peak of Mount Logan in the Yukon Territory. The first recorded sighting of the mountain was made in 1890. It wasn't until 35 years later that the first ascent was made to its highest peak.

Which countries are larger than Canada?
At 17,075,200 square kilometres (10,612,305 square miles) only Russia exceeds Canada in size. The largest countries after Canada are China, the United States, and Brazil.

Who were Canada's first farmers?
Native Canadians were the first to farm in Canada. The first European to farm in Canada was Louis Hébert, who began cultivating land outside Quebec City in 1617. An apothecary, Hébert is also considered to be Canada's first physician.

Where is "the Graveyard of the Atlantic"?
Sable Island, 300 kilometres (186 miles) off the coast of Nova Scotia, is famous for its shipwrecks. Fog, unpredictable currents, and frequent storms have challenged mariners for centuries. Since 1583 over 350 shipwrecks have been recorded around the island.

How many islands are in the Thousand Islands?
The area of the western reaches of the St Lawrence, known as the Thousand Islands, actually contains more than 1,500 islands.

What is known as "the Canadian Galapagos"?
The most isolated land mass in Canada, British Columbia's Queen Charlotte Islands are sometimes referred to as "the Canadian Galapagos." Like the Galapagos, the remoteness of the islands provides an ideal environment for studying evolution.

Mount Logan is named after Sir William E Logan, the first Director of the Geological Survey of Canada.

Which river did Europeans originally know as the "Rivière du Canada"?

THE ST LAWRENCE RIVER FIRST APPEARED ON MAPS OF NORTH AMERICA AS THE *Rivière du Canada*. In 1535, Jacques Cartier named the river, which he hoped would provide a Northwest Passage to Asia.

How much of the country is under water?

Nearly eight percent of Canadian territory – 755,165 square kilometres (469,338 square miles) – is covered by freshwater. Canada holds a quarter of the world's freshwater, enough to flood the entire country to a depth of more than 2 metres (6.6 feet).

Which is the country's longest river?

At 4,241 kilometres (2,635 miles) in length, Canada's longest river is the Mackenzie River in the Northwest Territories. It is named after Alexander Mackenzie, the first recorded person to have followed its full length. The only North American river to exceed the Mackenzie in length is the Mississippi River.

What gave Whitehorse its name?

The capital of the Yukon is named after the dramatic foaming rapids that used to be present in that area. In 1958, the rapids were submerged beneath Schwatka Lake, which was formed by the building of the Whitehorse hydroelectric dam.

Who said the Great Lakes were "great"?

IN 1665, PIERRE-ESPRIT RADISSON USED THE WORD IN DESCRIBING LAKE ONTARIO, Lake Erie, Lake Huron, Lake Michigan, and Lake Superior, the five lakes that make up the world's largest body of freshwater. One out of every three Canadians depends on the Great Lakes for their water.

When did Niagara Falls run dry?

In March 1898 an ice jam in Lake Erie cut off the water supply of the Niagara River. For over 24 hours souvenir hunters were able to pick up bayonets, muskets, tomahawks, and other artifacts of the War of 1812. The flow over the American Falls was stopped for several months in 1969 in order to determine the feasibility of removing a large volume of loose rock from the base. The goal, to enhance the appearance of the Falls, was abandoned when the expense appeared to be too great.

What was the original name of Lake Louise?

The body of water was known to the Stoney tribe as the Lake of Little Fishes. Tom Wilson, the first person of European descent to see the lake, named it Emerald Lake. The name was later changed to Lake Louise in honour of the fourth daughter of Queen Victoria, Princess Louise Caroline Alberta, after whom Alberta is also named.

Niagara Falls is considered one of the natural wonders of the world.

How many rivers are found at Trois-Rivières, Quebec?

Although *trois rivières* is French for "three rivers," only two rivers, the St Maurice and St Lawrence, are found in the city. The name is derived from the fact that the St Maurice forms a three-branch delta as it meets the St Lawrence.

Which is Canada's largest lake?

Covering an area of 31,800 square kilometres (12,275 square miles), the largest lake solely in Canada is Great Bear Lake in the Northwest Territories. Lake Superior is well over twice as large, but is shared with the United States.

What makes Mount Snow Dome unique in North America?

The glacier water that runs down the sides of the mountain flows into Canada's oceans, the Pacific, the Atlantic, and the Arctic. It is one of only two triple continental divides in the world, the other being in Siberia.

Which early explorer was a fool for gold?

IN 1576, MARTIN FROBISHER RETURNED TO ENGLAND CARRYING A SHINY BLACK ROCK FROM BAFFIN Island. When analysed, the rock was found to contain iron pyrites, known as "fool's gold." However, one assayer believed that the rock contained real gold dust, sparking off Canada's first gold rush.

Sir Martin Frobisher commanded a flotilla of 15 vessels carrying "fool's gold" to England.

How much fool's gold did Frobisher bring to England?

Frobisher returned twice to Baffin Island, mining over 400 tonnes of rock that he transported back to England. By 1578, it was recognized that Frobisher's black rock was indeed fool's gold, bringing Canada's first gold rush to an abrupt end.

When was Canada's first "real" gold rush?

The first significant Canadian gold find occurred in 1858 in the sands of British Columbia's Fraser River. The discovery led to the Caribou Gold Rush two years later.

What is a Gold Maple Leaf?

In 1979, the Royal Canadian Mint introduced the Maple Leaf series of bullion coins. The 99.99 percent pure gold coin was the purest in the world and was soon outselling the popular South African Krugerrand.

Which metals are used in circulating coins?

Nickel, aluminum, copper, bronze, and steel are used in making today's circulating coins. The five-cent coin, commonly known as the nickel, actually contains a very small amount of the metal!

Which city started with a bang?

THE ORIGINS OF SUDBURY, THE LARGEST CITY IN ONTARIO'S NORTH, CAN BE traced back almost two billion years to when a large meteorite fell to Earth. The collision damaged the Earth's crust creating a nickel deposit that covers an area of over 1,600 square kilometres (994 square miles). Although the site was not discovered until 1883, by the early 20th century Sudbury was providing up to 80 percent of the world's nickel supply.

The Big Nickel in Sudbury was erected in commemoration of nickel's discovery by Baron Axel Fredrik Cronstedt in 1751.

Which mineral serves as a plant nutrient?

Although it has several other uses, potash is most often employed as a plant nutrient. Canada has the largest potash deposit in the world and is the world's largest producer. Most of the country's mining activity is found in Saskatchewan, although New Brunswick also mines the mineral.

How important is Canada in terms of mineral production?

Canada ranks first in the world for the production of potash and uranium, is the second largest producer of nickel and asbestos, and ranks in the top five for the production of zinc, cadmium, titanium, aluminum, platinum, salt, gold, molybdenum, copper, gypsum, cobalt, and lead.

When were the first Canadian diamonds found?

Although Canada's mineral wealth exceeds all other countries, diamonds weren't discovered until 1991. The resulting mine, the Ekati Diamond Mine in Lac de Gras, Northwest Territories, began operations in 1998.

41

In what way did lumber replace furs?

IN THE VERY EARLY 19TH CENTURY DEMAND FOR FURS BEGAN TO WANE.

As the harvesting of trees quickly replaced furs as the dominant economic activity in Canada, many involved in the fur trade became lumberjacks.

In the late 19th century tree harvesting replaced the fur trade, and gangs of lumberjacks occupied the forests.

Which tree is sometimes called the "canoe birch"?
The paper birch, known for its easily stripped bark, was used by Native people of eastern Canada in the construction of canoes. The trees were also used in the construction of wigwams and for medicinal purposes.

Where is Canada's tallest tree?
The tallest tree in the country is "the Carmanah Giant," a 95 metre-tall (314 feet) Sitka spruce growing in the Carmanah Valley on the west coast of Vancouver Island.

Which tree provides good cough medicine?

The boiled pitch of the white spruce has been used for centuries to ease coughing. Chewing old pitch is said to be good for the gums.

How long has the maple leaf appeared on the penny?

The one-cent coin issued in 1920 featured separate maple leaves. In 1937, the leaves were changed to the two maple leaf twig design that Canadians are familiar with. However, most don't realize that in 1982 the design was again altered in order to aid the visually impaired.

Which provincial capital is considered "the City of Trees"?

Halifax is often referred to as "the City of Trees" for its many parks, the most important being the Halifax Public Gardens. Located in the heart of the city, the seven-hectare gardens (17 acres) were begun in the 1830s and are considered a unique example of Victorian landscaping and gardening.

Which provincial tree was once used to make chewing gum?

The red spruce, the official provincial tree of Nova Scotia, exudes spruce gum from wounds on its trunk. The gum was collected and used as a raw material for chewing gum from the last half of the 19th century until the early years of the 20th century.

Are maple trees found in every province?

Canada is home to a total of ten different species of maple: bigleaf, black, Douglas, Manitoba, mountain, red, silver, sugar, striped, and vine. At least one of these species grows naturally in every province.

Buckets are used to collect maple sap, which the Iroquois call "sweet water."

How much sap does it take to make a litre of maple syrup?

BETWEEN 30 AND 50 LITRES (6.5–11 GALLONS) OF SAP ARE BOILED in making one litre of syrup. The healthiest and largest trees can yield up to 180 litres during the four-to-six week season.

43

Which provincial flower was first proposed as the national flower of Canada?

The white trillium is native to southern Ontario and parts of southern Quebec.

AT THE END OF THE FIRST WORLD WAR, the trillium was proposed as the official flower of Canada; and was to be used on the graves of Canadians buried overseas. Although the proposal was not adopted, the white trillium was selected as Ontario's floral emblem in 1937.

Which provincial flower was not native to Canada?
In 1963, the Madonna lily, an Asian species, was selected as Quebec's official flower due to its resemblance to the fleur-de-lis. It was replaced by the Blue Flag Iris in 1999. The western lily is the floral emblem of Saskatchewan, and is found in meadows and clearings.

Which provincial flower does law protect?
The trillium requires 15 years of growth before it flowers and, for this reason, it is illegal to pick the flower within Ontario's borders.

Is the fleur-de-lis a real flower?
The stylized flower featured on Quebec's flag and coat of arms is based on a real flower, but not the lily as is generally thought. Historians believe that the fleur-de-lis is, in fact, based on an iris found along the banks of the Lys River in France.

What makes poison ivy itch?
All parts of poison ivy but the pollen contain an oil, urushiol, which reacts negatively to proteins in the human body. Contact made between skin and the oil causes inflammation.

Which Arctic plant produces crystals?
The purple saxifrage, the first Arctic plant to flower each spring, is known for sometimes depositing crystals on the tips of its leaves. This occurrence is quite unusual as the only other plants that do this live in warm deserts.

Which Canadian wheats form the backbone of production?

Until the late 19th century, farmers relied on European wheats that were often ill-suited to the Canadian climate. The Red Fife, developed in Ontario, was the first successful wheat cultivated for the country's farmers. The Marquis, developed at Ottawa's Experimental Farm in the early 20th century, was even better suited to the Prairie climate.

When was wheat first grown in Canada?

It is thought that the grass was first grown in Port-Royal, now Annapolis Royal, Nova Scotia, in 1605. The first Canadian wheat exports are known to have taken place in 1654.

What is Canada's most important wheat-producing province?

SASKATCHEWAN PRODUCES APPROXIMATELY 60 PERCENT of the wheat grown in Canada. The province's other major crops include canola, rye, oats, barley, and flaxseed.

Traditional wooden grain elevators are now a rare sight in Saskatchewan.

Where were the first dinosaur bones found in Canada?

IN 1874, GEOLOGIST GEORGE M DAWSON discovered several bones belonging to a hadrosaur near Wood Mountain, Saskatchewan. Later the same year, Dawson found several more hadrosaur bones in Alberta.

Which dinosaur is called "Lizard from Alberta"?

The Albertosaurus was discovered by Henry Fairfield Osborn near Drumheller, Alberta in 1884. The dinosaur was named Albertosaurus, meaning "lizard from Alberta," in 1905, the year in which the province was created. The dinosaur stood 3.5 metres (11.5 feet) tall, stretched 10 metres (33 feet), and lived in North America during the late Cretaceous Period.

What happened to the woolly mammoth?

Although the last woolly mammoth died 10,000 years ago, evidence indicates that the animal once existed in large numbers in the Canadian north. With a weight of up to 6,818 kilograms (15,000 pounds) and a height of nearly 4 metres (13 feet), they were prey to very few animals. It is thought that the mammoth was hunted to extinction, likely by humans.

Which dinosaur was recently identified at the Canadian Museum of Nature?

The *Chasmosaurus irvinensis* was identified at the museum in 2001. A new species of dinosaur, the first part of its name, Chasmosaurus, reflects the fact that it had large openings, or chasms, in its skull. The second part of the name, irvinensis, comes from the town of Irvine, Alberta, near where the fossil was found.

Who hunted the western camel?

The single-humped camel is known to have travelled in herds throughout North America until approximately 10,000 years ago. Although no one is certain as to the exact cause of the animal's extinction, it is known that they were being hunted by ancestors of today's Native people at about the time when the species died out.

When did crocodiles roam the Arctic?

Crocodile lizards, or champsosaurs, lived in the freshwater streams of North America and Europe from 140 million to 65 million years ago. Though long extinct, they were one of the few surviving reptiles of the mass extinction of dinosaurs. A champsosaur fossil was recently unearthed in the Canadian Arctic.

What horse was native to North America?

Though extinct, the Pleistocene horse was once one of the most common animals in northwestern North America. The last of the horses is thought to have died approximately 13,000 years ago.

What left tracks in Parrsboro, Nova Scotia?
In the Jurassic Period, about 205 million years ago, a baby coelophysis made the smallest dinosaur footprints ever found. The coelophysis may have been lucky, as it's thought that the adults often ate their young.

When did lions roam Canada?
Over 10,000 to 70,000 years ago, the American lion roamed the western hemisphere. Slightly larger than the African lion, it is thought that it became extinct due to the gradual disappearance of its large prey.

The Albertosaurus lived over 65 million years ago.

Which dinosaur may be found in Canada and Scotland?

SOME THEORIES HOLD THAT SCOTLAND'S LOCH NESS MONSTER IS ACTUALLY A LONG-NECKED plesiosaur. Whether the dinosaur lives in Loch Ness is a matter of debate, but we do know that plesiosaurs once lived in what is now Alberta. Equipment operators working in the Fort McMurray oil sands mines have found many of their remains.

Some people believe that plesiosaurs have survived into the 21st century.

In the 19th century the bison was nearly hunted to extinction.

Who first suggested the beaver as a symbol for Canada?

THE GOVERNOR OF NEW FRANCE, COUNT FRONTENAC, FIRST SUGGESTED THE beaver as an appropriate emblem for Canada in the late 17th century. In the proceeding 300 years, the mammal has adorned the shield of the Hudson's Bay Company, the armorial bearings of Quebec City and the City of Montreal, Canada's first postage stamp, and the five-cent coin.

What is the proper name of the "sea canary" found in the St Lawrence River?

Because of the birdlike sound it makes, the beluga whale is sometimes referred to as the "sea canary." Most belugas live in arctic and subarctic waters, but in summer months can be seen in the mouths of larger rivers. A small number of beluga whales live year-round in the St Lawrence River.

Why is a bison not a buffalo?

Although both the bison and buffalo are members of the cattle family, only the bison is native to North America. The buffalo is found only in Africa and Asia. Canada's largest land animal is the wood bison.

What are the Canadian dogs?

Four breeds are unique to Canada: the Newfoundland, considered one of the most intelligent and gentle breeds; the Nova Scotia duck-trolling retriever, a favourite among duck hunters; the Tahltan bear dog, a rare strain from the west coast; and the famous Canadian Eskimo dog, more commonly known as the husky. Although related to the Newfoundland, the Labrador retriever is not technically a Canadian breed.

How did Sable Island get its horses?

Popular belief holds that the approximately 300 wild horses on Sable Island descended from survivors of a shipwreck. In fact, they are the offspring of horses sent to graze on the island in the 18th century by a Boston merchant.

What is Canada's largest land-based carnivore?

Native to northern Canada and the Arctic, the polar bear is North America's largest land-based carnivore. At maturity, the male can attain a total weight of up to about 727 kilograms (1,600 pounds) and a length of nearly 3 metres (10 feet).

What were hunted so that women might have narrower waists?

The desire of Victorian women for an hourglass waist led to a great demand for corsets made of whalebone. The fashion gave a new impetus to whaling and led directly to the establishment of many whaling stations.

Male caribou use their antlers for fighting during the mating season but shed them in early winter.

Which animal has the largest herds?

THROUGH MUCH OF THE YEAR, CARIBOU TRAVEL IN HERDS OF 10 TO 50; however, during migration herds of up to 100,000 are common. Since 1937, the mammal has been depicted on the Canadian quarter.

Which females in the deer family have antlers?

Caribou are the only members of the deer family in which both sexes grow antlers. Females can weigh up to 102 kilograms (225 pounds), compared to the 181 kilograms (400 pounds) the heaviest males weigh. The breeding season is in October. They have a single calf born in May or June. Their birth weight is about 5 kilograms (12 pounds).

How do salmon return to their birthplace?

ALTHOUGH THE SALMON IS BORN IN FRESHWATER, USUALLY STREAMS, it spends the majority of its life in the ocean, returning only to spawn. It accomplishes its journey by swimming upstream using its sense of smell as a guide.

Which salmon follows another up the Yukon River?
Both the Pacific chinook and chum salmon start their migration in the Bering Sea and swim 3,000 kilometres (1,864 miles) up the Yukon River to spawn. The Pacific chinook salmon spawn from July to September, and are followed by the chum salmon in September and November.

What do salmon eat when returning to spawn?
On their journey upriver to spawn, the salmon do not feed, but live off reserves of fat that they have stored for the migration.

Which cannibal is found everywhere but the Maritime Provinces?
Primarily a freshwater fish, the pike feeds on minnows, frogs, mice, muskrats, ducklings, and other pike. They are found in all territories and provinces, with the exception of New Brunswick, Prince Edward Island, and Nova Scotia.

Which shark is known as "the sleeper shark"?
Known for its lethargic nature, the Greenland shark is considered "the sleeper shark." Inuit often catch the fish by simply dragging it out of the water by hand. Despite its sluggish nature it is able to catch squid, herring, salmon, and seals, although how it manages to do so remains a mystery.

Sockeye salmon

Atlantic salmon

What happened to the cod?

THIS QUESTION IS THE SUBJECT OF MUCH DEBATE. HOWEVER, IT IS GENERALLY AGREED THAT THE COD WAS A VICTIM OF mismanagement, overfishing, dumping, and adverse ocean conditions.

The Atlantic cod has been fished on the Grand Banks since the late 15th century.

Which endangered fish is found in only one river?

Although it is illegal to do so, New Brunswick's Saint John River is the only place in Canada where one can catch the shortnose sturgeon. Once more common in the United States, the fish has all but disappeared due to pollution and dams. Despite its rarity, the shortnose sturgeon is sometimes caught accidentally by commercial fishing operations.

Who pursued the cod?

Beginning in the 16th century, the English, Irish, French, Portuguese, Spanish, and Basques all established fishing settlements in Newfoundland in pursuit of the fish.

Do all salmon die after spawning?

Both the Pacific steelhead salmon and the Atlantic salmon are capable of surviving the spawning run.

Sockeye salmon swim upstream to spawn.

Which "Pacific" bird is found on the shores of Hudson's Bay?

Pacific loons breed on freshwater lakes and ponds in the tundra and northern forests of Canada, including northern Manitoba and northern Ontario along the coast of Hudson's Bay. The bird is only seen on the Pacific Coast during the winter months.

Who was "Wild Goose Jack"?

Conservationist Jack Miner earned the nickname for his work in protecting migrating birds. In 1904, he started a waterfowl sanctuary outside Windsor, Ontario. Through the use of aluminum bands, Miner was able to record the flight patterns and ages of the birds.

Where can you see Canada's smallest bird?

THE MOUNTAINS OF SOUTHERN BRITISH COLUMBIA AND SOUTHEASTERN ALBERTA are home to the tiny calliope hummingbird. Canada's smallest bird, adults measure between six and seven centimetres (approximately two inches) in length and weigh less than three grams.

Hummingbirds are the only birds capable of hovering and flying backwards.

Are Blue Jays only native to Ontario?

Although Toronto's major league baseball franchise is named after the bird, the blue jay is native to all the provinces and is the provincial bird of Prince Edward Island.

Which small bird migrates between the Arctic and Antarctic?

The arctic tern breeds in the Arctic tundra. In late summer it leaves the Arctic and flies southward to the edge of the Antarctic ice pack. The arctic terns of the eastern Canadian Arctic fly across the Atlantic Ocean before heading south along the coasts of Europe and Africa. The tern flies over 35,000 kilometres (21,752 miles) each year and spends most of its 20-year life span in the air.

Which American symbol is more common in Canada?

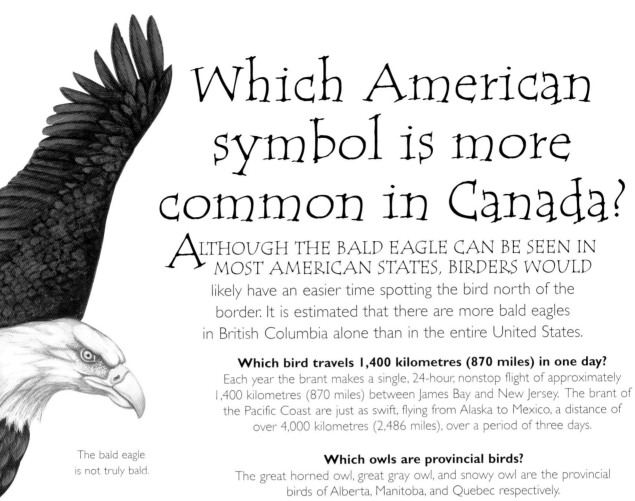

ALTHOUGH THE BALD EAGLE CAN BE SEEN IN MOST AMERICAN STATES, BIRDERS WOULD likely have an easier time spotting the bird north of the border. It is estimated that there are more bald eagles in British Columbia alone than in the entire United States.

The bald eagle is not truly bald.

Which bird travels 1,400 kilometres (870 miles) in one day?
Each year the brant makes a single, 24-hour, nonstop flight of approximately 1,400 kilometres (870 miles) between James Bay and New Jersey. The brant of the Pacific Coast are just as swift, flying from Alaska to Mexico, a distance of over 4,000 kilometres (2,486 miles), over a period of three days.

Which owls are provincial birds?
The great horned owl, great gray owl, and snowy owl are the provincial birds of Alberta, Manitoba, and Quebec respectively.

Which bird sees red?
The male robin will attack small red objects, even its own reflections in a mirror. It is thought that they react violently because they see the colour as representing an intruding male.

Which provincial bird is featured on the one-dollar coin?
The common loon, Ontario's provincial bird, has appeared on the one-dollar coin since it was first issued in 1987.

Why do Canada geese fly in a V-shaped formation?
Through flying in a group, Canada geese are able to take advantage of the updraft produced by the wings of the bird ahead, giving each bird better support when they are aloft. As a result, the geese expend far less energy to travel.

Why are Canada geese sometimes flightless?
Each summer, adult Canada geese lose their ability to fly for three to four weeks. During this time, the geese molt and regrow their feathers for flying. They often walk surprisingly long distances during this period.

The familiar sight of Canada geese in migration.

By what name is the milkweed butterfly better known?

THE MONARCH BUTTERFLY IS SOMETIMES REFERRED TO AS THE MILKWEED butterfly. Female monarchs lay their eggs – approximately 400 at any one time – only on milkweed plants. The milkweed is the only plant the monarch larvae are capable of eating.

How many species of moths and butterflies are native to Canada?
Of the 15,000 or so species of moths and butterflies, 293 are native to Canada. The largest of these is the crecopia moth, which can measure up to 15 centimetres (6 inches).

The monarch butterfly is native to every Canadian province and territory.

Which insect carries the West Nile virus?

The virus is carried by the mosquito and is transmitted by bites. Evidence of its existence in Canada was first discovered in 2001. It is thought that in areas where the virus is present, less than one percent of mosquitoes carry it. Fewer than one percent of those who are bitten by an infected mosquito will develop the disease.

Who said, "I'll die with the black fly pickin' my bones"?

Wade Hemsworth wrote *The Blackfly Song* about his experiences working in Northern Ontario in the mid-20th century. Although he recorded his ode to the irritating insect, it was a later recording by the Travellers that popularized the song.

Where do spiders go in winter?

Although most spiders die with the colder weather, as many as 55 species of spiders in Canada can live under the snow for up to six months. Of course, many spiders end up living in basements.

How did Native Canadians deal with insects?

The First Nations used a variety of herbs and plants to treat insect bites and as a repellent. The Huron, for example, used wild mint, which they called "quick smell," as an insect repellent.

Wasps eat the insects which would otherwise damage tomato plants.

How do wasps assist Canadian farmers?

WASPS PREY ON BUGS THAT THREATEN VEGETABLES GROWN IN CANADA. THE FLYING INSECT IS PARTICULARLY effective at protecting tomatoes and cucumbers.

What did the settlers of New France use to keep insects out of their homes?

Glass was often unavailable to the inhabitants of the French colony; the few who did have access usually did not have the means to pay for the goods. The more resourceful settlers kept insects out by using greased paper or oilskin as windows.

What is the mystery of the Lake on the Mountain?
Located on Quinte's Isle on the north shore of Lake Ontario, Lake on the Mountain has a constant flow of clean, fresh water, yet has no apparent source. With a surface nearly 62 metres (205 feet) higher than surrounding Lake Ontario, Lake on the Mountain defies all known geographical and geological theories.

Who named Percé Rock?

IN 1607, SAMUEL DE CHAMPLAIN, USED THE WORD PERCÉ – FRENCH FOR "pierced" – in describing the massive rock found off the shores of the Gaspé Peninsula. In Champlain's day there may have been as many as four holes in the rock; however, pictorial evidence indicates that there were only two.

What happened to Percé Rock in 1845?
In 1845, part of the monolith eroded, destroying one of the rock's openings. The dramatic event created a pillar of rock known as *L'Obelisque*. Today, only one opening, measuring 30 metres (100 feet) wide, remains.

What are reversing falls?
Reversing falls are caused by tidal action. At low tide, freshwater empties into the sea over a rocky shelf in a waterfall. As the tide rises above the falls, seawater forces its way against the river flow. The resulting turbulence makes the falls appear to have actually reversed. Canada has three reversing falls: at Saint John River in New Brunswick, and Wagner Bay and Barrier Inlet in Nunavut.

Percé Rock is a massive limestone island off the Gaspé Peninsula.

The Bay of Fundy features some dramatic rock formations.

What causes Nova Scotia to tilt?

LYING BETWEEN NOVA SCOTIA AND NEW BRUNSWICK, THE BAY OF FUNDY HAS the highest tides in the world. Twice daily, over 14 cubic kilometres (8.7 cubic miles) of sea water flow into the bay. The immense weight actually causes parts of the Nova Scotia countryside to bend. High tide can be as much as 16 metres (53 feet) higher than low tide, when more than 1,000 square kilometres (621 square miles) of ocean floor lie bare.

How much water flows over Niagara Falls?

Niagara Falls consists of two waterfalls, side by side, in close proximity to each other. The Canadian Falls, also known as Horseshoe Falls, are 675 metres (2,227 feet) wide and 52 metres (170 feet) high. Over 2,271,000 litres (499,560 gallons) flow over the Canadian Falls every second. The American Falls, at 305 metres (1,006 feet) wide and 56 metres (180 feet) high, carry over 567,000 litres (124,725 gallons) per second. The two waterfalls are separated by Goat Island, which is part of New York State. Together, the falls measure over 2,800 cubic metres (9,240 cubic feet), the world's greatest by volume.

How big is the Big Rock?

Deposited by a glacier over 10,000 years ago, the Big Rock is a massive boulder located near Okotoks, Alberta. Its size is often compared with that of an ocean freighter.

What are hoodoos and where can you find them?

Hoodoos, which Native peoples referred to as "hills on hills," are pillars of sediment that are created by wind and water erosion. Although hoodoos can be seen throughout the Prairies, the very best place to see them is in the Alberta Badlands.

Is Niagara Falls Canada's highest waterfall?

Though not nearly as famous as Niagara Falls, British Columbia's Takakkaw Falls leads the country in height. With a vertical drop of 503 metres (1,650 feet), Takakkaw Falls is well over eight times higher than the Canadian and American Falls. At 979 metres (3,230 feet), the world's highest waterfall is Angel Falls in Venezuela.

Who were interned in Banff National Park?

DURING THE FIRST WORLD WAR, OVER 8,000 "ENEMY ALIENS" WERE interned in 24 internment camps across Canada. The camps at Banff National Park, Castle Mountain, and the Cave and Basin housed up to 600 prisoners, two-thirds of whom were Ukrainian immigrants. The internees provided cheap labour to carry out park development projects, including the construction of a railway intended to bring tourists to Lake Louise.

Why is Lake Louise turquoise?
The lake's unique colour is caused by minute particles of rock powder – known as rock flour – found in the water. The powder is caused by surrounding glaciers as they scrape and grind nearby rocks. Meltwater then carries the rock flour into the lake.

Where is the world's largest park?
With a total area of over 44,840 square kilometres (27,868 square miles), Wood Buffalo National Park in northern Alberta and the Northwest Territories is the largest park in the world. It was established in 1922 to protect the last known herd of wood bison.

Which province has the most provincial parks?

British Columbia has over 400 provincial parks covering over 12 percent of its land base. The province was the third, after Ontario and Quebec, to create parks.

Which province established the first provincial parks?

Ontario established the first Canadian provincial parks, beginning in 1893 with Queen Victoria Park at Niagara Falls. The province now has 265 provincial parks.

What was the purpose of Rocky Mountains National Park?

When established in 1885 as the first national park in Canada, it was designed to preserve the Banff Hot Springs. As the park grew in size, the name was changed to Banff National Park.

Which province has the fewest provincial parks?

Though the country's largest province, Quebec has only 17 provincial parks, 13 fewer than Prince Edward Island. The total area covered by the province's provincial park system is 4,248 square kilometres (2,640 square miles), less than 0.3 percent of its territory.

What distinction does Ellesmere Island National Park hold?

Approximately 700 kilometres (435 miles) south of the North Pole, Ellesmere Island National Park is the world's most northern park. Covering a territory of 37,775 square kilometres (23,477 square miles), the park is Canada's second largest.

Canada's most famous park is Banff National Park in Alberta.

Whose cabin is located in Dinosaur Provincial Park?

JOHN WARE'S CABIN IS A POPULAR DESTINATION FOR THOSE VISITING THE PARK. AN AFRICAN- American born into slavery, Ware was freed at the end of the American Civil War. He came to Alberta in 1882 and soon achieved fame for his exceptional skills as a cattle driver and rancher.

Alberta's Dinosaur Provincial Park is the source of the country's richest fossil discoveries.

The First Nations

Chuki Peninsula

SIBERIA

Bering Strait

Seward Peninsula

ALASKA

Bering Sea

Kamchatka Peninsula

Aleutian Islands

Alaska Peninsula

It is thought that the first people arrived in North America by crossing the Bering Straight.

Who discovered Canada?

W HILE THERE IS NO RECORD AS TO WHO FIRST STOOD ON CANADIAN SOIL, IT is thought that people travelled from Siberia to Alaska between 10,000 and 25,000 years ago. Today's Native Canadians are their descendants.

What is the difference between the Inuit and the Eskimo?
The names Inuit and Eskimo refer to the same people, however the former is preferred. Eskimo is an Algonquian word, translated roughly as "eaters of raw meat." Its use is considered both derogatory and a misnomer as the Inuit cook their fish and game. The word Inuit means, simply, "the people."

What are the languages of Native Canadians?
The languages of Native Canadians are usually grouped into 13 linguistic families: Algonquian, Athapascan, Beothukan, Chinookan, Haidan, Inuktitut, Iroquoian, Koluschan, Kootenayan, Salishan, Siouan, Tsimshian, and Wakashan. Beothukan and Chinookan are considered extinct languages.

Who were the Thule?
The Thule were the ancestors of today's Inuit people. They came to Canada approximately 1,000 years ago, and over the proceeding century spread across the north to Greenland.

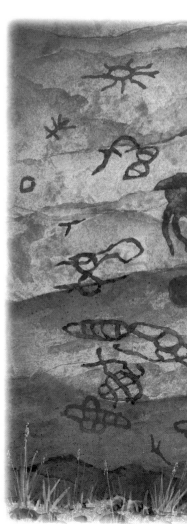

What is a pictograph?

PICTOGRAPHS ARE PREHISTORIC

illustrations painted with fingers and using red ochre. Together with petroglyphs, which are ancient images carved on cliffs, boulders, and other surfaces, pictographs present the earliest Canadian images.

In what ways are the Inuit different from the rest of Canada's Native Peoples?
Though the Inuit are spread out over many hundreds of thousands of square kilometres, they all share the language, Inuktatuk, share the same culture, and can be traced back to the Thule in terms of ancestry.

Petroglyphs and pictographs are the earliest visual records of the First Nations' history and culture.

Why were the people of the First Nations called "Indians"?
When Christopher Columbus first came upon North American land, he believed he had achieved his goal of discovering a new route to the Orient. He thought that the people he encountered were from India.

Which early Europeans figure in Canadian Inuit legends?
Several legends handed down over the centuries detail trade with the Vikings. While it is known that the Norse explored Labrador and Baffin Island, recent evidence indicates that they travelled as far north as Ellesmere Island.

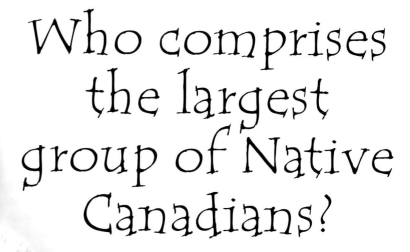

Who comprises the largest group of Native Canadians?

A Cree female in traditional dress.

NUMBERING OVER 208,000, CREE PEOPLE MAKE UP THE LARGEST group of the First Nations in Canada. They also have the greatest geographical distribution of the First Nations. Traditionally the Woodland Cree have lived in northwestern Manitoba and the forests of northern Saskatchewan, the Plains Cree in the prairies of Saskatchewan and Alberta, and the Swampy Cree on land stretching from Lake Winnipeg to northern Quebec.

Who were the real Red Indians?

Although the term was often used until the early 20th century, its use can be traced back to the Beothuk. A now-extinct people who lived on the island of Newfoundland, the Beothuk would often use ochre to dye their skin red.

Who are the Wendat?

The Huron referred to themselves as the Wendat, most often translated as "people of the peninsula." It was the French missionaries and traders in the early 17th century who named the tribe the Huron. Derived from the French word *hure*, meaning "head of a boar or pig," the name may have been inspired by the distinctive haircut worn by male members of the tribe.

How did the Métis get their name?

The French Canadians called the Métis the *bois-brûlés*, or charred-wood people. The name Métis is also French, meaning "half-breed." The Métis trace their heritage back to Cree and Ojibwa women and European fur traders.

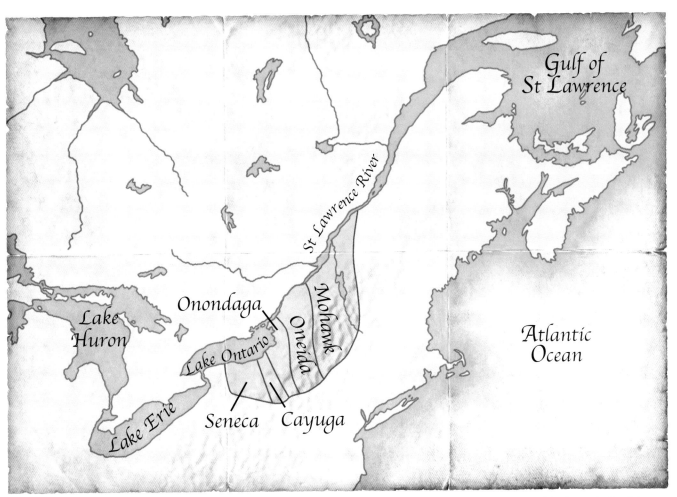

Gulf of St Lawrence

St Lawrence River

Onondaga

Mohawk

Oneida

Lake Huron

Lake Ontario

Atlantic Ocean

Seneca

Cayuga

Lake Erie

Map of the Five Nations of the Iroquois Confederacy.

What was the Iroquois Confederacy?

ALSO KNOWN AS THE HAUDENOSAUNEE, THE LEAGUE OF THE FIVE NATIONS, and the League of the Iroquois, the confederation was composed of five Native bands inhabiting the northern part of present-day New York State to the St Lawrence River and Lake Ontario. In the early 18th century, the Mohawk, Oneida, Onondaga, Cayuga, and Seneca were joined by the Tuscarora, becoming the Six Nations.

When was the Iroquois Confederacy established?

Considerable debate surrounds the date of the Confederacy's founding. While some scholars argue that the league can be traced back to the 12th century, it is known to have existed since at least the mid-15th century.

Which tribe gave Canada's capital its name?

The name of the nation's capital is derived from the Algonquian word *Adawe*, meaning "to trade." English-speakers have also used the word for the Ottawa people, also known as the Odawa, of the Three Fires Confederacy. The Ottawa call themselves the Ashinabe, meaning "the people."

What is Gayanashagowa?

The constitution of the Iroquois Confederacy is known as *Gayanashagowa*, or the Great Binding Law. The centuries-old agreement has proved so effective that it served to influence the American Constitution and the United Nations Charter.

Who were named by their enemies?

The peoples of the original Five Nations were given the name Iroquois by their foes, the Algonquian-speaking people of the St Lawrence. The name is derived from *iroqu*, the Algonquian word for "rattlesnake" and the French suffix *-ois*.

Who used knives made of slate?
Slate was often used by the Inuit as a cutting tool. Knives were often sharpened through the use of a whetstone made of fine sandstone. Many knives had their own small whetstone attached with a cord.

Which peoples developed snow shovels?
The Inuit used snow shovels consisting of a triangular frame of antlers, together with sinew, hide, and bone. The shovels were usually employed in the construction of snowhouses.

The Iroquois male had sole responsibility for the hunt.

How did the nomadic tribes transport their belongings?
Tribes from the Prairies used an A-framed device called a *travois*, consisting of two or more long poles tied together with a carrying basket in the middle. Depending on its size, the *travois* was designed to be pulled by a horse or dog.

Who was responsible for food in the Iroquois Confederacy?

THE ROLES IN PROVIDING FOOD WERE DIVIDED ALONG THE LINES OF GENDER. WOMEN WERE RESPONSIBLE for farming and gathering, while only men were involved in hunting.

Who equipped their canoes with three masts?

Measuring as long as 20 metres (66 feet), the three-mast Haida canoe was capable of carrying five tonnes of cargo. Work started on the dug-out canoes in the autumn, beginning at sites where the very best red cedars stood.

With the onset of winter, the Haida would slide their partially completed canoes over snow to the nearest water. It would then be towed to the village and would be completed over the winter.

What was the Sacred Run?

The Sacred Run was the method by which messages or objects were sent from one community to another. Unless the distance was very great, a single man would cover the run. Before setting out, the runner or runners would take part in a ceremony in their honour.

What is the role of Iroquois Clan Mothers?

The Clan Mothers, known as *Gontowisas*, have traditionally held vast powers. They conferred citizenship, declared war, appointed and impeached officials, and set the agenda of the Grand Council of the Iroquois Confederacy. The Clan Mothers were also responsible for choosing the *Sachem*, or chief, a male relative who would lead the tribe. If the *Sachem* proved unworthy, the Clan Mothers had the power to take his title away and bestow it upon another male member of the tribe.

Which tribes used the canoe?

ALMOST ALL OF CANADA'S FIRST NATIONS USED CANOES OR KAYAKS. BECAUSE of the country's abundant water, the boats were an integral part of hunting, fishing, and transportation.

How did the Inuit obtain wood for their kayaks?

The wood used in making frames for kayaks was sometimes cut from available timber near the tree line. However, as most Inuit lived farther north it was much more common to gather driftwood.

The canoe was a mode of transportation shared by nearly all Native peoples.

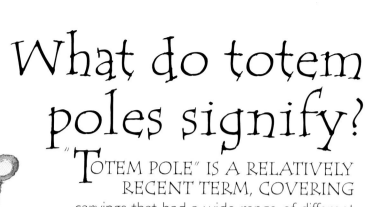

What do totem poles signify?

"TOTEM POLE" IS A RELATIVELY RECENT TERM, COVERING carvings that had a wide range of different functions. For example, the Haida used elaborately carved poles in the construction of houses, as posts holding up the interior beams of houses and as frontal poles that also served as the doorway. Of greater importance were poles that were carved as grave monuments and memorial columns.

A ceremonial totem pole from the West Coast.

Are tipis the same as wigwams?
Tipis are often confused with wigwams and vice versa. In fact, the wigwam is a dome-shaped structure constructed of flexible branches, often willow and birchbark.

Whose houses were long?
The Iroquois peoples lived in longhouses made of wood and elm bark. Their structures were called longhouses because they were much longer than they were wide. The houses had openings at both ends that were covered with skins during the winter months. There were no windows, with light coming from indoor fires, door openings, and small holes in the roof.

What did the traditional Huron villages look like?
The Huron village consisted of a dense concentration of various-sized longhouses. Middens, or refuse heaps, often separated the structures, and are now considered invaluable archeological resources. A two-to-six row palisade protected each village. As the village grew, portions of the palisade would be removed and rebuilt to enclose a larger area.

The Haida lived in impressive houses constructed of western red cedar planks. Measuring up to 15 by 18 metres (50 by 60 feet), they would have been occupied by as many as 80 people, usually close relatives and slaves. Sleeping compartments and privacy were provided by elaborately decorated plank partitions.

Which Iroquois village lies beneath Montreal?

In 1535, Jacques Cartier became the only European to visit Hochelaga, a village of approximately 500 people on the island of Montreal. According to the explorer, the fortified settlement consisted of some 50 longhouses and subsisted on farming, fishing, and hunting. Europeans next visited the island in 1603, by which time the village had completely disappeared.

A typical igloo. Due to its structural strength, parts could be dismantled allowing additional domes to be attached.

What did the Inuit use for light?

The Inuit used soapstone lamps that burned caribou fat or seal oil. These were usually placed beneath suspended soapstone pots, providing both light and heat. The lamps were especially important during the shortened periods of sunlight experienced in the Arctic winter.

Which Inuit lived in log homes?

The Inuvialuit, traditional Inuit of the mouth of the Mackenzie River, lived in houses made of logs and sods. In larger Inuvialuit communities, these structures were often large multi-family dwellings shaped like clover leafs. Each family was allowed one of the three alcoves and shared a common living area in the middle.

How do the Inuit cut ice when building igloos?

CONTRARY TO POPULAR BELIEF, IGLOOS ARE NOT MADE OF ice but are constructed of blocks of hard snow using a special knife. Although they are always built as temporary shelters, igloos are extremely strong with domes that have been known to support over 1,500 kilograms (3,300 pounds).

Who were the first Canadian farmers?

THE IROQUOIS BEGAN FARMING APPROXIMATELY 3,000 YEARS AGO. THEIR MAIN CROPS, CORN, beans, and squash, were planted in thousands of small mounds called corn hills. Grown around their villages, the vegetables would be harvested in the fall, and stored in longhouses to provide food for the winter.

Food preparation in an Iroqu- village. Traditionally women farmed and prepared all foo including that hunted by me

What were buffalo pounds?
Used in the hunting of bison, buffalo pounds were large fenced-in pens usually made of brush and hides. Hunters would drive small herds of bison into a funnel-shaped corridor leading to the entrance of the pound. Once inside, the bison were trapped and killed. Poundmaker, the famous Cree Chief, was so named for his skill in constructing buffalo pounds.

How did Native peoples treat scurvy?
The Iroquoians of Stadacona used a remedy called *annedda*, made from boiled white cedar bark, to treat the illness. In 1536, members of Jacques Cartier's crew became the first Europeans to receive the medicine.

Which food was considered to be food from the Great Spirit's garden?
Wild rice was referred to by the Ojibwa elders as *Manitou gi ti gahn*, which can be translated as "food from the Great Spirit's garden." Used as a food staple by indigenous peoples throughout much of North America, wild rice is known by several different names.

How is pemmican made?

An important staple of Plains First Nations people, pemmican consisted of a dry meat, usually bison, which was pounded and shredded into a coarse powder. The meat was then mixed with an equal amount of animal fat, and occasionally other edibles. The ease with which the mixture could be stored and shipped made it ideal for transient tribes and, later, for those involved in the fur trade.

What is k'aaw?

A Haida delicacy, *k'aaw* is herring roe on kelp. It is one of the many foods derived from the Pacific Ocean, including salmon, halibut, and seaweed, that are part of the traditional Haida diet.

What medicinal uses did the bunchberry have?

The Mi'kmaq used to apply the plant's leaves to wounds in order to stop bleeding and promote healing. The leaves were also boiled, making a tea that was given to children to prevent bed-wetting.

Who hunted through breathing holes?

In pursuing food during the winter months, the Inuit used a technique known as "breathing hole hunting." The hunter would maintain a watch over holes in the sea ice. When a seal or other sea mammal would approach for a breath of air, the hunter would stab the mammal with his harpoon.

What vessel was used in hunting whales?

THE INUIT OFTEN USED UMIAKS, BOATS MADE OF DRIFTWOOD AND WALRUS or seal skins when pursuing whales. The vessel differed from the kayak in that it was deeper, wider, and had no decking.

The Inuit whale hunt. Ceremonies and feasts take place when a whale is landed.

Who are known for their embroidery?

THE MI'KMAQ WERE TALENTED AT THE ART OF EMBROIDERY

long before the first arrival of Europeans to their shores. After contact, the women quickly incorporated European-sourced materials into their designs.

Which shirts were said to protect against bullets?

Ghost dance shirts were first worn by the Sioux in the late 19th century. Made of deerskin, they were sometimes decorated with a small moon and one or two stars. Legend held that bullets could not pierce a ghost dance shirt.

How were Inuit women's parkas designed to take care of their young?

While the women's parka, like the men's, was made of caribou skin, there were many design elements that differed between the two. The most notable difference was a back pouch in which children were carried for the first two to three years of their lives. The parka's large hood provided the child protection, while allowing air to circulate. Extremely wide shoulders allowed for breastfeeding without the infant having to leave the parka's warmth and protection.

Mi'kmaq embroidery is recognized nationwide for its creativity and beauty.

Which people invented the snowshoe?

Worn to prevent sinking in deep snow, snowshoes were developed by the Innu, Montagnais, and Cree of the St Lawrence River region.

What article of clothing did Cree brides present to their husbands?

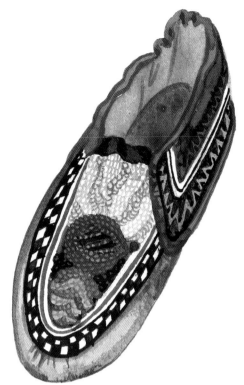

CREE WEDDINGS WOULD TAKE PLACE IN A NEW TIPI built by the bride's family. Inside the tipi, the bride would offer a pair of moccasins to her groom. If accepted, the marriage was sealed and the couple would adopt the tipi as home.

The gift of moccasins is used in traditional Cree marriage ceremonies.

Which people wore clothing made of bark?
Before contact with Europeans and those of European descent, Coast Salish clothing was woven from red or yellow cedar bark. Long strips would be taken from the trees and processed until soft enough to be sewn or woven. The resulting fabrics were either dense and watertight, or soft and comfortable.

Who wore Mohawk haircuts?
The Mohawk is a misnomer. The first people to wear the Mohawk were male Hurons, who are known to have been wearing the hairstyle at the time of first contact with Europeans in the early 17th century.

Who wore a crown made of grizzly bear claws?
The Haida *shaman* might wear one of three pieces of headgear: a wedge-shaped or pointed hat, or a crown made of grizzly bear claws or goat horns. His hair, always worn long, would be worn in a bun on top of his head.

How did an Inuit man's parka reflect his role as hunter?
The parka of an Inuit male had a tight-fitting hood so as not to interfere with vision. During a hunt, arm movement was facilitated by the coat's broad shoulders. A concealed knife was often tied to the inside of the sleeve.

What is a transformation mask?

Three masks of the Haida of British Columbia.

THE HAIDA USED MANY DIFFERENT KINDS OF masks in ceremonial dances. The most complex, the transformation mask, usually featured an animal and could be opened through the use of cedar-bark string to reveal a humanlike face.

Who went on a "Vision Quest"?

A Cree boy would leave his people for a "Vision Quest" at the onset of puberty. He would travel with his father or other close male relative to a remote place. After the two had built a shelter, the boy would be left alone to pray and fast until he experienced a vision of one or more spirit helpers. The spirit, or spirits, would present rituals and gifts that would be used throughout the boy's life.

Was "Old Man Buffalo" a man or a buffalo?

Neither. "Old Man Buffalo" was the name the Cree and Blackfoot gave to a 175-kilogram (386-pound) meteorite. Both tribes considered it a sacred object and feared repercussions when Christian missionary George McDougall moved it in 1869. The following year, three of the missionary's children died of smallpox.

Which tribal myth held that the first people emerged from a clam shell?

According to the Haida the world's first people were originally held in a gigantic clam shell on the beach at Rose Spit in British Columbia. Although they were afraid, the people were coaxed out by Raven. In another Haida myth, Raven disguises himself and steals the sun, moon, and stars from the House of the Sky Chief. He later gives them to the people.

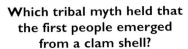

According to the Iroquoian creation story, Earth was created on the back of a great turtle.

What is Kitchi-Manitou?

Kitchi-Manitou, an Algonquian word meaning "mystery," is the name of the supernatural force that Algonquian peoples believe pervades the natural world.

Were there women shaman?

While in most Native cultures only men could be *shaman*, there were exceptions. For example, the Haida had a minority of women *shaman*, who usually focussed their work on curing the sick and on the difficulties of childbirth.

What was special about the Lake on the Mountain?

The Mohawks called the Ontario lake *Onokenoga*, meaning "Lake of the Gods," and believed that spirits dwelled within it. Early settlers believed the unusually deep lake to be bottomless.

Where is Turtle Island?

A CCORDING TO THE IROQUOIAN CREATION STORY, EARTH WAS created on the back of a great turtle swimming on an endless black sea. While some Iroquois refer to the entire planet as "Turtle Island," others use the name as a designation for North America only.

What was the purpose of the Smoke Feast?

The First Nations of the Pacific Coast believed that the souls of their deceased would enter the sky for the first part of their cycle of reincarnation. It was thought that a soul could be helped on its journey through the use of prayer and smoke rising from the central hearth of a house or through pipe smoking.

Who sacrificed themselves for humans?

The tribes of the Pacific Coast believed that salmon were supernatural beings who lived beneath the sea in human form. At the start of the salmon run these supernatural beings would transform themselves into fish and sacrifice themselves for human beings.

What was the potlatch?

CELEBRATED BY NORTHWEST COAST TRIBES, THE POTLATCH ANNOUNCED a major event in the community, often the birth, marriage, or death of a member of high rank. It was also used in the naming of a new chief. During the potlatch, a considerable amount of wealth, in the form of objects, was given to guests. The potlatch was illegal from 1885 to 1951.

The potlatch was held in celebration of a significant event, such as the claiming of hereditary privileges or an important marriage.

Which ceremonial dance was prohibited under Canadian law?

The Sun Dance was celebrated annually as well as on special occasions. Sun Dances were profoundly religious and social occasions. Christian missionaries frowned on the Sun Dance and set out to suppress it. In 1884, legislation was passed making it a criminal offense to practice the Sun Dance. It wasn't until 1951 that the ceremony was once again legal.

When were rattles used in ceremonies?

The Haida used raven rattles in ceremonies to mark the beginning of the annual salmon run. The noise of the rattles was similar to the sound of the fish breaking the water's surface and was thought to encourage the salmon.

How did the potlatch build prestige?
The family hosting the potlatch would contribute to the wealth that was given away by their chief to the guests. The prestige granted to the chief depended heavily on the wealth he displayed and gave away. It was expected that the host chief would receive even more wealth than he had distributed at a rival chief's next potlatch.

What motivated the Drum Dance?
The Drum Dance is held by the Inuit in celebration of a successful hunt or to welcome travellers. Singing also plays an important role in the celebration. Decorative dance hats, coats, pants, and boots are worn during the celebration.

What was the Ghost Dance?

FIRST PERFORMED IN THE LATE 19TH CENTURY, THE GHOST Dance was created during the period of encroachment by American settlers and the United States military. The dance was believed to be a method of renewal through which Native Americans could bring back the time before the arrival of settlers.

The Ghost Dance shirt was believed to be impervious to bullets.

What is an ikarig?
The Inuvialuit Inuit of northwestern Canada held their dances and ceremonies in *ikari*, large community buildings made of wood and sod. More northerly Inuit held their celebrations in temporary snow buildings that could hold up to 60 people.

Who saw the winter as a supernatural season?
The long wet winters of the Pacific Coast were considered supernatural by the Haida. Families and guests celebrated the season with feasting, storytelling, and dancing.

Which tribe celebrated thanksgiving twice a year?
The Ojibwa celebrated two thanksgivings each year. The spring celebration marked the end of winter and the rising of the sap. The autumn celebration was in gratitude for the fall harvest.

When was the first conflict between indigenous people and Europeans?

Approximately 1,000 years ago Norse trader Thorfinn Karlsefni launched an expedition to North America, which is thought to have included as many as 150 men and women. They spent several summers exploring and gathering a cargo of lumber, pelts, and other things for sale in Greenland and Europe. Eventually, clashes broke out between the Norse and the indigenous people, forcing the expedition to return to Greenland.

Who were enemies of the Inuvialuit?

At the time of European contact, in the late 18th century, the Inuvialuit and Dene had shared a history of violence that extended back for centuries. Archeologists have unearthed evidence of massacres that took place as early as the 14th century.

An Iroquois warrior.

How did a game of lacrosse disguise an act of war?

In 1763, Odawa Chief Pontiac and his warriors captured Fort Michilimackinac by pretending to play a game of lacrosse outside its gates. When one of the players threw the ball into the fort, the rest rushed in to retrieve it. Once inside, Native women handed concealed weapons to the warriors.

What type of warfare did the French adopt?

IN THE MID-17TH CENTURY, SEVERAL FRENCH SETTLEMENTS FELL
victim to raids carried out by small tribes of Iroquois warriors. The French adopted these strategies, which they called *la petite guerre*. Today, the same tactics are known as guerilla warfare.

Which warriors wore leather armour?

Tsimshian warriors of the Pacific Coast wore both armour and helmets made of leather when going into battle. Their primary weapons consisted of the bow and arrow.

What was the Haldimand Proclamation?

At the end of the American Revolution, the majority of Mohawk land, notably the Mohawk Valley in New York State, became part of the United States. Governor Frederick Haldimand rewarded the Mohawk with the Haldimand Proclamation, granting the territory 10 kilometres (6 miles) on either side of the Grand River to the Mohawk and other members of the Iroquois Confederacy.

Why were the Mohawk refused their promised land?

Governor Haldimand's term ended before the Confederacy received the title. Although the Iroquois eventually received land on the Grand River, it was less than 10 percent of what was originally promised.

Which First Nations were at war during the founding of New France?

The Algonquians and the Iroquois Confederacy had been at war for generations when Samuel de Champlain founded the French colony. Desiring trade, Champlain formed an alliance with the Algonquian tribes, most notably the Huron. In return, the Algonquians asked for French support in their war with the Confederacy.

Many Native warriors were allied with the Canadians and British against the Americans in the War of 1812.

Why are the drawings of Shawnandithit particularly valuable?

THE LAST OF THE BEOTHUK, THE EXTINCT BAND OF THE ISLAND OF

Newfoundland, Shawnandithit's drawings provide the only visual record of Beothuk culture by one of their own.

What does a sacred birchbark record?
The Ojibwa utilized rectangular pieces of bark, ranging in size from mere centimetres to many metres in length, upon which intricate, almost imperceptible designs would be cut. The records often served as memory aids to be referred to in preparation for sacred rituals.

What was the difference between the embroidery of Mi'kmaq men and women?
Traditionally, embroidery created by women was two-dimensional and employed moosehair, quills, and beads. Mi'kmaq men worked with less delicate material, including wood and stone, to create three-dimensional pieces.

Drawings by the last of the Beothuk, Shawnandithit, also known as Nancy or Nance April.

An Inuit soapstone carving.

Who carved in soapstone?

ALTHOUGH THE STONE IS MOST OFTEN ASSOCIATED WITH THE INUIT, IT WAS also used by many tribes of Native people to the south. The earliest known pieces date back 7,500 years.

What are False Faces?

The Iroquois use masks, known as False Faces, for ceremonial purposes. Carved out of wood, the masks were painted red or black or both. False Faces have eyes made of metal and a wide variety of mouth types. The masks represent mythological figures, such as Crooked Face, so called because his nose was broken when he challenged the Creator.

What were wampum?

Wampum were strings of purple and white shells, often several metres in length. They were traded among the Iroquois as a visual record of various historical events and treaties.

What special purpose did images hold on the shields of the Plains warriors?

The Blackfoot, Blood, and Assiniboine painted images of their personal guardian spirits on their shields. They believed that the paintings would protect them in battle and assist while hunting.

Whose art depicts Vikings?

Many surviving Thule culture art objects feature elongated faces with heavy brows topped by what appear to be helmets. They are thought to be images of Norse traders.

Who united the Iroquois?

Dekanawida, known as "The Heavenly Messenger," was the founder of the Iroquois Confederacy. Believing that there had been too much bloodshed among the Iroquois, Dekanawida worked for four decades in establishing a constitution that would unite the Mohawk, Onondaga, Seneca, Cayuga, and Oneida.

E Pauline Johnson, the author of *Flint and Feather* and *Legends of Vancouver*.

Who was Nanook of the North?

Alakarialak, an Inuit from Inukjuak, became internationally famous as the subject of the movie *Nanook of the North*. Considered the first feature-length documentary, the film sought to capture the daily life of Alakarialak and his family. Alakarialak died of starvation in 1923, the year following the film's release.

Who sought a confederacy of Iroquois and American tribes?

Mohawk War Chief Joseph Brant, or Thayendanega, a veteran of the Seven Years' War and the American Revolution, worked to expand the Iroquois Confederacy among the Ohio Indians in an effort to block American expansion. British betrayal, tribal infighting, and American aggression doomed his efforts to failure.

Who billed herself as the Mohawk Princess?

ONE HUNDRED YEARS AGO, E PAULINE Johnson was one of the country's most popular and successful writers and entertainers. The daughter of a Mohawk father and an English mother, she developed an international reputation, giving recitals of her poetry in Canada, Great Britain, and the United States. She was the first Native poet published in Canada, and was one of very few female writers at the time who could make a living by writing and performing.

Who was the fastest man in the world?

I̶N THE EARLY 20TH CENTURY, TOM LONGBOAT OF THE

Six Nations Reserve in Ontario was considered the greatest long-distance runner in the world. Among his many triumphs was winning the Boston Marathon in 1907, one of 14 Canadians to have achieved the feat.

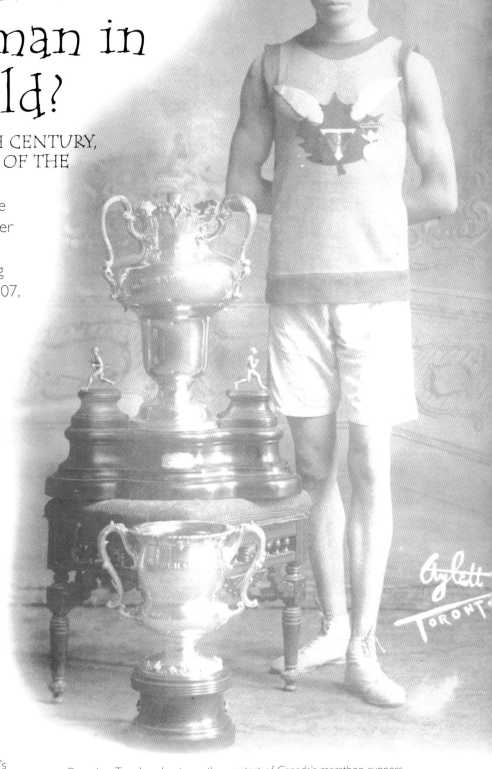

Onandaga Tom Longboat was the greatest of Canada's marathon runners.

What is Spirit of Haida Gwaii?

Located at the Canadian Embassy in Washington, *Spirit of Haida Gwaii* is Haida artist Bill Reid's largest and most complex sculpture. One of Canada's most accomplished sculptors, Reid studied jewellery-making and engraving. He was also known for his paintings, prints, and books. The original plaster pattern used to cast the bronze sculpture can be seen at the Canadian Museum of Civilization in Hull.

Who was the first Native Canadian to become a published author?

In 1847, Ojibwa George Copway's autobiography, *The Life, History and Travels of Kah-ge-ga-gah-bowh*, became the first published book by a Native Canadian. Copway went on to write several more books, including *The Traditional History and Characteristic Sketches of the Ojibway Nation*.

Which former longshoreman was nominated for an Academy Award?

Dan George, Chief of the Tsleil-Waututh band from 1951 to 1963, was employed as a longshoreman and a logger until the age of 60. He began his acting career in 1959, earning an Oscar nomination for his role as Old Lodge Skins in the 1970 film *Little Big Man*.

Who always paid for coffee at the Dead Dog Café?

THOMAS KING, AUTHOR OF "MEDICINE RIVER" AND "TRUTH AND BRIGHT WATER," always paid for coffee at the Dead Dog Café. King played himself in the popular radio show *Dead Dog Café Comedy Hour*. The show, which was actually only 15 minutes in length, also featured Floyd Favel-Starr as Jasper Friendly Bear and Edna Rain as Gracie Heavy Hand. The café made its first appearance in King's novel, *Green Grass, Running Water*.

Writer Thomas King is the editor of *All My Relations* – an anthology of Native Canadian literature.

Which member of The Band was raised on the Six Nations Reserve?

The son of a Jewish father and a Mohawk mother, Robbie Robertson was raised on the Ontario reserve. He began playing music professionally at the age of 15. Two years later he joined a group that would eventually become The Band. Among his many accomplishments is the soundtrack for *The Native Americans*, a six-hour television documentary.

Whose work is known as "x-ray art"?

The work of self-taught Ojibwa painter, printmaker, and illustrator Norval Morrisseau is the originator of a style referred to as "x-ray art" or "legend painting." Among his most notable works was the mural for the Indians of Canada Pavilion at Expo '67.

What is the purpose of the Christmas and Winter Relief Association, founded in 1988?

The association is dedicated to raising money to help homeless people. Its founder, singer, actor, writer, director, and producer Tom Jackson, was once himself homeless. At the start of each winter, his show, *The Huron Carole*, crosses the country raising thousands of dollars for the charity.

Whose name appears six times on the Stanley Cup?
Born to a father of Cree and Chippewa heritage, forward Bryan Trottier was a member of the New York Islanders during their four consecutive wins of the Stanley Cup. He later won the cup two more times as a member of the Pittsburgh Penguins. The winner of the Hart Memorial Trophy and the Conn Smythe Trophy, Trottier is among the ten greatest National Hockey League scorers of all-time.

Which acclaimed filmmaker is also a sculptor?
Zacharias Kunuk, the producer and director of *Atanarjuat*, first achieved fame for his soapstone carvings. He is also co-founder of Igloolik Isuma Productions, Canada's first Inuit-owned independent production company.

Who helped draft the Constitution Act of 1982?
Senator Charlie Watt first gained national attention as a chief negotiator in the James Bay and Northern Quebec Agreement. He later played an important role in creating Canada's constitution, including section 35, recognizing the rights of Native people in Canada.

Who designed the Canadian Museum of Civilization?

The Canadian Museum of Civilization in Hull, Quebec, was completed in 1989.

THE POPULAR MUSEUM WAS DESIGNED BY DOUGLAS Cardinal, and is an excellent example of his "organic style" of architecture. More recently, he designed an entire community for the Oujé-Bougoumou Cree of northern Quebec.

Explorers
and Settlers

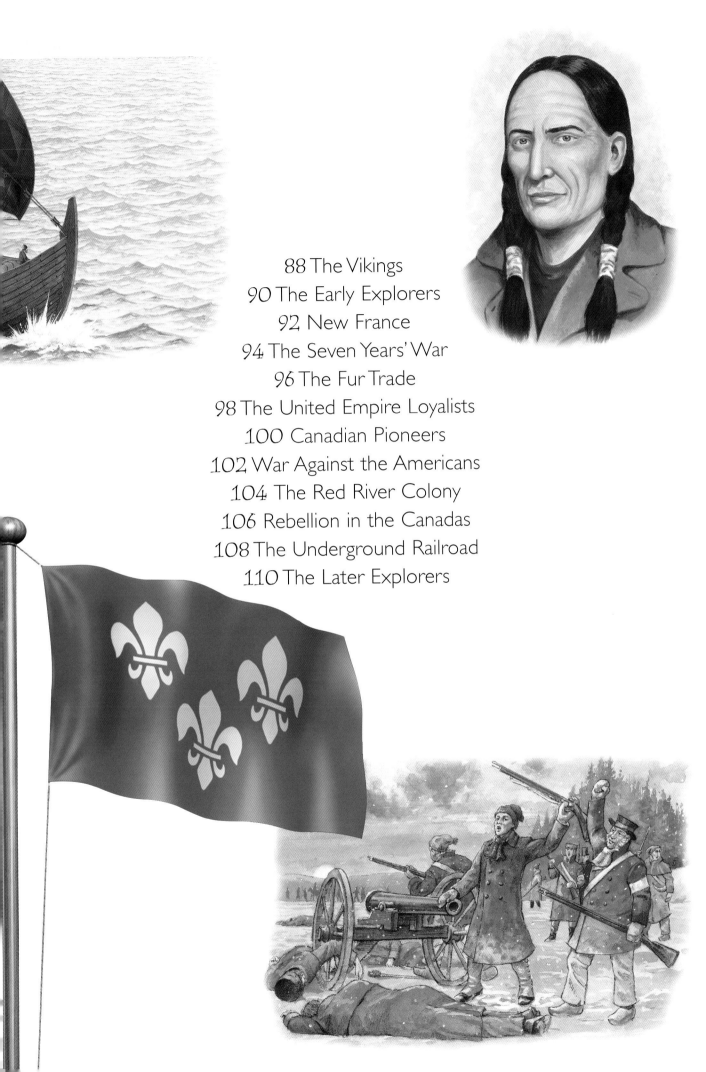

How large were Leif Ericson's ships?

LEIF THE LUCKY'S SHIPS WOULD HAVE BEEN TYPICAL VIKING VESSELS. SIZE depended on use. Trading ships, which may have been used exclusively by Leif Ericson, were approximately 15 metres (50 feet) in length. The other class of Viking vessels, warships called long ships, could measure as long as 29 metres (96 feet).

This is an example of a typical Viking ship used to explore the Canadian coast.

Who was Leif the Lucky?
The son of Eric the Red, Leif Ericson, or Leif the Lucky, was the first European to set foot on North American soil. Eric the Red had recommended that his son undertake an expedition to find land to the west of Greenland.

What prevented Eric the Red from voyaging to North America?
Leif's father had intended to accompany his son, but fell off his horse on the way to the ships. Considering the fall a bad omen, Eric the Red chose to remain behind.

L'Anse aux Meadows in Newfoundland is now recognized as a World Heritage Site.

Where are Helluland, Markland, and Vinland?

The three lands were discovered and named by Leif Ericson during his voyage of AD1001. Baffin Island is the territory Leif referred to as Helluland, while Labrador is Markland. Although there is still considerable debate, most believe that Vinland, where Leif the Lucky finally landed, was the northern tip of the island of Newfoundland.

Who was the first European to reach Canada?

Although Irish legends indicate that Saint Brendan, an Irish monk, may have sailed to North America in the sixth century, it is likely that the Vikings were the first Europeans to sight Canadian shores. Norse saga records that Bjarni Herjolfsson followed the coasts of Newfoundland, Labrador, and Baffin Island in AD986.

Who was Snorri Thorfinnsson?

Snorri Thorfinnsson is thought to have been the first non-Native child born in North America. It is likely that he was born in Newfoundland sometime between AD1005 and 1013.

What did the Norse build at L'Anse aux Meadows?

ALTHOUGH THE VIKINGS MAY HAVE STAYED AT L'ANSE AUX MEADOWS for only a few years, they left behind a substantial settlement. The community consisted of several houses, workshops, and a small forge.

Who were the Skraelings?

The Native People encountered by trader Thorfinn Karlsefni and members of his expedition were referred to as the Skraelings. An Icelandic trader, Karlsefni learned of Leif Ericson's discoveries while visiting Greenland.

Which murderer founded a colony?

In about AD985, Eric Thorvaldson and approximately 450 colonists settled Greenland. Better known as Eric the Red, several years prior Thorvaldson became the first European to sight and set foot on the immense island. At the time, the explorer was under a sentence of exile from Iceland for several quarrels and killings.

89

What happened to the first explorers to winter in Canada?

JACQUES CARTIER AND HIS MEN WERE THE FIRST TO EXPERIENCE a Canadian winter. Cartier was ill-prepared as he had expected the season to be similar to that of France. Twenty-five of his men died before spring.

Who lied when claiming Canada?
In 1534, Jacques Cartier erected a 9-metre (30-foot) cross in claiming Canada for France. When questioned by Donnacona, the Chief of Stadacona, Cartier described the cross as an insignificant landmark carrying no meaning.

The intrepid 16th-century explorer, Jacques Cartier, led three expeditions to Canada and may have participated in as many as three others.

Which Italian explorer first claimed land for France?

In 1524, Giovanni da Verrazzano explored the coastline from Cape Breton Island to Florida. During his voyage he claimed the entire eastern coast of North America for his patron, King François I of France.

Which explorer suffered a mutiny?

In search of the Northwest Passage, English explorer Henry Hudson made two trips to North America. During his first trip, he narrowly avoided a mutiny while searching for the passage in the Hudson River. In his second voyage, the explorer wasn't quite so lucky. After having spent a winter in icebound James Bay, Hudson insisted that his men continue their search for the elusive passage. Hudson was grabbed. He and several men, including his son, were set adrift in a small open boat.

The New World was explored using vessels such as this.

Who first claimed land in the New World for England?

In June 1497, less than two months after leaving England in search of the Northwest Passage, John Cabot landed at either the island of Newfoundland or Cape Breton Island. The explorer claimed the land for King Henry VII of England. Cabot never did find the passage, and he perished after his ship was lost in either 1498 or 1499.

What was "the Kingdom of the Saguenay"?

The main objective of Jacques Cartier's second voyage to North America was the exploration of the St Lawrence River and the Kingdom that the Iroquois had told him about. He was frustrated to reach the island of Montreal and to find that he could go no further due to the Lachine rapids. The Kingdom remains undiscovered to this day.

Who were the Sea Dogs?

IN ORDER TO OBTAIN ENGLISH SUPREMACY AT SEA, QUEEN ELIZABETH I RELIED ON the "sea dogs," a group of daring merchant seamen. Among her sea dogs were several men who played great roles in exploring Canada, including Sir Humphrey Gilbert, Sir Martin Frobisher, John Davis, and Henry Hudson.

Why is a large area of Montreal named after China?

Convinced that he would one day discover a route to China, explorer and trader René-Robert Cavelier, Sieur de La Salle, named his estate in Montreal *La Chine*, the French name for China. The area of the island is now known as Lachine.

How did Italians name New France?

The origin of "New France" can be traced back to explorer Giovanni da Verrazzano, who, in 1524, used the name Francesca to designate lands situated in the interior of the Atlantic coast. Born and raised in his family's castle, Catello Verrazzano near Florence, the explorer's expedition was funded by King François I of France and several Italian bankers and merchants. The explorer's brother, cartographer Giovanni da Verrazzano, mapped the voyage and used the name *Nova Gallia* to cover the territory of New France.

Who was "The Father of New France"?

ALSO KNOWN AS "THE FATHER OF CANADA," Samuel de Champlain earned the title for having established the first European settlements in Acadia and Quebec. In 1612, he was made the first Governor of New France. At the time of his death, in 1635, the population of New France was only 150 people.

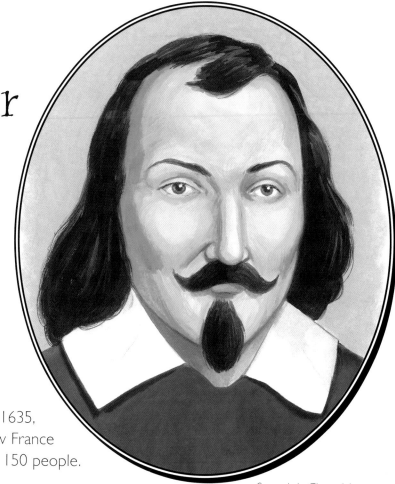

Samuel de Champlain.

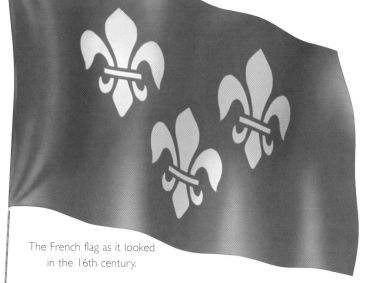

The French flag as it looked in the 16th century.

Who were the Kirke brothers?

Sir David Kirke and his four brothers were French-born adventurers of English descent. In 1628, they seized Tadoussac in New France and demanded that Champlain surrender Quebec. When the Governor refused, the brothers captured supply ships, bringing about famine in the capital of New France. In the summer of 1629, the Kirkes and their men took possession of Quebec. Champlain was forced to return to France, and was unable to return to the town until 1632, when the Treaty of Saint-Germain-en-Laye returned Quebec to France.

What did France lose in the Treaty of Utrecht?

The Treaty of Utrecht was one of several treaties that ended the War of the Spanish Succession. Although the 11-year war broke out in Europe, fighting had spread to Newfoundland, Acadia, and New England. In signing the 1713 treaty, King Louis XIV of France ceded Acadia, his possessions in Newfoundland and mainland Nova Scotia, and his claims to Rupert's Land.

Who were *les Filles du Roi*?

Les Filles du Roi, which can be translated as "the King's girls" or "the daughters of the King," were a group of 770 young French women who emigrated to New France in the mid-17th century. Primarily composed of orphans, *les Filles du Roi* were considered wards of the King of France. It was hoped that their presence would encourage population growth in a colony composed of over 85 percent men. When marrying one of the *filles*, male settlers were presented with a considerable dowry.

How large was New France?

In 1712, at its greatest, New France occupied well over two-thirds of North America. Newfoundland, Acadia, the Gulf of St Lawrence, the St Lawrence River, the Great Lakes, and the entire Mississippi Valley were all under French rule. The territory was so vast that it was divided into three administrative zones: Canada, Louisiana, and the Atlantic Coast.

How many French citizens settled in New France?

Although it is difficult to know the exact number, it is thought that over 3,000 people left France for life in its North American colony.

How many people lived in New France?

In 1666, Governor Jean Talon conducted the first census. He travelled from door to door and counted 3,215 persons. Native peoples were not included in Talon's census.

What was the capital of New France?

The colony was governed from Quebec City, the largest settlement in New France. Montreal, founded as Ville Marie in 1642, was many times smaller than the capital.

Who were the habitants?

The habitants were the farmers of New France. Although the habitants cleared and farmed the land, it was owned by the Seigneur, to whom the farmers paid annual dues.

Who planted a cross on Mount Royal?

In 1643, Paul de Chomedy de Maisonneuve, the founder of Montreal, carried a wooden cross to the summit of Mount Royal. He was fulfilling a promise that he would do so if colonists survived the threat of flooding. The present-day cross was built in 1924.

What was "The Gibraltar of Canada"?

NAMED IN HONOUR OF KING LOUIS XIV OF FRANCE, LOUISBOURG IS LOCATED on Cape Breton Island. North America's largest fortress, it was built to house 4,000 soldiers. The bastion took 25 years to build and, at the time of completion, was considered impenetrable. However, Louisbourg was twice captured by the British and was destroyed in 1760. Work began on reconstructing the site in 1961.

The fortified town of Louisbourg was the major French settlement on Cape Breton.

A map of New France in 1759.

What sale marked the end of New France?

THE NAME "NEW FRANCE" FELL OUT OF USE AFTER THE END OF THE SEVEN YEARS' War. However, France held a considerable amount of territory in North America until 1803 when Louisiana was sold to the United States.

What was the motivation behind the establishment of Lunenburg, Nova Scotia?

Originally known as Merliguesche, a small Acadian settlement, Lunenburg was created in 1743. That year, the British government brought over 1,400 German, Swiss, and French Protestants to the town in an effort to reduce the French Catholic presence in Nova Scotia. Over 250 years later, the population of Lunenburg is less than twice what it was at its founding.

What was Louis-Joseph Montcalm's greatest victory?

In 1756, at the onset of the Seven Years' War, Montcalm took the British fort at Oswego, in present-day New York State. In doing so, he captured 1,600 men and won control of the Great Lakes.

How many troops fought on the Plains of Abraham?

APPROXIMATELY 4,500 BRITISH SOLDIERS TOOK PART IN THE BATTLE.
Montcalm's French forces were of an equal number, but could have been more – the Lieutenant-General chose to attack the British before he had amassed all the troops at his disposal.

Who was Abraham?
The Plains of Abraham are named after their first owner, Abraham Martin, who was granted the deed to the land in 1635.

Where did Montcalm and Wolfe die?
Although many paintings depict the two adversaries dying on the battlefield, only General James Wolfe died on the Plains of Abraham. Montcalm returned to the city after having been shot in the groin and thigh. He died from his wounds the next day.

Who attempted to recapture Quebec?
In the spring of 1760, the Duc de Lévis was defeated in his attempt to take back the capital in the Battle of Sainte Foy.

Were both Montcalm and Wolfe aware of the battle's outcome?
Wolfe was told of the victory shortly before his death. When Montcalm was informed that he had only hours to live, he replied, "So much the better, I shall not see the surrender of Quebec."

The Battle of the Plains of Abraham took place on September 13, 1759. Quebec surrendered five days later.

Who were the Nor'westers?

The Hudson's Bay Company had a fleet of ships to transport Canadian goods back to England.

THE NICKNAME WAS GIVEN TO THE NORTH WEST COMPANY, FORMED IN 1783 by fur traders from Montreal. Rivals of the Hudson's Bay Company, Nor'westers tended to be French-speaking Canadians or Scottish immigrants. Although the resulting fur war was costly for both companies, the Nor'westers weakened first. In 1821, the North West Company became part of the Hudson's Bay Company.

Who were Radishes and Gooseberries?

Often credited with the true beginning of the fur trade in the 17th century, Pierre-Esprit Radisson and Médard Chouart des Groseilliers are also remembered as explorers. The two men, who were related by marriage, have been known to generations of schoolchildren as "Radishes and Gooseberries." They eventually became founding members of the Hudson's Bay Company.

Which canoe was designed specifically for the fur trade?

The Algonquin-style Montreal canoe was considered the freighter of the fur trade. Made of birchbark, cedar, white ash, rawhide, spruce roots, and spruce gum, the 11-metre-long (36-feet) canoe was capable of transporting more than three tonnes of goods and people, and would travel as far as 80 kilometres (50 miles) a day.

What brought about the decline in the fur trade?

MUCH OF THE FUR TRADE WAS FUELLED BY A HIGH DEMAND FOR BEAVER HATS. HAVING BEEN POPULAR FOR generations, the hats finally fell out of fashion in the very early 18th century when silk hats came into vogue. In addition, new fur treatments were being developed which made beaver less necessary and more costly.

Why did Radisson and Groseilliers fight against France?

After travelling far inland in search of furs, Radisson and Groseilliers returned to the colony with nearly 100 overflowing canoes. However, as they hadn't obtained a license before their departure the furs were confiscated, Groseilliers was put in jail, and both were given fines for breaking the law.

Which language was most useful to fur traders?

Although the French and English were both involved in the fur trade, the most commonly used language was Cree. Knowledge of Machif, the Métis language using a combination of Cree verbs and French nouns, was also useful to traders.

Who were the Voyageurs?

The name "Voyageurs" was first used in the 16th century to describe men seeking opportunity in New France. Over the centuries, the term changed meaning, but is most often associated with a merchant or hired hand involved in trading expeditions. By the 19th century, the word was being applied to hunters, trappers, and lumberjacks.

How far did the Voyageurs voyage?

The Voyageurs travelled thousands of kilometres, many covering as much as 70 kilometres (44 miles) per day on a diet of corn and fat. Many Voyageurs adopted a Native Canadian lifestyle, often marrying First Nations women.

Many First Nations people were active participants in the fur trade.

What happened to the Black Loyalists?

At THE END OF THE AMERICAN REVOLUTION, MANY BLACKS WERE

returned to slavery before they could flee the United States. Some went to England, others to Florida and the West Indies, but most went to the North American colonies to the north, in what is now Canada. Those who made it to Florida were largely abandoned to the Spanish. Most black Loyalists who made it to what is now Canada settled in Nova Scotia, where they had been promised land.

Which war helped bring about the American Revolution?
Arguing that the Seven Years' War was fought, in part, to defend the Thirteen Colonies, the British government looked to the colonists to help pay off the war debt. It imposed new taxes on newspapers, tea, sugar, and other items. The taxes were greatly resented and are frequently cited as being among the chief causes of the American Revolution.

How did the Loyalists divide Quebec in two?
The influx of thousands of Loyalists to the western half of Quebec had created a semi-British, Protestant society. In contrast, the eastern-half of the colony was largely populated by the Catholic, French-speaking Canadians who, though British subjects, maintained their own civil law. The Constitutional Act of 1791 sought to address these differences by creating Upper and Lower Canada.

Who were the United Empire Loyalists?
The Loyalists were inhabitants of the Thirteen Colonies who remained loyal to Great Britain. It's thought that over 70,000 Loyalists fled the Colonies during or immediately after the American Revolution. Although some emigrated to Great Britain, the vast majority settled in what are today Nova Scotia, Quebec, and Ontario.

Black Loyalists were granted freedom in exchange for their support of the British forces.

Which Loyalists were former slaves?
During the revolution, the badly outnumbered British promised freedom to slaves of the rebels, provided they helped in the war effort. Approximately 30,000 slaves escaped and worked beside the British as soldiers, labourers, cooks, and musicians.

What caused Quakers and Pennsylvania Germans to flee the United States?

As PACIFISTS, QUAKERS AND PENNSYLVANIA GERMANS WERE DISLIKED BY SUPPORTERS OF THE AMERICAN Revolution because they chose to remain neutral during the war. Many decided to emigrate to avoid religious persecution, the very same reason that had encouraged their ancestors to come to the Thirteen Colonies.

Who encouraged her tribe to side with the British?

Although her tribe was neutral at the beginning of the American Revolution, Mohawk Molly Brant sided with the British. She sheltered the first Loyalists, supplied arms to British supporters, and passed intelligence on to the British Army. Molly Brant's support of her brother, Chief Joseph Brant, aided his ability to end Mohawk neutrality.

Who was "the Town Destroyer"?

George Washington, future President of the United States, was known to the Iroquois Confederacy as "the Town Destroyer." During the American Revolution, Washington sent an army into the Mohawk Valley to destroy the villages of all Iroquois siding with the British.

Many Loyalists fled violence, intimidation, and persecution at the hands of their fellow colonists.

Whose motto is a reference to the Loyalists?

The motto of the province of Ontario, "Ut incepit fidelis sic permanet" – Latin for "Loyal it began, Loyal it remains" – is an allusion to the Loyalists. More Loyalists settled in Ontario than in any other area of Canada.

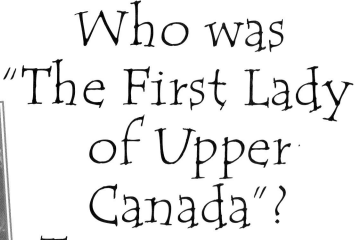

Who was "The First Lady of Upper Canada"?

Four watercolour sketches painted by Elizabeth Simcoe in the late 18th century.

THE WIFE OF UPPER CANADA'S FIRST LIEUTENANT GOVERNOR, Elizabeth Simcoe earned the title during her five years in the colony. She is remembered today for her diaries and sketches, which provide some of the earliest records of what is now Ontario.

When was Toronto known as York?

The first Parliament of Upper Canada was held in 1792 at Newark, now known as Niagara-on-the-Lake, then recognized as the capital of the colony. However, the Lieutenant Governor John Graves Simcoe, a veteran of the American Revolution, felt that the city was too vulnerable to American attack. The following year he chose Toronto as the new capital, changing its name to York. The city was renamed Toronto in 1834.

Who first banned slavery?

In 1793, John Graves Simcoe, Lieutenant Governor of Upper Canada, passed a law banning slavery in the colony. Though his legislation did not free those who were already slaves, Upper Canada became the first territory in the British Empire to end the slave trade.

What was Canada's first bestseller?

In 1835, Thomas Chandler Haliburton began submitting a series of comical sketches about a Yankee peddlar named Sam Slick to the *Novascotian* newspaper. The next year the pieces were collected and published as *The Clockmaker*. The book went through many editions in Nova Scotia, the United States, Great Britain, and Germany. Today, Haliburton is often described as the father of North American humour.

Susanna Moodie was one of the country's earliest and most-enduring writers.

What was the Family Compact?

The disparaging name was applied to a small group of elites who dominated governmental, bureaucratic, and judicial positions in Upper Canada. The origins of the group can be traced back to Lieutenant Governor Simcoe's attempts to establish an Upper Canadian aristocracy. By 1837, the exclusiveness of the group provoked a growing number of people to demand responsible government.

Who published the "Colonial Advocate"?

William Lyon Mackenzie began publishing the paper in 1824. Viewed as the mouthpiece of the reform movement in Upper Canada, the *Colonial Advocate* ceased publication when his press was destroyed and his type was thrown in Lake Ontario.

Who was Samuel Strickland?

Often overshadowed by his famous sisters, Susanna Moodie and Catharine Parr Traill, Samuel Strickland was a successful pioneer in Upper Canada. He encouraged and supported his sisters and their husbands in their emigration to Canada. Strickland published his own memoir, *Twenty-seven Years in Canada West*.

Which two sisters became famous for their pioneer memoirs?

Susanna Moodie and Catharine Parr Traill were born into a family of writers in 19th-century England. In 1832, they emigrated with their husbands to Upper Canada, settling in the backwoods of what is now Ontario. The sisters wrote several books recording their experiences as pioneers. Susanna Moodie's *Roughing It in the Bush* and Catharine Parr Traill's *The Backwoods of Canada* are seen as cornerstones in Canadian literature.

Who joined the British side to fight for a Native homeland?

HAVING STRUGGLED FOR YEARS WITH AMERICANS WHO HAD ENCROACHED in his tribe's territory, Shawnee chief Tecumseh allied himself with the British in the war. He believed that a British victory would help him achieve his goal of a large-scale Native confederacy that would be strong enough to withstand aggressive American troops and settlers.

Who won the war?
Although both sides claimed victory at the end of the war, it is usually accepted that the Canadians and British won the War of 1812. The United States failed to achieve their objective of gaining new territory.

Who was Wacousta?
Wacousta is the main character in John Richardson's novel of the same name set during the War of 1812. Some believe that Wacousta is based on John Norton, Teyoninhokorawen, a Mohawk chief.

Tecumseh was one of the greatest military heroes in Canadian history.

Who said that taking Canada would be "a matter of mere marching"?
Former US president Thomas Jefferson made the bold claim. His words came back to haunt him after the first battle ended in defeat for the Americans.

What sparked the war?
The official reason for the American declaration of war was British treatment of American ships during the Napoleonic Wars. However, many historians believe that the United States saw an opportunity to expand their territory while the British Army and Navy were occupied on the European continent.

Sir Samuel Cunard's transatlantic steamship line led the way in bringing visitors to Canada from abroad.

When was the War of 1812?
Despite its name, the War of 1812 lasted from June 18, 1812 until December 24, 1814.

What was the battle that saved Canada?
The Battle of Crysler's Farm, fought in Upper Canada on November 11, 1813, is often considered the most serious defeat in American plans to take Canada. A greatly outnumbered Canadian and British force was victorious over 8,000 American troops, the largest army assembled by the United States prior to the American Civil War.

Whose house was burnt to the ground?
On August 24, 1814, troops invaded Washington DC, burning several government buildings including the official residence of the President of the United States. The house wasn't rebuilt until 1817.

Which War of 1812 veteran founded a steamship line?

NOVA SCOTIAN SIR SAMUEL CUNARD FOUNDED THE CUNARD LINE, ONE OF the leading passenger lines. In the early 19th century, Cunard became wealthy by building sailing ships that he used for trade. He soon abandoned sail for steam, becoming the leading operator of transatlantic steamships.

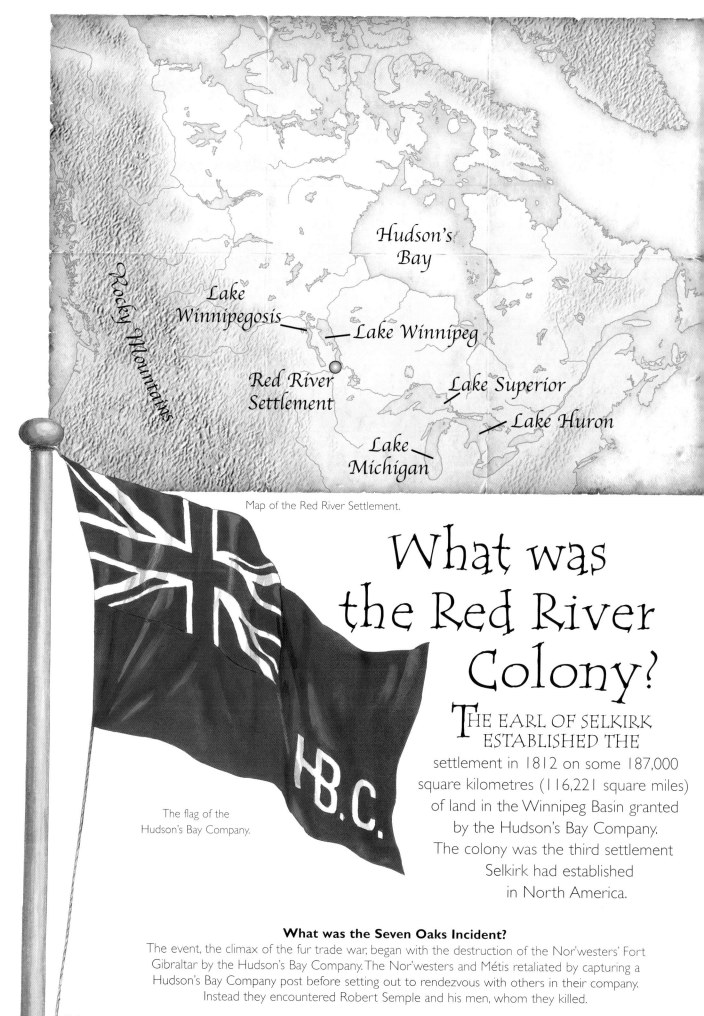

Map of the Red River Settlement.

The flag of the
Hudson's Bay Company.

What was the Red River Colony?

THE EARL OF SELKIRK ESTABLISHED THE

settlement in 1812 on some 187,000 square kilometres (116,221 square miles) of land in the Winnipeg Basin granted by the Hudson's Bay Company. The colony was the third settlement Selkirk had established in North America.

What was the Seven Oaks Incident?

The event, the climax of the fur trade war, began with the destruction of the Nor'westers' Fort Gibraltar by the Hudson's Bay Company. The Nor'westers and Métis retaliated by capturing a Hudson's Bay Company post before setting out to rendezvous with others in their company. Instead they encountered Robert Semple and his men, whom they killed.

Who saved the settlers?

ILL-PREPARED AND UNSUITED FOR THEIR new environment, the Red River Colony settlers suffered. It was only through the assistance of the Nor'westers and Saulteaux Chief Peguis that they were able to eke out a subsistence.

Who was Miles Macdonnell?

Selkirk's choice as Governor for his new colony, Macdonnell led the initial settlers to the Red River in 1812. An emotionally unstable man, Macdonnell's belligerent attitude led immediately to conflicts with the Nor'westers and Métis in the region.

Chief Peguis was also known as William King.

Who was Robert Semple?

Semple was a travel writer whose work caught the attention of the Earl of Selkirk. Although he was clearly unqualified for the demands of the position he was made the second Governor of Selkirk's colony.

Why did the Nor'westers view the settlement with suspicion?

Although they initially assisted the settlers, the Nor'westers believed that the Red River Colony might be a base from which the Hudson's Bay Company was intending to penetrate their territory.

What was the Pemmican Proclamation?

Just over a year into the settlement's life, Governor Macdonnell issued a proclamation prohibiting the export of provisions from the colony. Unable to function under the new law, the Nor'westers retaliated by encouraging many colonists back to Upper Canada. Later, they arrested Macdonnell, causing the remaining settlers to leave. The settlement was then burned to the ground.

What happened to the Red River Colony?

After the battle at Seven Oaks, a series of retaliations and lawsuits was launched. The death of Selkirk brought about a cessation of hostilities between the two companies, allowing them to become one. The colony was gradually populated by retired fur traders and Métis. Selkirk's family eventually transferred the land back to the Hudson's Bay Company.

Publisher William Lyon Mackenzie was the leader of the rebellion in Upper Canada and first Mayor of Toronto.

Which Canadian women were the first to win the right to vote?

Between 1809 and 1849, women who owned property in Quebec could vote in municipal elections. After the right was withdrawn, no Canadian women had the right to vote for over five decades. In January 1916, women in Manitoba received the right to vote in provincial elections. Although most other provinces soon followed Manitoba's lead, women in Quebec weren't able to vote in provincial elections until 1940.

What was the Annexation Manifesto?

In 1849, a group of Montreal businessmen and merchants drew up the Annexation Manifesto, advocating that the Canadian colonies sever their ties with Great Britain and join the United States. Although the threat was a rather obvious attempt at trying to extract concessions from Great Britain, it later haunted future Prime Minister Sir John Abbott, one of its signatories.

What were the Rebellions of 1837?

THE REBELLIONS WERE STRUGGLES BETWEEN REFORM-MINDED CITIZENS IN THE Canadas and their respective governors and elites. Led by Louis-Joseph Papineau, the rebellion in Lower Canada was particularly bloody, resulting in the deaths of over 100 men. In Upper Canada, the rebellion led by William Lyon Mackenzie was much more modest in size.

What is "responsible government"?

A responsible government is one that is answerable to its electors. Neither Upper or Lower Canada had enjoyed such a government as they were ruled by a colonial authority.

How did the economy contribute to the Rebellions?

Beginning in 1836, North America suffered almost two years of depression. The effects were particularly harsh in Upper and Lower Canada, where the market for farming goods dwindled, leading to further discontent.

Which side won in the Rebellions?

Although both Papineau and Mackenzie were defeated and went into exile, the momentum for change could not be stopped. Responsible government was achieved within a decade and the two men returned to Canada shortly thereafter.

Which American President used a slogan to threaten Canada?

In 1848, President James Polk wanted to make southern Canada part of the United States by moving the border north to the 54th parallel, 40th minute. He used the cry "54.40 or Fight!" as part of his campaign.

The rebellion in Lower Canada. Fighting broke out in November 1837 and ended one month later.

What was the Durham Report?

THE DOCUMENT WAS THE RESULT OF AN INVESTIGATION BY JOHN GEORGE

Lambton, first Earl of Durham, into the causes of the Rebellions of 1837. In his report, Durham made a number of recommendations, including the union of Upper and Lower Canada, the granting of responsible government, and the unification of municipal institutions. While many of Durham's recommendations can be seen as enlightened, he has gone down as something of a villain in Canadian history for proposing the assimilation of French Canadians.

What was the Province of Canada?
In 1841, Upper and Lower Canada were once again united, forming the Province of Canada. The union put French-speaking Canadians in a minority, and ultimately proved unworkable. In 1867, Ontario and Quebec again became separate provinces when they joined with Nova Scotia and New Brunswick in forming the Dominion of Canada.

Which British colony first achieved responsible government?
In 1848, Nova Scotia was granted responsible government. Prior to this, a governor chosen by the British government held almost all of the power.

With the passing of the American Fugitive Slave Act, slaves' attempts to escape became more dangerous.

When did slavery end in Canada?

ALTHOUGH JOHN GRAVES SIMCOE ABOLISHED SLAVERY IN UPPER Canada in 1793, his legislation failed to free those who were already slaves. It wasn't until 1834, when an act of the British Parliament abolished slavery throughout the Empire, that Canadian slaves became free.

What was the Underground Railroad?
The Underground Railroad was an informal network of shelters and people who assisted fugitive slaves. Initially, assistance was given to slaves escaping the slave states of the American South to the northern states.

What was the American Fugitive Slave Act?
Passed in 1850, the American Fugitive Slave Act made it illegal to harbour runaway slaves anywhere in the United States. As a result, Canada became the last stop on the Underground Railroad.

What was the "Provincial Freeman"?

Established in 1853 in Windsor, Ontario, the "Provincial Freeman" was a weekly newspaper that covered the lives of Canadian blacks and promoted the cause of black refugees. Its founder, Mary Ann Shadd, was the first woman to edit a North American newspaper.

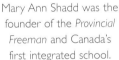
Mary Ann Shadd was the founder of the *Provincial Freeman* and Canada's first integrated school.

How many slaves escaped to Canada?
Although it's not possible to know the exact number, it's estimated that 30,000 to 40,000 slaves managed to escape to Canada between 1800 and 1860.

Who was Josiah Henson?
A slave in Maryland, Henson escaped to Canada with his wife and children in 1830. He founded the black settlement of Dawn, Ontario, and served as its spiritual leader. Henson's 1849 autobiography, *The Life of Josiah Henson*, was allegedly read by Harriet Beecher Stowe, inspiring her best-selling novel, *Uncle Tom's Cabin*.

What prompted Shadd to return to the United States?
Born a free black in the United States, Shadd only left for Canada after the passage of the Fugitive Slave Act. During the American Civil War, she returned to the United States and became a recruiter in the Union army.

Which woman was known as "Moses"?
Arguably the most famous conductor on the Underground Railroad, Harriet Tubman became known as "Moses" for leading her people to freedom. Born into slavery, she escaped at the age of about thirty. Over a period of nearly two decades she helped hundreds flee slavery. For eight of those years she used St Catharines, Ontario as her base.

Who was the "first across the continent"?

Sir Alexander Mackenzie.

IN 1793, EXPLORER ALEXANDER MACKENZIE BECAME THE first known person north of Mexico to reach the Pacific by crossing overland.

Which river did Mackenzie name "River Disappointment"?
Mackenzie's disappointing river is the one that was eventually named after him. The explorer was frustrated that the Mackenzie River led to the Arctic Ocean and not the Pacific Ocean, as he had hoped.

The doomed Franklin Expedition was last sighted in late July 1845.

Whom did a horse kick?

Sir James Hector, a medical doctor and member of the Palliser expedition, was kicked in the chest by a packhorse as he struggled to lead it out of a river. The accident gave Kicking Horse Pass its name. Two decades later, the pass was the route chosen through the Rocky Mountains by the Pacific railway.

Who were killed by their food?

Although the fate of John Franklin's men remains a mystery, it is known that several died of lead poisoning from canned foods. A relatively new process at the time, the cans had been soldered with lead.

Whose ships were the Terror and the Erebus?

In the early 19th century, great Britain continued to pursue the dream of a Northwest Passage across North America. In 1845 the HMS *Erebus* and HMS *Terror*, under the command of John Franklin, set out to look for the elusive passage. The ships were never seen again.

Who is known as "The Greatest of Canadian Geographers"?

David Thompson earned the honour for having spent 34 years exploring and mapping the main trading routes between the St Lawrence River and the Pacific Ocean. Much of what we know of the geography of western Canada was first recorded by Thompson.

Who finally travelled the Northwest Passage?

The passage remained elusive until 1906 when Norwegian adventurer Roald Amundsen completed his three-year journey from the Atlantic to the Pacific Ocean.

Where is "the open polar sea"?

Well into the 19th century, explorers who searched for the Northwest Passage were convinced they would find the "open polar sea," an ice-free body of water through which they could reach the Pacific Ocean. Unfortunately, the open polar sea only existed in their imaginations.

Building a Nation

WESTERN CANADA
THE NEW ELDORADO

THIS IS YOUR OPPORTUNITY TO BUY
YOUR OWN FARM

DECIDE ON CANADA NOW!

Who were the Fathers of Confederation?

The fathers are the men who attended the three

conferences that led to Confederation. Among the 36 men were George Brown, George-Étienne Cartier, Sir John A Macdonald, Thomas D'Arcy McGee, Oliver Mowat, Sir Étienne-Pascal Taché, and Charles Tupper.

Why was the first conference held on Prince Edward Island?

The first conference was held in Charlottetown because the delegates from Prince Edward Island were not interested enough in the discussions to leave the island.

Why is Canada a "Dominion"?

At the time of Confederation, Sir John A Macdonald had proposed that the new country be called the Kingdom of Canada, but some feared offending America's anti-monarchist sentiments. Like the country's motto ("From sea to sea"), the word "dominion" comes from a Biblical psalm: "He shall have dominion also from sea to sea …" Until 1982, Canada Day was known as Dominion Day.

The more prominent Fathers of Confederation:
Front row, left to right: Robert Dickey, Alexander Galt, George Coles, William Henry, Edward Palmer, and William Steeves.

Middle row, left to right: Alexander Campbell, George Brown, John A Macdonald, Jonathan McCully, John Gray, John Hamilton Gray, Edward Barron Chandler, and Samuel Leonard Tilley.

Back row, left to right: William McDougall, Hector-Louis Langevin, Charles Tupper, Andrew Archibald Macdonald, William Henry Pope, Thomas D'Arcy McGee, John Mercer Johnston, Adams G Archibald, and George-Étienne Cartier.

What names were considered for the new country?

Although Canada was always the most popular, New Britain, Britannia, Borealia, Cabotia, Laurentia, Superior, Acadia, Hochelaga, Colonia, Canadia, Columbia, Norland, Transatlantia, and Victorialand were among the many proposed names. Perhaps the most unusual suggestions were Tuponia (an acronym for The United Provinces of North America) and Efsiga (which uses the first letters of England, France, Scotland, Ireland, Germany, and Aboriginal lands).

What did Macdonald fear would happen to Rupert's Land?

THE NEW PRIME MINISTER BELIEVED THAT THE VAST TERRITORY TO THE WEST and north could fall into American hands, destroying his vision of a country stretching from the Atlantic to the Pacific. He sent his friend and political ally George-Étienne Cartier to England to seek the purchase of Rupert's Land.

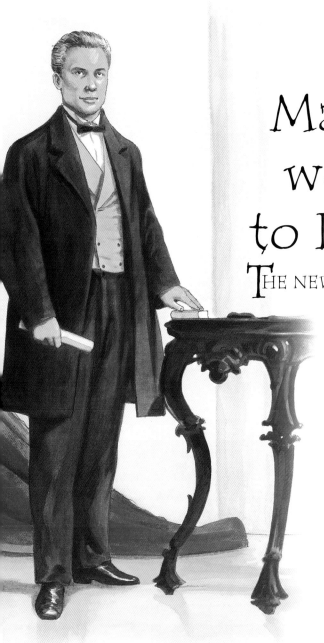

Father of Confederation Sir George-Étienne Cartier was the leading French Canadian politician of his day.

What reminder of the Father of Canada was discovered at the time of Confederation?

In 1867, the astrolabe of Samuel de Champlain was unearthed by a 14-year-old farmer ploughing a field near Cobden, Ontario. The explorer would have used the instrument to tell time and measure latitude over 150 years earlier.

What were the conferences leading to Confederation?

The conferences were named after their locations: the Charlottetown Conference, the Quebec Conference, and the London Conference. The Charlottetown Conference was held at Province House, the seat of Prince Edward Island's government.

Who are the "Confederation Poets"?

Bliss Carman, Wilfred Campbell, Archibald Lampman, Sir Charles G D Roberts, and Duncan Campbell Scott were prominent poets in the late 19th century. All five men were born in the years leading up to Confederation.

Who was the first Prime Minister?

Sir John A Macdonald was Canada's first prime minister. He held office from 1867 to 1873 and again from 1878 to 1891. Macdonald was born on January 11, 1815 in Glasgow, Scotland and died in office on June 6, 1891.

Why wasn't Prince Edward Island one of the original provinces?

At the time of Confederation, Prince Edward Island was an extremely prosperous colony with lucrative fishing, forestry, and shipbuilding industries. It did not join Canada until six years later, having accumulated a large debt from the construction of a railway across the island. The most important condition of Prince Edward Island entering into Confederation was that the Canadian government would take over the debt.

How did Ottawa become Canada's capital?

Prior to Confederation several cities, Kingston, Montreal, Toronto, and Quebec City, served as the capital of the Province of Canada. In 1857, on the advice of the Canadian Parliament, Queen Victoria chose Ottawa as the permanent capital. The small lumber city was chosen primarily because it was considered easy to defend against American invasion. Construction of the Parliament Buildings took six years and was not completed until 1866. The following year, Ottawa became the capital of the new Dominion of Canada.

Donald Smith drives the last spike of the Pacific Railway.

Who was Sir William Cornelius Van Horne?

An American with extensive experience in building railways, Van Horne was hired by the Canadian Pacific Railway to supervise its construction. He later served as president and chairman of the board of the railway. Van Horne founded Canadian Pacific Hotels and, as an amateur architect, assisted in the planning of the Banff Springs Hotel and the Château Frontenac.

Who made the trains run on time?

Sir Sanford Fleming was a chief surveyor for the Pacific railway. He was also a leading inventor, scientist, and engineer during a period in which every major centre set its own time. Frustrated after missing a train, Fleming proposed that the world be divided into 24 equal time zones. The idea, which he called "standard time," was adopted in 1884.

What was the Last Spike?

THE LAST SPIKE WAS THE FINAL SPIKE USED IN THE CONSTRUCTION OF the Canadian Pacific Railway. It was struck by Donald Smith, the principal shareholder in the railway, at Craigellachie, British Columbia on November 7, 1885. After the ceremony, the spike was presented to the president of the Canadian Pacific Railway, Edward Beatty, but was later stolen.

What promise was made to British Columbia?

The country's western-most province joined the Confederation after being assured that a Pacific railway would be started within two years and completed within ten.

What was the Pacific Scandal?

In 1872, a contract for the construction of the Pacific railway was awarded to a syndicate headed by Sir Hugh Allan, a Canadian shipowner and financier. Allan had been a heavy contributor to Sir John A Macdonald's successful campaign in the 1872 general election. Macdonald's opponents accused him of having awarded the contract in return for this financial support. In 1873, the charges led to the resignation of the Conservative government and to the cancellation of the contract.

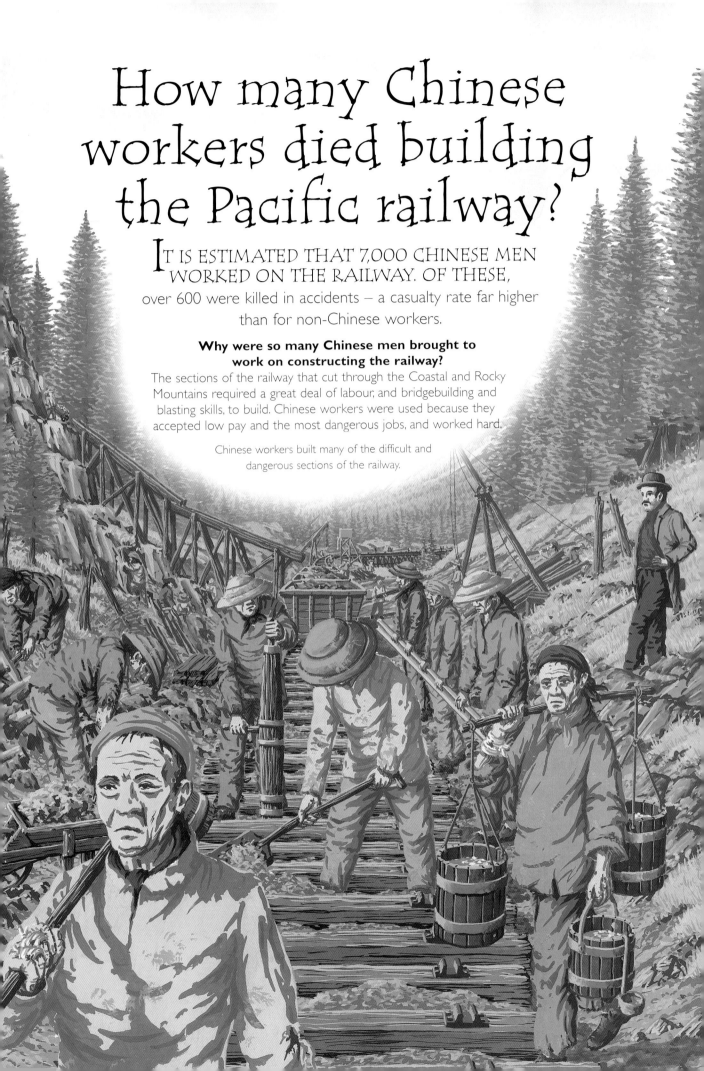

How many Chinese workers died building the Pacific railway?

It is estimated that 7,000 Chinese men worked on the railway. Of these, over 600 were killed in accidents – a casualty rate far higher than for non-Chinese workers.

Why were so many Chinese men brought to work on constructing the railway?
The sections of the railway that cut through the Coastal and Rocky Mountains required a great deal of labour, and bridgebuilding and blasting skills, to build. Chinese workers were used because they accepted low pay and the most dangerous jobs, and worked hard.

Chinese workers built many of the difficult and dangerous sections of the railway.

What is the motto of the force?
The RCMP motto is *Maintiens le droit*. While there is no official English version, it is commonly translated from the French as "Maintain the right" or "Uphold the law."

What horrific event led directly to the creation of the force?
Although Sir John A Macdonald's idea of a national police force had been under consideration since 1869, the North-West Mounted Police came into being as a result of the 1873 murder of 36 Assiniboine by American and Canadian hunters. The incident has come to be known as the Cypress Hills Massacre.

What was the original name of the RCMP?

The force was to be called the North-West Mounted Rifles, but this was changed by Sir John A Macdonald to the North-West Mounted Police. In 1904, King Edward VII honoured the force with the prefix "Royal." The Royal North-West Mounted Police became the Royal Canadian Mounted Police in 1920.

Who was the Lion of the North?
Sir Samuel Steele earned the title "Lion of the North" during his years serving with the North-West Mounted Police. A veteran of the Fenian Raids and the Red River Rebellion, he was part of the March West and is often credited with its success. In 1885, he became Superintendent of the force and later played an important role in establishing order during the Klondike Gold Rush.

A participant in the Long March in an early NWMP uniform.

How long was the Long March?

The march began in Dufferin, Manitoba, on July 8, 1874 when approximately 275 Mounties and an unknown number of Métis began moving west. The column, which also consisted of as many as 310 horses, 181 wagons and carts, 90 cows, and 142 oxen, often stretched out over several kilometres. The force arrived at their destination, Fort Whoop-Up in present-day southern Alberta, three months later in October.

Who was Jerry Potts?

A Métis, Jerry Potts was the force's guide through the unfamiliar Canadian west. He proved himself indispensable and was offered a permanent position with the force. His career with the North-West Mounted Police lasted 22 years.

What was Fort Macleod?

BUILT BY THE MOUNTIES AT THE END OF THE LONG MARCH, FORT MACLEOD was the first North-West Mounted Police post. It was named after James Macleod, the force's second in command.

What was Charles Dickens' connection to the force?

Francis Dickens, a son of the famous English novelist, was an early member of the North-West Mounted Police. As the result of pressure placed by Lord Dufferin, the Governor General of Canada and a family friend, Dickens joined the force in 1874. His career was marred by ineptitude, directly leading to the death of one of his men and the abandonment of Fort Pitt to Chief Big Bear during the North West Rebellion. He was discharged in 1886, leaving behind one of the sorriest records in the history of the force.

Fort Macleod was located in present-day Alberta.

What caused the Red River Rebellion?

C ALLED THE RED RIVER RESISTANCE
BY MANY MÉTIS, THE 1870 EVENT
was precipitated by the Hudson's Bay Company's
sale of Rupert's Land to the government of
Canada. Negotiations between the two parties
had ignored those living in the Red River
Colony. Before the Métis were consulted,
a governor and non-elected council were
appointed to rule the territory.

To which political party did Louis Riel belong?
Although Riel was elected as a Member of Parliament
in an 1873 by-election and again in the federal election
of 1874, he belonged to no party. However, he later
joined the Republican Party during his second period
of self-imposed exile in the United States.

Was Riel insane?
During Riel's trial on the charge of high treason,
the Métis leader's lawyers argued that he
was insane. However, Riel's eloquent
address to the jury appeared to
indicate a man in full possession
of his faculties. Riel was hanged
on November 16, 1885.

Why did Riel return to Canada?
In 1884, Riel was asked to return
by the Métis of Saskatchewan to
take up their cause. The Métis had
been unsuccessful in their
attempts at achieving Canadian
government recognition of their
traditional land.

Louis Riel (shown ab
on trial for high trea

How did Riel become leader of the Métis?

In 1869, the people of the Red River settlement formed a provisional government, choosing Riel as its leader. The following year, the provisional government formed the territory of Assiniboia, and declared its intention to negotiate with Canada to join Confederation as a fully fledged province. A year later, it did join as the Province of Manitoba.

Who considered himself "The Prophet of the New World"?

During his time as a patient in a Quebec asylum, Louis Riel began referring to himself as "The Prophet of the New World." Riel believed that he had been chosen by God to lead the Métis people.

Who was Sir William McDougall?

Appointed first Lieutenant Governor of Rupert's Land, McDougall is often blamed for sparking the Red River Rebellion by authorizing a survey of the area that ignored the property lines of the Métis farms.

Chief Big Bear was the leader of the Plains Cree during the North West Rebellion of 1885.

Who rejected an alliance with Riel?

CREE CHIEFS BIG BEAR AND POUNDMAKER rejected the Métis leader's overtures, primarily because they did not like his strategy of resorting to arms in order to achieve his goals.

Which North West Rebellion leader was a star in Buffalo Bill Cody's Wild West Show?

Gabriel Dumont was the most accomplished strategist of the Rebellion, winning the battles at Duck Lake and Fish Creek in 1885. He fled to the United States as the Rebellion failed and performed as a marksman in Buffalo Bill Cody's show. He returned to Canada in 1888 after an amnesty was granted for the rebels.

What was discovered at Bonanza Creek?

GOLD! THREE PROSPECTORS, SKOOKUM JIM, TAGISH CHARLIE, AND GEORGE Carmack, discovered the precious metal on August 17, 1896, sparking the Klondike Gold Rush – the greatest gold rush in Canadian history.

These two Klondike goldseekers are panning for gold.

How many people took part in the Klondike Gold Rush?
Although accurate numbers were not kept, it is certain that over 100,000 amateur goldseekers left for the Yukon in the 24 months that followed the initial strike. During that period, more wealth was spent in an effort to reach the Klondike than would be mined for the next five years.

Who signed the Numbered Treaties?

From 1871 to 1921, the Canadian government negotiated a series of eleven numbered treaties with the country's Native Peoples. The treaties allotted reserve land and covered agreements concerning education, health, agricultural equipment, gifts, annuities, and protection against famine.

What was the Alaska Boundary Dispute?

In the late 19th century, there was considerable disagreement involving the border between the Alaska Panhandle and British Columbia. In 1903, an international tribunal of three Americans, two Canadians, and a British jurist, Lord Alverstone, resolved the dispute. In the final decision, Alverstone endorsed the American claim, sparking a nationwide wave of protest.

Who became an Italian opera singer?

Quebecer Marie-Emma Lajeunesse was internationally famous as Dame Emma Albani. She first performed in Montreal at the age of nine. In 1869 she made her Italian operatic debut and soon achieved international fame as "the queen of song." Dame Albani sang on all the great opera stages before her retirement.

Which Prime Minister died while dining with Queen Victoria?

Sir John Thompson died of a heart attack in 1894 as he sat down to dine with the Queen at Windsor Castle. Sir John A Macdonald is the only other Prime Minister to die in office.

Which Premier was the son of a Prime Minister?

Sir Hugh John Macdonald, the son of Sir John A Macdonald, led the Manitoba Conservative Party to victory in the 1899 provincial election. A talented lawyer, he also served in the House of Commons when his father was Prime Minister.

The government used posters as a means of luring farmers to Western Canada.

Who encouraged the settling of the west?

THE VICTORY OF WILFRID LAURIER IN 1896 BROUGHT WITH IT A HUGE INFLUX OF immigrants to the Prairie provinces. An aggressive advertising campaign directed toward experienced farmers was implemented.

Which is Canada's all-time bestselling book?

Prince Edward Island's L M Montgomery.

L M MONTGOMERY'S "ANNE OF GREEN GABLES" WAS first published in 1908. The novel about an unwanted orphan has been translated into over 15 languages. The book has never been out of print and is now available in more editions than at any other time in its history.

What was Canada's first feature film?
Evangeline, based on Henry Wadsworth Longfellow's long narrative poem, was the first feature film shot in Canada. The film premiered in Halifax in 1913. Unfortunately, no known copies of the film have survived.

What is "the champagne of ginger ales"?
Canada Dry is described as the champagne of ginger ales. Toronto pharmacist John J McLaughlin created the popular drink in 1907. He used the word "dry" to indicate that his ginger ale was not sweet.

Which sporting goods company made an electric car?
In 1903, the Canada Cycle and Motor Company of Toronto began making an electric car called the Ivanhoe. Today, the company is better-known by its initials – CCM.

Which two provinces share the same birthday?
Alberta and Saskatchewan were created as the eighth and ninth provinces through an act of Parliament on September 1, 1905. Their territories were previously covered by the districts of Athabaska, Alberta, Saskatchewan, Assiniboia, and the Northwest Territories.

What kicked off the Calgary Stampede?
The first Stampede was launched on September 2, 1912 with a parade of cowboys, cowgirls, and Native Canadians. Although it was a great success, the second Stampede was not held until 1919.

Which shipwreck was worse than the *Titanic*?
On May 29, 1914, 1,014 people died when *The Empress of Ireland* sank in the St Lawrence River. Surrounded by a dense fog, the ocean liner was struck by a Norwegian coal steamer bound for Quebec City.

What were silk trains?
From the 1890s until the Second World War, silk trains carried raw silk from the Vancouver docks to silk mills on the American East Coast. Because their contents were so valuable, the trains carried armed guards and rarely stopped. To prevent the silk cocoons from spoiling, the trains travelled at very high speeds and were given the right of way over all others.

Which doctor became famous for her work in heart disease?

Born in 1869, Maude Abbott was one of Canada's earliest female doctors. Although prejudice against women practicing medicine limited her opportunities, she achieved an international reputation as a leading heart specialist.

Who was "America's Sweetheart"?

Although she was born in Toronto in 1892, "America's Sweetheart" was silent film star Mary Pickford. She began her acting career at the age of eight and made her first film in 1909. She continued to play children's roles well into adulthood, long after she'd earned her nickname.

Who was the first Canadian airplane pilot?

On March 12, 1908, engineer Frederick Walker flew a biplane at Hammondsport, New York. Walker was one of five men, including fellow Canadian John McCurdy, who built the plane. The following year, McCurdy became the first to pilot a plane on Canadian soil at Baddeck, Nova Scotia.

Why did Halifax become the City of Sorrow?

As the closest major port city, Halifax became headquarters of retrieval efforts after the 1912 sinking of the *Titanic*. Ships departing from the port recovered the bodies of 328 victims, burying 119 at sea. The remaining bodies were returned to Halifax where they were placed in a temporary morgue set up in a curling rink. In the end, 150 of the *Titanic's* victims were buried in Halifax cemeteries.

Who believed in "Power at Cost"?

Millionaire industrialist Sir Adam Beck fought to create a publicly owned electric utility. In 1906, the Hydro-Electric Power Commission of Ontario was created, with Beck as chairman. Ontario Hydro, as it became known, was the first publicly owned electric utility in the world.

Who claimed the north?

IN 1909, CAPTAIN JOSEPH-ELZÉAR BERNIER UNVEILED A TABLET ON MELVILLE ISLAND, proclaiming Canadian sovereignty over the entire Arctic Archipelago, from the mainland to the North Pole.

Although the Arctic Islands had long been considered Canadian territory, it wasn't until 1909 that they were officially claimed.

Suffragettes led the struggle for women's voting rights.

Mrs. Nellie L. McClung

LECTURE

On Womans Suffrage

THURSDAY, JUNE

Who was the first woman elected to Parliament?

Agnes Macphail was elected to the House of Commons in the 1921 general election, the first in which women could run for public office. Of the four women candidates in the election, only Macphail was successful. For 14 years she was the only woman Member of Parliament. She later served in the Ontario Legislature.

When was Canada's only General Strike?

The Winnipeg General Strike began on May 15, 1919 and lasted for 42 days. At its height, over 22,000 workers walked away from their jobs. The strike ended after its leaders were imprisoned. Four days later, the RCMP fired into a crowd of demonstrators, killing two men.

When did women first vote in federal elections?

IN THE 1917 FEDERAL ELECTION, FEMALE NURSES IN THE ARMED FORCES, women related to those fighting overseas, and women with considerable property were granted the vote. The next year, the vote extended to all women over the age of 21 and older. They first exercised their right to vote in the 1921 federal election.

Who was "The Canadian Hemingway"?

Morley Callaghan was compared to his friend, American writer Ernest Hemingway in an advertisement from his first publisher. Callaghan's first book, *Strange Fugitive*, was published in 1928.

Which house burnt in 1916?

The House of Commons, indeed the entire Centre Block of the Canadian Parliament, was destroyed by fire on February 3, 1916. The Parliamentary Library, its priceless collection of books, and several Members of Parliament were saved by closing heavy metal doors which separated it from the Centre Block. The House of Commons and the Senate were moved to the Victoria Museum – now the Canadian Museum of Nature – during the four years of reconstruction that followed.

When did Native Canadians first vote in federal elections?
Although the election of 1921 was the first in which Native Canadians could vote, they had to give up their treaty rights and registered Indian status to do so. The condition wasn't removed from election legislation until 1960.

What was the Persons Case?
In 1929, the English Judicial Committee of the Privy Council of the House of Lords, then Canada's final court of appeal, overturned a Supreme Court of Canada decision that women were not "qualified persons" within the meaning of the constitution.

When did the NHL begin moving south?
On November 1, 1924, the first NHL game was played in the United States. The Boston Bruins defeated the Montreal Maroons by a score of 2 to 1, but ended the season in last place.

Who was the "kid who couldn't miss"?
Billy Bishop, one of the greatest fighter pilots of the First World War, earned the nickname for shooting down 72 enemy planes. Only Germany's Manfred von Richthofen, nicknamed the Red Baron, shot down more planes.

What "temporary" measure was put into place during the First World War?

ON SEPTEMBER 20, 1917, INCOME TAX CAME INTO FORCE THROUGH THE INCOME TAX War Act. The tax was originally meant to assist only in paying for Canada's war effort.

Which future Governor General led a battalion?
Georges Vanier was one of the most decorated Canadians during the First World War. Enlisting as an officer he rose through the ranks and, in 1918, was made commander of the 22nd Battalion. After the war, Vanier had a brilliant military and diplomatic career. In 1959 he was appointed Governor General, the first French Canadian to hold the office.

Canadian soldiers fought in Europe during the First World War.

Who did the Prime Minister welcome to Quebec?

In 1943 and 1944, Prime Minister Mackenzie King played host to Prime Minister Winston Churchill and President Franklin Delano Roosevelt in Quebec City. The Quebec Conferences were the only chances that the latter two leaders had to discuss the war in person.

Who was the "Voice of Doom"?

CBC newscaster Lorne Greene was dubbed the "Voice of Doom" for his reports during the Second World War. Born and raised in Ottawa, Greene began a career in public performance while studying chemical engineering at Queen's University. He is best remembered outside the country as Ben Cartwright in *Bonanza*, a long-running television western.

Which province elected North America's first socialist government?

The Co-operative Commonwealth Federation became the first social democratic government after winning 47 of 53 seats in the 1944 Saskatchewan provincial election. Under the new Premier, Tommy Douglas, the government introduced public hospitalization and Medicare, removed taxes on food, and eliminated the provincial debt.

Which bestseller concerns the Halifax Explosion?

Published during the Second World War, *Barometer Rising* takes place during the time of the tragedy. The author, Hugh MacLennan, witnessed the explosion and its aftermath as a 10-year-old.

What was Operation Jubilee?

THE AUGUST 19, 1942 RAID ON DIEPPE, WHICH INVOLVED nearly 5,000 Canadians and over 1,000 British paratroopers, was code-named Operation Jubilee. One of the darkest episodes in Canadian history, the raid on the German-held French seaport was ill-planned and lacked the element of surprise. Over 900 Canadians were killed, with a total of 3,367 casualties, and 1,946 prisoners of war taken by the Germans.

A Canadian soldier in Second World War uniform.

Who drove Bennett Buggies?

BENNETT BUGGIES WERE CARS PULLED BY HORSES OR OXEN.

Prairie farmers who could not afford gasoline during the Great Depression drove them. The buggies were named after Prime Minister R B Bennett, whom many blamed for their economic hardships.

What was Trans-Canada Air Lines?

What was Trans-Canada Air Lines?
Founded in 1937, Trans-Canada Air Lines was a crown corporation established to provide air passenger and mail service. In 1965, the airline changed its name to Air Canada. The company was privatized by the Mulroney government in 1989.

What made the nickel copper?
During the Second World War Canada's nickel production was devoted to the war effort. In 1942 and 1943, the composition of the five-cent coin was changed from 99 percent nickel to a combination of copper and zinc. In 1944, the composition was again changed to chrome-plated steel. After the war, the nickel was again made from 99 percent nickel for a number of years. Since 2000, the coin has been made of steel and copper with nickel plating.

What caused the Great Depression?
The worst economic depression in Canadian history began on Black Tuesday, October 29, 1929, in New York. Shareholders in the market, realizing that their stocks were overvalued, panicked and sold their holdings for whatever they could get. The selling quickly spread to Montreal and Toronto, setting off a chain of events which resulted in a decade-long period of economic trial.

Prairie farmers were among the hardest hit during the Great Depression, and returned to their horses for transportation.

Which Newfoundland and Labrador airport was once the busiest in the world?
For much of the Second World War the airport at Happy Valley–Goose Bay, in Labrador, was the world's busiest. Constructed in 1941, it was used by the Canadian, British, and American governments as a transatlantic aircraft ferry facility.

Who was the last living Father of Confederation?

Although he was born in 1900, decades after the Charlottetown, Quebec, and London conferences, Joseph Smallwood was often referred to as a Father of Confederation for his work at bringing Newfoundland into Confederation. He later served as Premier of the newest province until 1972. Smallwood died in 1991.

When was Canada's first subway built?
Toronto's Yonge Street subway opened in 1954. At the time, the subway consisted of just one line and was little more than 7 kilometres (4.5 miles) long. Although only one line has been added in its five-decade history, it is now nearly nine times longer. Today the subway runs over 62 kilometres (38.5 miles) in length. The country's only other subway system, Montreal's Metro, opened in 1966. Several stations in Edmonton's Light Rapid Transit system and Vancouver's Skytrain are located underground.

Which question was asked of Newfoundlanders on July 22, 1948?
Voters were asked to choose between becoming a colony with a responsible government or Confederation with Canada. The Confederation option carried the day with just 52 percent of the votes.

When did Newfoundland join Confederation?
Newfoundland became a Canadian province on March 31, 1949. The original date selected was April 1, but this was changed so that the event wouldn't be taking place on April Fool's Day.

When were the last executions in Canada?
On December 11, 1962, two men were hanged at Toronto's Don Jail. Although no further executions were carried out, capital punishment wasn't abolished until 1976.

What was the Avro Arrow?

Considered by many to be one of the finest achievements in aviation history, the Avro Arrow was a delta-wing, supersonic, all-weather interceptor. Started with a program initiated in 1949, the Arrow incorporated dozens of advanced technical innovations that would be adopted in later planes. Less than a year after the first flight of a prototype, the Diefenbaker government, citing high costs, cancelled the program, and ordered the destruction of both planes and plans.

Early CBC dramas were broadcast live.

Which Canadian was the United States ambassador to India?

An adviser to a number of American Presidents, economist John Kenneth Galbraith was appointed ambassador by John F Kennedy. Among Galbraith's influential books are *The Affluent Society*, *Anatomy of Power*, and *The Culture of Contentment*.

What was the purpose of the St Lawrence Seaway?

Opened in 1959, the seaway allowed ocean-going ships and tankers to travel beyond Montreal to Canadian and American ports in the Great Lakes.

Which new political force was referred to as "the third party"?

In 1961, the New Democratic Party was formed out of the Co-operative Commonwealth Federation. Over the next three decades, the party held the third largest number of seats in the House of Commons. It often held the balance of power in minority government situations.

What went on the air for the first time in 1952?

On SEPTEMBER 6, 1952, THE CANADIAN BROADCASTING CORPORATION AIRED the country's first television programs from CBFT in Montreal. Initially a bilingual station, CBFT now broadcasts in French. The city's CBC English-language station is CBMT.

What was the Diefenbunker?

During the Cold War, the Central Emergency Government Headquarters, a four-storey subterranean office building, was built in 1959–61 outside Carp, Ontario. Nicknamed the Diefenbunker, the headquarters was designed to house key government figures – including then-Prime Minister John Diefenbaker – in the event of a nuclear war. The Diefenbunker was closed in 1994 and is now protected as a National Historic Site.

Canadian troops in Montreal during the October Crisis.

What was the October Crisis?

THE OCTOBER CRISIS IS THE NAME GIVEN TO THE EVENTS OF OCTOBER THROUGH December 1970, beginning with the October 5th kidnapping of British Trade Commissioner James Cross by the FLQ. The crisis intensified five days later when Quebec cabinet minister Pierre Laporte was kidnapped and killed. Eventually, Cross's kidnappers were discovered and, after a period of negotiation, were promised passage to Cuba. Laporte's murderers were later captured, tried, and convicted. They served prison terms of varying length.

What was the War Measures Act?

The Act, first implemented during the First World War, allowed for the limiting of personal liberties. Ottawa applied the Act during the October Crisis at the request of the Quebec government and the City of Montreal. Approximately 7,500 troops were deployed in Ottawa, Montreal, and Quebec City.

What was the Official Languages Act?

The 1969 Act declared English and French to be Canada's official languages. Among its many provisions, the Act ensured that both languages had equal status and privileges in all federal institutions.

Who were "The Boat People"?

The 1975 fall of the Thieu regime in Vietnam led many Vietnamese to flee the country. Over the next 10 years over 130,000 Vietnamese refugees found new homes in Canada.

What was the "Front de libération du Québec"?

Established in 1963, the FLQ was an organization dedicated to an independent, socialist Quebec. Over an eight-year period it used bombs, armed robbery, kidnapping, and murder as a means of meeting its objectives.

When did 18-year-olds receive the right to vote in federal elections?

In 1970, the Canada Elections Act lowered the voting age and the minimum age to be a candidate from 21 years. The first election in which 18-year-olds exercised their votes occurred in 1972. The closest in Canadian history, the election returned the Liberals to power with 109 seats, two more than the opposition Progressive Conservatives.

Who won the Nobel Prize for Literature?

Canadian-born Saul Bellow was the 1976 recipient of the prize. Bellow was born to Russian immigrant parents in Lachine, Quebec in 1915. His family moved to Montreal before relocating in the United States when Bellow was nine years old.

The Canadian Pavilion at Montreal's Expo '67 featured a dramatic pyramid called Katimavik, or "meeting place."

What is Canada's most expensive building?

Although original estimates for the cost of Montreal's Olympic Stadium were set at 120 million Canadian dollars, the total cost is expected to be just under 3 billion. Intended for the 1976 Summer Olympic Games, the construction was plagued by difficulties and was not completed until 1983. The debt for the building is scheduled to be paid off in 2006, in time for the 30th anniversary of the games.

What was the original site for Expo '67?

ALTHOUGH MONTREAL WAS IN THE RUNNING FOR THE WORLD FAIR in 1967, it was originally awarded to Moscow. The Soviet Union had intended Expo '67 as a celebration of the fiftieth anniversary of the October Revolution. Montreal won the right to hold the fair after Moscow pulled out for financial reasons.

What question was asked on May 20, 1980?

Quebec's Parti Québécois government asked Canadian residents of the province for a mandate to negotiate "sovereignty association" with the rest of Canada. A portion of the 108-word question assured voters that no changes would actually be made without approval in another referendum. Nearly 60 percent of voters rejected the request.

What was "sovereignty association"?

The term covered a Parti Québécois proposal in which Quebec would become an independent country while maintaining economic ties with the rest of Canada.

What was the "Shamrock Summit"?

Held in Quebec City in March 1985, the summit was a meeting between Prime Minister Brian Mulroney and President Ronald Reagan. It was at the Shamrock Summit that the idea of the Free Trade Agreement between Canada and the United States was first discussed. The Summit was so named because of the leaders' Irish heritage.

Where was the country's worst terrorist attack?

In 1985, 329 people were killed after a bomb exploded on an Air India flight. The plane, which was en route to New Delhi from Vancouver, Toronto, and Montreal, went down off the coast of Ireland. The event was the worst single terrorist attack prior to September 11, 2001.

What is the Assembly of First Nations?

Established in 1982, the assembly is the national representative organization of the First Nations.

Whose signatures appear on the 1982 Constitution Proclamation?

QUEEN ELIZABETH II, PIERRE ELLIOTT TRUDEAU (AS PRIME MINISTER), JEAN CHRÉTIEN (AS ATTORNEY GENERAL), and André Ouellet (as Registrar General) signed two copies of the proclamation of the repatriated Constitution. Signed during an outdoor ceremony on Parliament Hill, some of the signatures are smeared by raindrops.

Prime Minister Pierre Elliott Trudeau and Queen Elizabeth II sign the Constitution Proclamation.

Who coined the term "cyberspace"?

WILLIAM GIBSON FIRST USED THE WORD "cyberspace" in his 1984 debut novel, *Neuromancer*. Considered one of the finest contemporary science-fiction writers, Gibson is also the author of *Count Zero*, *Mona Lisa Overdrive*, and *Virtual Light*.

When did Canada achieve true independence?

Although most Canadians would agree that the country achieved sovereignty in 1867, the British Parliament retained the right to pass legislation affecting Canada. In 1931, the passage of the Statute of Westminster recognized Canada as equal to the United Kingdom, but permitted future acts to extend to Canada with the Dominion's consent. It wasn't until the Constitution Act of 1982 that British parliamentary power in Canada was brought to an end.

American-born William Gibson emigrated to Canada in 1969.

Who ran the Marathon of Hope?

On April 12, 1980, Terry Fox began a run from the Atlantic to the Pacific in an effort to raise money for cancer research. Fox had lost most of his right leg to cancer. On September 1, outside Thunder Bay, Ontario, he was forced to end his run. Although he died the following year, Fox's work continues through annual runs held in his name both in Canada and around the world.

What was the Meech Lake Accord?

Officially called the Constitutional Accord, the 1987 Meech Lake Accord was an attempt at obtaining Quebec's signature on the Constitution. The effort resulted in failure when it was not passed by the Manitoba and Newfoundland legislatures. A second attempt, popularly known as the Charlottetown Agreement, was defeated when put to a national referendum in 1992.

When did the country hold its breath?

In the second Quebec referendum in 1995, voters rejected the sovereignty option by a vote of 50.6 percent. The vote was much closer than federalists had predicted at the beginning of the campaign.

Who was the first woman to play in the National Hockey League?

In 1992, Manon Rheaume played goal for the Tampa Bay Lightning team in a pre-season game.

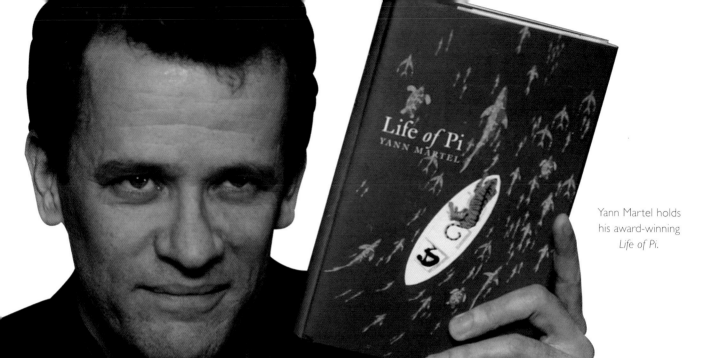

Yann Martel holds his award-winning *Life of Pi*.

Who won the 2002 Man Booker Prize?

CANADIAN YANN MARTEL WON THE PRIZE WITH HIS SECOND NOVEL,
Life of Pi. He was the third Canadian author to win the Man Booker, after Michael Ondaatje and Margaret Atwood.

Who is Canada's first parliamentary poet laureate?
In 2002, British Columbian George Bowering was chosen as the country's first poet laureate. A prolific writer, Bowering is one of the few writers to have won Governor General's awards for poetry *and* fiction.

What is Canada's most popular festival?
Attracting well over one million people each year, the Festival International de Jazz de Montréal is one of the largest jazz festivals in the world. Each summer several downtown streets are blocked off to accommodate hundreds of indoor and outdoor concerts.

What is the importance of the Nisga'a Treaty?
Implemented in 2000, the treaty ended a 114-year effort by the Nisga'a of British Columbia to regain some of their traditional lands. The treaty, the first in over a century, provided the tribe with approximately 2,000 square kilometres (1,243 square miles) of the Nass River Valley in the northern part of the province, rights to the surface and subsurface resources, and a share of the salmon from the Nass River.

Which party dominated federal politics in the 20th century?
From Wilfrid Laurier to Jean Chrétien, the Liberals were in power for a total of over 67 years. The party won 19 of the 29 federal elections held last century.

Which parties are currently represented in the House of Commons?
There are currently five political parties with seats in the House of Commons: the Liberal Party, the Canadian Reform Conservative Alliance, the Bloc Québécois, the New Democratic Party, and the Progressive Conservative Party. All five parties have the minimum fourteen seats required for Official Party Status. The Liberal Party has been in power since November 1993.

Which film won the 2001 Camera d'Or?
The award was won by *Atanarjuat*, also known as *The Fast Runner*, the first feature film written, produced, directed, and acted by Inuit. It was the first time a Canadian film had won the award.

Which "Canadian" is building the International Space Station?

IN 2001, THE FIRST CANADARM2 WAS INSTALLED ON THE International Space Station. An essential component, the Canadarm2 will be employed during every mission used in the station's construction. The original Canadarm first went into space upon the space shuttle *Columbia* in 1981. Including the Canadarm2, there are currently five Canadarms; a sixth was destroyed in the 1986 *Challenger* disaster.

What is the importance of "The Seventh Generation"?

The majority of Canada's First Nations hold the concept of the "Seventh Generation." In the decision-making process, consideration is placed as to how the decision will affect current and future members of the tribe seven generations hence.

Who is the first woman Chief of the Six Nations Confederacy?

Roberta Jamieson, the first aboriginal woman to earn a law degree in Canada, was elected Chief of Confederacy in 2001. She is the first woman to hold a position thought to be at least 450 years old.

Which Canadian cities have lost National Hockey League teams?

Since the establishment of the National Hockey League in 1917, a total of five Canadian cities have had teams either move or fold: Hamilton (the Tigers), Montreal (the Wanderers and Maroons), Ottawa (the original Senators), Quebec (the Bulldogs and the Nordiques), and Winnipeg (the Jets).

The Canadarm2 is a permanent part of the International Space Station.

War and Peacekeeping

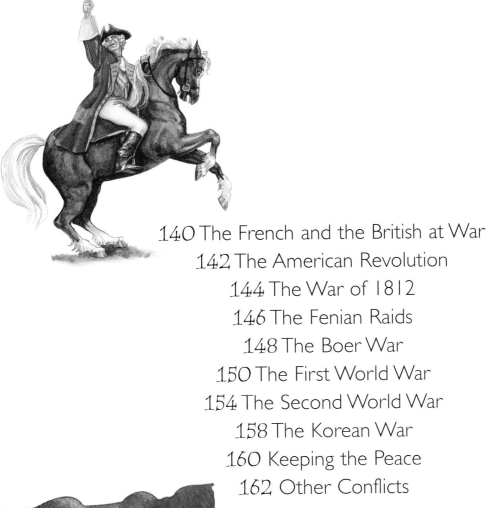

ROYAL CANADIAN
AIR FORCE

Come and
join us!

James Wolfe was commander of the British expedition that captured Quebec.

Lasting roughly from 1688 to 1763, the French and Indian Wars is the name given by some historians to fighting between Great Britain and France in their North American colonies. The hostilities were often extensions of major European wars: the War of the Grand Alliance (1688–97), the War of the Spanish Succession (1702–13), the War of the Austrian Succession (1739–48), and the Seven Years' War (1756–63).

When was Saint John's captured?

The French attacked the city during the War of the Spanish Succession in 1705. Three years later, the French captured Saint John's. It was France's greatest North American victory in the war.

What made Quebec so difficult to capture?

The settlement sat on a plateau bordered by a rocky cliff that was thought to be inaccessible from the St Lawrence River. Prior to the Battle of the Plains of Abraham, the city had been captured only once, by the Kirke brothers in 1629. In the century that followed, Quebec had grown more than a hundred times over and had become the only walled city on the continent.

Which treasure-seeker attacked New France?

Born to a poor family, as a young man William Phips married a wealthy widow. His fortunes increased greatly when he recovered 32 tonnes of silver from a shipwreck in the Caribbean. In 1690, he was ordered to attack Port-Royal and Quebec City. Although the latter campaign was a failure, Phips lived on to become Governor of Massachusetts. He held the office during the famous Salem witch trials of 1692.

How old was James Wolfe?

ALTHOUGH THE GENERAL WAS ONLY 32 YEARS OLD WHEN HE WAS KILLED ON the Plains of Abraham on September 13, 1759, he'd spent nearly two decades in the military. Born into a military family, at the age of fourteen Wolfe was appointed Second Lieutenant in his father's regiment of marines. He first saw the action of battle at the age of sixteen.

Why was the capture of Quebec considered so important?

Quebec was the political, administrative, and military centre of New France. The British correctly predicted that the capture of the settlement would lead to the fall of New France.

Which island did the French seek to retain at the end of the Seven Years' War?

During the treaty negotiations that brought an official end to the war, the French hoped to hold on to Cape Breton, but were forced to settle for the small islands of Saint-Pierre and Miquelon to the south of Newfoundland.

What was "The Indian Magna Carta"?

Also referred to as "The Indian Bill of Rights," the Royal Proclamation of 1763 established a framework for government in the lands the French had lost in the Seven Years' War. The document also set aside lands for First Nations peoples to the west of the Thirteen Colonies.

Which people were expelled during the French and Indian Wars?

After Acadia on the Bay of Fundy was ceded to Great Britain in 1713, work began on setting up a number of French forts along the border. The British grew increasingly concerned that France would attempt to take back the territory. In 1755, the Acadians were asked to swear an oath of allegiance to the British Crown. The great majority refused. Over 8,000 Acadians were deported.

What French feud worked in favour of the British?

What happened to the expelled Acadians?

The great majority of Acadians were scattered throughout the Thirteen Colonies and the British West Indies; others ended up in the French West Indies and Great Britain. However, most exiled Acadians managed to return home. Some undertook their return journeys within months of expulsion, while others had to wait several years.

A QUARREL BETWEEN LOUIS-JOSEPH MONTCALM AND THE MARQUIS de Vaudreuil-Cavagnal, the Governor of New France, contributed to the fall of Quebec. Although Montcalm was favoured in the French court, his request for an additional army of veterans was denied.

A painting of Montcalm's death. He actually died in bed behind city walls on September 14, 1759.

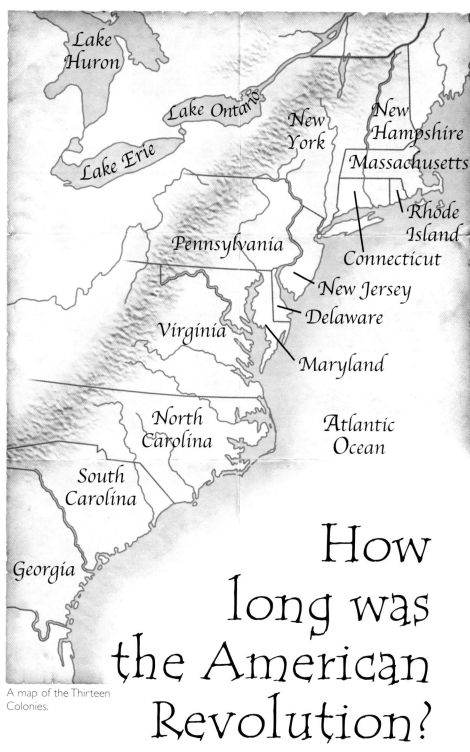

A map of the Thirteen Colonies.

How long was the American Revolution?

ALSO KNOWN AS THE AMERICAN WAR OF INDEPENDENCE, THE WAR BEGAN in Lexington, Massachusetts in 1775 and lasted until 1783. In 1783 American independence was officially recognized with the ratification of the Treaty of Paris.

What were the Thirteen Colonies?
The Thirteen Colonies refer to the British colonies to the south of Canada that united in revolution against the mother country. They were New Hampshire, Massachusetts, Rhode Island, Connecticut, New York, New Jersey, Pennsylvania, Delaware, Maryland, Virginia, North Carolina, South Carolina, and Georgia. Together they formed the thirteen original states of the United States of America.

What were the causes of the Revolution?
The American colonists had a number of grievances with Great Britain. Some colonies felt that the lands set aside for First Nations people in the Royal Proclamation of 1763 prevented westward expansion of their territories. The Thirteen Colonies were also angry over matters of taxation, administration, and the implementation of the Quebec Act.

What was the Continental Army?
Formed in 1775, the Continental Army and local militia were the main fighting forces of the Thirteen Colonies. The army was under the command of George Washington.

Why were the Thirteen Colonies opposed to the Quebec Act?
The 1774 act extended the southern and western boundaries of Canada to the Ohio and Mississippi rivers, territory desired by the colonies of Connecticut, Massachusetts, and Virginia. The act also legalized Catholicism and French civil law in the new British colony, both strongly opposed by many Protestants in the Thirteen Colonies.

Why did Canadians reject the Revolution?
In 1775, the Thirteen Colonies used a variety of means to encourage the French-speaking Canadians to join the Revolution; the church, Seigneurs, and a majority of merchants opposed the war. American forces later captured two forts in Canadian territory, sowing seeds of distrust amongst the Canadians.

Which governor assisted fleeing Loyalists?

SIR GUY CARLETON, LORD DORCHESTER, WAS GOVERNOR of Quebec during the outbreak of the American Revolution. In 1782, as the conflict was drawing to a close, he was appointed Commander-in-Chief of British forces at New York. Despite growing danger of an overwhelming American assault, Carleton refused to evacuate the city until the last Loyalists had been sent to safety.

Which city fell to the Americans?
The Continental Army under General George Montgomery captured Montreal in November 1775. That New Year's Eve, Montgomery and his top officers were killed in a failed attempt to take Quebec City. The Americans continued to hold Montreal until May 1776.

Which future traitor led the attack on Quebec?
Benedict Arnold was hand-picked by George Washington to lead an assault on the capital city of Montreal. Although Arnold was one of the great military minds of the Revolution, weather and disease worked against him. Despite the loss, Arnold's efforts were considered heroic. For five years he provided the Revolution with a number of important and impressive victories, before turning traitor in 1780.

Why were many Nova Scotians sympathetic to the Revolution?
Although the colony sided with the British, most of Nova Scotia's 20,000 citizens were immigrants from the Thirteen Colonies. At the Revolution's outbreak, many Nova Scotians met secretly to express their support for the Americans.

What turned Nova Scotia against the Thirteen Colonies?
Between 1776 and 1779, American privateers, owners of vessels who were licensed to wage war, raided nearly every outpost in Nova Scotia. In doing so, the privateers destroyed the private property of many who had previously been supportive of the Revolution.

Sir Guy Carleton was Governor of Quebec at the beginning of the American Revolution.

How many American states voted against the war of 1812?

SIX OF THE THEN-SEVENTEEN AMERICAN STATES VOTED AGAINST GOING TO WAR with Great Britain. Those that voted against had nothing to gain in terms of territory in the event of an American success.

What led the Americans to believe that the war would be easily won?

The United States believed British military forces would be too occupied with fighting Napoleon's armies in Europe to defend Canada properly. An ally of the United States, France acted in concert with the Americans during the opening days of the North American war.

What led to fires in Washington?

Public buildings, including the White House, were set alight in direct retaliation for the United States Army's 1813 looting of York – now known as Toronto – the capital of Upper Canada.

What reception did the Americans expect?

The government of American President James Madison believed that the Canadians would support their invaders. Their Secretary for War, William Eustis, declared: "We can take the Canadas without soldiers, we have only to send officers into the province and the people ... will rally round our standard."

Charles-Michel de Salaberry leads his troops into battle.

Who was "The Heroine of the War of 1812"?

While attending to her ill husband, Laura Secord overheard American invaders discussing a planned surprise attack 32 kilometres (20 miles) to the west. She walked the distance to warn the Canadians, enabling the 46 soldiers and 70 Mohawk warriors to capture over 500 American soldiers.

Who were Les Voltigeurs?

Les Voltigeurs Canadiens was a corps of French Canadians formed by Captain-Lieutenant Charles-Michel de Salaberry in 1810. Although the corps was disbanded after the War of 1812, a regiment in the Canadian armed forces continues its name.

Laura Secord warns Lieutenant James FitzGibbon of an imminent American attack.

Who was the first Canadian-born novelist?

The first Canadian novelist, John Richardson, was a veteran of the War of 1812. His most famous novel, *Wacousta*, is set during the war. Richardson was also the author of a history of the conflict.

Which territories were held by foreign armies at the end of the war?

When the Treaty of Ghent was signed, officially ending the war, Canadian forces occupied Fort Niagara, most of Maine, the Lake Michigan area including Wisconsin, and part of Georgia. The American army held the Canadian side of the Detroit River.

Which battle occurred after the war had ended?

The Battle of New Orleans occurred on January 8, 1815, fifteen days after the Treaty of Ghent ended the war. Unfortunately for those involved, the news of peace arrived too late to prevent the hostilities. Over 2,000 soldiers, mostly British, were killed or wounded in the battle.

What was the most impressive victory of the war?

At the Battle of Chateauguay on October 26, 1813, a force of 1,700 Canadians, including 250 under the command of Charles-Michel de Salaberry, defeated 3,500 invading soldiers of the United States Army. Salaberry's victory is often credited with having saved Montreal and Lower Canada from American occupation.

Which war hero disobeyed orders?

In the early days of the war, Canadian Governor Sir George Prevost hoped that a diplomatic solution could be found. He ordered his forces not to provoke the enemy. However, learning that American General William Hull had invaded Upper Canada, General Isaac Brock marched his troops to confront the United States Army.

The Fenians hoped that in attacking her remaining North American colonies, Great Britain would be drawn into a war with the United States. They believed that the large allocation of British troops to North America would give Ireland the opportunity to rise for independence.

Who were the Fenians?

THE FENIAN BROTHERHOOD, FOUNDED IN THE

US in 1858, was a group of approximately 10,000 Irish-Americans, many veterans of the American Civil War, whose goal was to achieve Irish independence through attacking British North America.

How long did the raids last?

The first raid was on April 10, 1865, when the Fenians captured Campobello Island in New Brunswick. The last occurred on October 5, 1871 when Fenian troops occupied the Hudson's Bay Company post at Pembina, Manitoba.

Which future Prime Ministers served during the Fenian Raids?

Alexander Mackenzie, Sir John Abbott, Sir Mackenzie Bowell, and Sir Wilfrid Laurier joined the Militia to defend British North America.

The Fenians carried the flag of the Finnia, who were an early group of Celtic knights.

What was the worst raid?

The first raid, which culminated in the Battle of Ridgeway, was the worst. In 1866, 1,500 Fenians crossed the Niagara River and captured Fort Erie. They then proceeded farther inland where they were met by 840 members of the Militia. The Fenians defeated the Militia, killing ten men, before returning to American territory.

Who turned his back on the Fenians?

IRISH-BORN FATHER OF CONFEDERATION THOMAS D'ARCY McGEE HAD LOBBIED for Irish independence as a young man. He had been forced to flee Ireland due to his involvement in the Irish Rebellion of 1848. However, opinions changed over the years and he grew strongly opposed to Irish republicanism. In 1868, McGee was shot and killed while returning home from an evening session of the House of Commons. It is believed that McGee was the victim of a Fenian plot.

In what way did the raids contribute to Confederation?
The raids would have been a footnote in Canadian history were it not for the fears they raised in the Canadas, New Brunswick, and Nova Scotia. Many in the colonies came to believe that they could best defend themselves through political union.

Who were expected to join the raids?
The Fenians believed that Montreal's large Irish population would rise to support them, as would French-speaking radicals.

Militia members preparing to confront the Fenians.

How did Louis Riel reject the Fenians?
The final raid took place in 1871 when a small group of Fenians crossed into Manitoba. Although they believed the Métis could be encouraged to rebel against Ottawa, Riel stated that neither he nor his friends would ever join the Fenians.

Which important American was sympathetic to the Fenians?
After American President Andrew Johnson met with the Fenian leadership, he agreed to release John Mitchel, who had been imprisoned as a result of his support for the Confederate States in the American Civil War. A prominent member of the brotherhood, Mitchel was dispatched to France to raise money for the raids. Although Johnson initially allowed the cross-border raids he eventually issued a proclamation against them.

Who won the only Victoria Cross on Canadian soil?
In 1866, Irish soldier Timothy O'Hea struggled for over an hour to put out a fire in a boxcar containing 910 kilograms (2,000 pounds) of ammunition to be used in fighting the Fenians. The train was also carrying 800 German immigrants who would certainly have perished if he had failed. O'Hea remains the only recipient of a Victoria Cross awarded for action taken on Canadian soil.

Who fought against sending troops to the Boer War?

LIBERAL HENRI BOURASSA ARGUED THAT CANADA

had no obligation to send troops overseas. After the Liberals failed to consult Parliament over the decision to send Canadians to South Africa, he resigned his House of Commons seat to protest. Bourassa won back his seat in an uncontested by-election.

Henri Bourassa was a politician and founder of Montreal's *Le Devoir* newspaper.

How many Canadians participated in the war?
Over 7,000 Canadians volunteered to serve in the Boer War. Many did not see action as the fighting ended before they reached South Africa.

What caused the war?
The British wanted to rule a unified South Africa, something the Boers opposed. Tensions grew when gold and diamonds were discovered on land held by the Boers, leading to war in October 1899. The fighting lasted until May 1902.

How did the Government resolve the debate?
Sir Wilfrid Laurier's Liberals agreed to support Great Britain by providing volunteers, equipment, and transportation to South Africa. The British would be responsible for paying the troops and returning them to Canada. The Boer War marked the first time that Canadians served in an overseas war.

Who was a "Daughter of Confederation"?
Georgina Pope was the daughter of William Pope, a Father of Confederation from Prince Edward Island. Educated as a nurse, she left for South Africa in 1899, one of 8 Canadian women to care for the troops.

How did the war divide Canada?
Most Canadians saw the Boer War as an attack on the British Empire and wanted the country to participate. However, some citizens, particularly French Canadians, viewed the conflict as Great Britain's war, one in which Canada should not become involved.

Who were the Boers?

The descendants of Dutch settlers, the Boers were farmers who lived in the northern part of South Africa.

How did the war end?

The four-year war ended in 1902 with the signing of the Treaty of Vereeniging. The Boers surrendered their independence, but were given promises of future self-government and relief for the victims of war.

Which famous Mountie commanded a British Army Unit?

Former Superintendent Sam Steele volunteered for overseas service and was given command of Lord Strathcona's Horse regiment. The mounted force, which contained many members of the North West Mounted Police, drew considerable praise for its abilities in scouting out enemy positions.

What was the greatest cause of death in the conflict?

ALTHOUGH CANADA LOST 277 MEN IN THE BOER WAR, ONLY 89 WERE KILLED in the fighting. Most died of disease. In fact, thousands of lives were lost in the war due to poor sanitation, disease, and inadequate medical care.

Which famous poet served in the Boer War?

John McCrae volunteered to fight at the outbreak of the war, leaving his medical studies at McGill University. Although he spent one year in South Africa leading an artillery battery, he had mixed feelings about the war. While he supported the war's goals, he was critical of the treatment received by sick and injured soldiers. McCrae left military service, but again volunteered in 1914 to participate in the First World War. The following year, he wrote *In Flanders Fields*, his most famous poem.

Canadian volunteers in South Africa during the divisive Boer War.

Why didn't Canada declare war?
Under its obligations at the time, Canada was automatically drawn into the conflict when Great Britain declared war on Germany on August 4, 1914. The first troops left for England two months later.

How many Canadians died in the war?
The First World War was the worst for the country in terms of casualties. Death took more than one in ten of the 619,636 Canadians who saw service.

What was the Canadian Expeditionary Force?
The CEF was the name given to the Canadian force serving overseas. The first contingent, numbering over 33,000 men, arrived in England in the autumn of 1914. The force included the Canadian Corps, the Canadian Cavalry Brigade, the Canadian Railway Troops, and others.

Who was Canada fighting in the First World War?

CANADA FOUGHT ALONGSIDE GREAT BRITAIN, FRANCE, RUSSIA, AND their allies against Germany, the Austro-Hungarian Empire, and other smaller nations.

What happened at Ypres?
Ypres was the location of the first major Canadian battle of the war. Taking place on April 22, 1915, the battle marked the first use of chlorine gas by the Germans. Two days later, at the Battle of Saint Julien, gas was again used. In both battles the Canadians held their ground, but lost a total of 6,035 men in the process.

What was Canada's greatest accomplishment?
In April 1917, 100,000 men of the Canadian Corps captured Vimy Ridge. The victory at the ridge, which was thought to have been impregnable, heightened Canada's stature in the eyes of the world. The Canadian Corps maintained an undefeated record during the remainder of the war.

Which famous runner was declared dead?
In 1916, Tom Longboat of Ontario's Six Nations Reserve, at the time the world's fastest man, enlisted. He continued running as a dispatch carrier with the 107th Pioneer Battalion in France, carrying messages and orders between units. Longboat was wounded twice and was once declared dead. He was one of the fortunate ones, returning to Canada in 1919.

Canadian troops following the Battle of Vimy Ridge.

Which two great air aces met on April 30, 1917?

ON THAT APRIL MORNING, BILLY Bishop and a colleague encountered Manfred von Richthofen – the Red Baron – and four of his squadron. Bishop described the ensuing battle, which ended as a draw, as unlike any other he had experienced.

Who shot down the Red Baron?
Although it is uncertain as to who shot down the greatest ace of the First World War, many credit Ontario fighter pilot Arthur Roy Brown with the kill. Australian ground troops were shooting at von Richthofen at the same time as Brown.

William "Billy" Bishop was the greatest Canadian flying ace of all time.

What was the Ross rifle?
The invention of British aristocrat Sir Charles Ross, the Ross was the standard issue rifle of Canada's armed forces. Despite a decade-long history of problems, the rifle was sent with Canadians serving overseas. It quickly developed a reputation for jamming in battle. It was considered responsible for the deaths of a great number of Canadian soldiers.

Why was the conflict referred to as "The War to End All Wars"?
The First World War was greater than all previous wars. For the first time, fighting extended beyond Europe into Asia, Africa, and the Atlantic and Pacific oceans. Over 65 million men took part in the fighting and more than 10 million soldiers and citizens lost their lives. The large-scale destruction and great loss of life led many to believe that there could never be another war.

Which war poem is featured on a bank note?

An excerpt of "In Flanders Fields," the best-known Canadian poem, is featured on the

Canadian 10-dollar bill. The poet, John McCrae, was a medical doctor who enlisted at the beginning of the First World War. He saw his first fighting in 1915, the same year as the poem's composition. McCrae died of pneumonia ten months before the end of the war.

John McCrae during the First World War.

Who were the Bluebirds?
The nickname was given to nurses because of their starched white veils and blue cotton dresses. More than 3,000 Canadian women served as nurses in the First World War.

Which future Prime Ministers participated in the war?
John Diefenbaker and Lester B Pearson were veterans of the First World War. Diefenbaker achieved the rank of Lieutenant in the 105th Saskatoon Fusiliers. Pearson left his studies at the University of Toronto to enlist in the war. He served in the Canadian Army Medical Corps and the Royal Flying Corps.

What novel set during the war won a Governor General's Award?
Published in 1977, The Wars by Timothy Findley won the Governor General's Award for Fiction. The author made use of war-time letters of his uncle, Thomas Irving Findley, in researching the novel. The Wars was eventually adapted to film with a score by Glenn Gould.

Which hockey hero was killed during the war?
Although he only had one eye, Ottawa-born Frank McGee scored fourteen goals for the Ottawa Silver Seven in a 23 to 2 win over the Dawson Nuggets. The record for the most goals scored in a Stanley Cup play-off game will likely never be broken. McGee was killed in 1916 at the battle of the Somme. His uncle was Thomas D'Arcy McGee.

Which Canadian company lost ships during the war?

With a fleet of almost 300 ships, the Hudson's Bay Company played an important role, transporting troops and supplying food, fuel, and ammunitions to Great Britain, France, and Russia. A third of the company's fleet was sunk by the enemy.

Which university was founded in memory of soldiers who had died in the war?

In 1925, Memorial University was founded in memory of Newfoundlanders who had lost their lives in the First World War. The conflict claimed over 300 of the nearly 12,000 Newfoundlanders who served overseas.

Who were the war artists?

A number of the country's finest painters, including William Beatty, Maurice Cullen, A Y Jackson, Charles Simpson, and Frederick Varley, were sent to the front lines in France and Belgium. There they would sketch Canadians in battle, often completing their work in their London studios. Some painters were commissioned to record scenes of the home front in Canada. Although Canadian war artists continue to be sent to conflicts, those of the First World War were particularly distinguished.

What was trench warfare?

EARLY IN THE FIRST WORLD WAR, SOLDIERS ON BOTH SIDES OF THE CONFLICT DUG a series of trenches running approximately 760 kilometres (472 miles) along the Western Front. Soldiers were surrounded by mud, lice, rats, and, sometimes, the dead bodies of their comrades.

What was the Treaty of Versailles?

Signed on June 28, 1919, the peace treaty officially brought the First World War to an end. It was also the first multilateral treaty to be signed by Canada. Although the country had no choice in entering the war, Canada's signatory status helped end it.

Who were "enemy aliens"?

Over 80,000 Canadians who were formerly citizens of Germany and the Austro-Hungarian and Turkish empires were required to register as "enemy aliens." Those who didn't comply were interned in camps and weren't released until 1920.

Where is "The Tower of Victory and Peace"?

The Tower of Victory and Peace is the original name for the Peace Tower, the dominant feature of the Centre Block of the Parliament Buildings. It was constructed after the original Centre Block was destroyed by fire in 1916.

An example of the muddy terrain that Canadian forces and their allies had to contend with.

ROYAL CANADIAN
AIR FORCE

Come and
join us!

Recruitment posters appeared across the country days after war was declared.

When did Canada enter the Second World War?

THE COUNTRY DECLARED WAR ON GERMANY ON SEPTEMBER 10, 1939. The declaration, which occurred seven days after Great Britain and France had entered the war, was the first made by Canada as an independent country.

Who were the Nazis?
A Nazi was a member of the German National Socialist Party. Led by Adolph Hitler, the party held power in Germany from 1933 until the end of the Second World War. During the war, the word was used loosely to mean a German.

In which way did the First World War lead to the Second?
Most historians agree that the Treaty of Versailles, which ended the First World War, was in part responsible for the outbreak of the Second World War two decades later. The treaty imposed extremely harsh conditions upon Germany, leading to a period of extreme economic instability.

What delayed Canada's declaration of war?
Although there was never any doubt that Canada would enter the conflict, Prime Minister William Lyon Mackenzie King intentionally delayed the declaration of war. Mindful of French-Canadian resentment concerning conscription in the First World War, King hoped that the slight delay would emphasize that Canada was joining the conflict as an independent nation.

How long was the war expected to last?
While those in 1914 had expected the First World War to reach its end by Christmas, those entering the Second World War were more realistic. The British and Canadian governments expected the war to last at least three years. In fact, the war didn't end until the surrender of Japan in August 1945, just one month short of the sixth anniversary of the beginning of the conflict.

How many Canadians served in the war?
Over 1,000,000 Canadian men and women served in the Second World War; of these over 45,000 died and 55,000 were wounded.

What was "The Phony War"?

The Phony War, which lasted from October 1939 to April 1940, was a period of apparent inactivity along the Western Front. Both sides utilized this period to prepare for the fighting to come. The lull in fighting came to a sudden end when Germany invaded Denmark and Norway.

What was the Victory Coin?

Between 1943 and 1945 the nickel became known as the Victory Coin. Usually copper coloured, the coin's design was changed from the beaver to a torch. The message "We Win When We Work Willingly" was engraved in Morse code on the Victory Coin's edge.

Who were the "Wrens"?

Established in 1942, the Women's Royal Canadian Naval Service, or "Wrens," was a group that served in non-combatant roles in Canada, Newfoundland, the United States, and the British Isles. The Wrens comprised approximately 7,000 of the more than 45,000 Canadian women who volunteered for military service during the war.

How did the war change the role of women in Canada?

As the war progressed, women were employed in increasingly large numbers in factories and machine shops. They manufactured the guns, artillery shells, airplane parts, and other equipment that were essential to the war effort. After the war, these same women were expected to vacate their jobs to return to what were considered traditional female occupations.

A woman working on parts to be used in the war effort.

Which sea battle lasted almost the entire war?

THE BATTLE OF THE ATLANTIC WAS THE STRUGGLE TO PROTECT VESSELS CROSSING THE NORTH ATLANTIC FROM GERMAN U-boats during the Second World War. Canadian warships and aircraft were essential in protecting merchant ships as they carried much-needed supplies from Halifax and other North American ports to Great Britain.

A deadly German U-boat, one of many that patrolled Canada's East Coast during the war.

What was Camp X?

A large school in the Ontario towns of Whitby and Oshawa, Camp X was established by the British Intelligence Service to train Americans in espionage. Although the school functioned only between 1941 and 1944, the camp continued as a military installation for a further two decades.

What was the effect of the Battle of the Gulf of St Lawrence?

In 1942, the battle forced the Canadian government to close the gulf and the St Lawrence River to overseas shipping. The closure of the major supply route to Great Britain delayed goods from the manufacturing centres in Ontario and Quebec. It wasn't until 1944 that anything other than coastal convoys and warships were allowed to enter or exit the two bodies of water.

Which battle took place in Canada's inland waters?

Between 1942 and 1944 German U-boats roamed the Gulf of St Lawrence, disrupting traffic and inflicting loss of life. A total of 23 ships were lost during what became known as the Battle of the Gulf of St Lawrence. The two-year battle marked the first time since the War of 1812 that war was fought in Canadian waters.

Who said, "Conscription if necessary, but not necessarily conscription"?

Prime Minister William Lyon Mackenzie King used the words as his slogan during the 1944 plebiscite on conscription. King asked voters to release his government from a promise not to invoke conscription. He wasn't saying that conscription would be a certainty, rather that, if conscription was necessary to end the war, the Government would need permission to invoke it.

Who was known as "Screwball"?

Quebec's George "Buzz" Beurling was the greatest Canadian flying ace of the Second World War. He downed a total of 31 planes during the war, making him a national hero. Beurling's nickname, "Screwball," was considered inappropriate by the Royal Canadian Air Force, who instead promoted the use of "Buzz." He died under mysterious circumstances after having been recruited as a mercenary by Israel.

Who wrote a novel set in an internment camp?

Poet and novelist Joy Kogawa's most popular work is *Obasan*, a semi-autobiographical account of a child's experiences in an internment camp. Kogawa and her Japanese family were placed in a camp during the war.

Who were placed in camps during the war?

Over 22,000 Japanese Canadians living in British Columbia were sent to camps during the Second World War. Their land, businesses, and other assets were confiscated by the government and sold. It wasn't until four years after the war that Japanese Canadians were permitted to return to Vancouver.

Where is "The National Monument to the Canadian Liberators"?

The statue, titled *"De man met de twee hoeden,"* meaning "The Man with Two Hats," is located in the Netherlands near Het Loo Palace. It was commissioned to mark the 55th anniversary of the liberation of the Netherlands by Canadian forces.

What was Canada's role on D-Day?

CANADIANS LANDED AT JUNO BEACH BEFORE MOVING ON TO CAPTURE the city of Caen. The battle ended in August when they took an important German communications centre 32 kilometres (20 miles) inland at Falaise. In total, 5,021 Canadians were killed and 13,423 were injured.

What was D-Day?

D-Day is commonly used in reference to the allied invasion of Normandy on June 6, 1944. The successful campaign marked the first step in the liberation of northwest Europe from the German forces that had held the territory since the summer of 1940.

Tens of thousands of Canadians took part in the D-Day invasion.

Under which flag did Canadians fight?

Canada was one of 16 countries to send forces under the United Nations Command. The first Canadians to be sent to the war were the crews of the destroyers HMCS *Cayuga*, HMCS *Athabaskan*, and HMCS *Sioux*.

What was the Canadian Army Special Force?

Five years after the end of the Second World War, Canada's armed forces were in a weakened state. The CASF was created on August 17, 1950 to carry out the country's obligations by training volunteers as part of the regular army.

Canadian soldiers serving in Korea.

How many Canadians served in the Korean War?

BETWEEN JULY 1950 AND JULY 1953, OVER 26,000 CANADIANS SERVED IN THE war under the flag of the United Nations. A total of 1,558 Canadians lost their lives in the hostilities.

What was the cause of the Korean War?

The war began on June 25, 1950 when North Korea invaded South Korea. The first act of aggression since the establishment of the United Nations, the organization called for countries to come to the aid of South Korea.

Why did the first Canadians not expect to fight?

Due to the early success by South Korea and the United Nations Command, the first Canadian soldiers expected to perform a role as occupiers. However, by the time they landed in Korea, the war had dramatically changed due to the intervention of China in support of North Korea.

How did the Korean War end?

North and South Korea are still officially at war. The fighting ended on July 27, 1953 with the signing of the Korea Armistice Agreement, which failed to bring about a permanent peace. In the half-century that has followed, both sides have violated the terms of the agreement tens of thousands of times.

What were the government's greatest fears during the war?

The leader of the United Nations Command, American General Douglas MacArthur, felt the use of nuclear weapons should be considered in the war. He also expressed his desire to expand the war into China. Less than a year into the war, MacArthur was dismissed.

Who promoted Canada's participation in the war?

Lester B Pearson, then Secretary of State for External Affairs, was the government's strongest proponent for entering the conflict under the flag of the United Nations.

Who was a "peacemonger"?

The son of a Russian count, George Ignatieff was one of Canada's most distinguished statesmen. Among his many positions was Ambassador to the United Nations. His biography, *The Making of a Peacemonger*, was published in 1985.

What are the Books of Remembrance?

The Books of Remembrance commemorate the lives of 114,710 Canadians who died while serving in battle after Confederation in 1867. Over 500,000 people view the books, housed in the Memorial Chamber of the Peace Tower, each year.

How many Books of Remembrance are there?

Numbering six in total, four books are dedicated to those who gave their lives in different conflicts: the Boer War and Nile Expedition, First World War, Second World War, and Korean War. A fifth book lists those who died while serving in the Merchant Navy. The final book is dedicated to Newfoundlanders who lost their lives before the province joined Confederation.

Which great Canadian warship saw service in Korea?

LAUNCHED IN 1943, DURING THE SECOND WORLD WAR, THE DESTROYER HMCS HAIDA SANK MORE ENEMY vessels than any other Canadian warship. Dubbed "Canada's Fightingest Destroyer," in the Korean War HMCS *Haida* destroyed two North Korean supply trains with an off-shore bombardment.

HMCS *Haida* is now located in Hamilton, Ontario.

When were the first peacekeepers used?
The word "peacekeeper" was first used to describe the first international peacekeeping force sent to the Suez Canal. In 1956, the United Nations passed a resolution to send an emergency force to secure and supervise the cessation of hostilities. The proposal, drawn up by Lester B Pearson, is acknowledged as the main reason he received the Nobel Peace Prize.

What was Canada's longest peacekeeping effort?
In 1964, Canadian peacekeepers were sent to the Mediterranean to prevent further fighting between Greek and Turkish Cypriots on Cyprus. Twenty-nine years later, the last Canadian peacekeepers left the island. More than 12,000 Canadian peacekeepers served on Cyprus.

How many Canadians have participated in peacekeeping missions?
Beginning with troops sent to the Suez Canal in 1956, over 125,000 Canadians have served in over 70 different missions. Over 100 Canadian peacekeepers have died in the line of duty.

Who won the Nobel Peace Prize?

FUTURE PRIME MINISTER LESTER B PEARSON was the 1957 recipient of the prize. Pearson was the head of the Canadian delegation to the United Nations and, in 1951 and 1952, served as the president of the United Nations General Assembly. The prize was seen as recognition of Pearson's role in international policymaking during the post-war period.

Maryon Pearson and Lester B Pearson at the Nobel Prize ceremony.

What body was awarded the 1988 Nobel Peace Prize?
The prize was awarded to the United Nations Peacekeeping Forces, including those from Canada, in recognition of their collective contribution to world peace.

Canadian peacekeepers have served in Europe, Africa, and Asia.

What was the Trudeau Peace Initiative?

In 1983, during a heightened period of tension in the Cold War, Prime Minister Pierre Elliott Trudeau visited the major nuclear and military powers. He proposed a comprehensive nuclear test ban, a ban on testing high-altitude weapons, and the implementation of a consultative process. The mission received a great deal of attention from the media, but was met with resistance in Washington and Moscow.

What is the purpose of the Ottawa Protocol?

The Protocol is a ban on the use of anti-personnel mines, more commonly known as land mines. In recognition of his work on the treaty, Foreign Minister Lloyd Axworth was nominated for a Nobel Peace prize.

Where can one visit the world's only monument to peacekeepers?

Ottawa is the location of "Reconciliation." Unveiled in 1992, it is the world's first and only monument to peacekeepers.

What role does the RCMP play in peacekeeping?

SINCE 1989, THE RCMP'S CIVILIAN POLICE PEACEKEEPING OPERATIONS HAVE played a major role in training police forces as part of the United Nations peacekeeping missions. The force has served in Namibia, Yugoslavia, Kosovo, Haiti, Bosnia/Herzegovina, East Timor, Guatemala, and Croatia.

Which international structures celebrate peace between Canada and the United States?

Built in the early 20th century, over 100 hundred years after the end of the War of 1812, both the Peace Bridge and Peace Arch commemorate the end of hostilities between the two nations. The Peace Bridge spans the Niagara River between Fort Erie, Ontario and Buffalo, New York. The Peace Arch, located on the boundary shared by British Columbia and the State of Washington, is the only international gateway erected in celebration of peace between nations.

In which war did Canada suffer no casualties?
Over 1,900 Canadians served overseas in the Gulf War, a multinational effort prompted by the 1990 Iraqi invasion of Kuwait. Fighting broke out early in 1991, and ended when a cease-fire was called 42 days later.

How many Canadians served in the Spanish Civil War?
More than 1,500 Canadian men and women served in the conflict. Among the better-known participants were surgeon Norman Bethune and novelist Ted Allan. Nearly half of those who served died in action.

Who were the Mac-Paps?

THE MACKENZIE-PAPINEAU BATTALION WAS FORMED IN 1937 TO FIGHT against the fascists in the Spanish Civil War. Named after William Lyon Mackenzie and Louis-Joseph Papineau, the leaders of the Rebellions of 1837, the Battalion was comprised entirely of volunteers and received no support from the Canadian government.

What is Operation Apollo?
Apollo is the name of Canada's military contribution to the War in Afghanistan. The operation went into effect four weeks after the events of September 11, 2001.

Members of the Mackenzie-Papineau Battalion supported the Spanish government in the Spanish Civil War.

Canadians protesting against American participation in the Vietnam War.

Who were the draft dodgers?

THE TERM IS USUALLY USED IN REFERENCE TO THOSE WHO FLEE RATHER THAN be forced to participate in a war. The first known draft dodgers to enter Canada did so to avoid fighting in the American Civil War. Perhaps the most famous draft dodgers are the 50,000 Americans who fled to Canada in order to avoid participating in the Vietnam War.

What did Igor Gouzenko reveal?

Gouzenko's documents revealed a large spy ring operating in Canada. Among other things, the agents were attempting to obtain required knowledge for making an atomic bomb.

Which war began in Ottawa?

Although there were already tensions between the Soviet Union and the West, the defection of Igor Gouzenko is often sited as the beginning of the Cold War. On September 5, 1945, Gouzenko, a Russian cipher clerk at the Soviet Embassy in Ottawa, defected, taking with him over 100 sensitive documents.

How did Canadians serve in the Vietnam War?

Although Canada was officially neutral during the war, as many as 30,000 Canadians joined the American forces to fight in Vietnam.

Canadian Leaders

LAURIER OUR NEXT PREMIER

LAURIER HUN GLADSTONE GLADSTONE

Who foresaw his own death?
Before participating in the 1813 Battle of Moraviantown, Tecumseh had a vision in which he saw death. Although it is certain that he was violently killed during the battle, his burial place has never been found.

Joseph Brant was one of the great chiefs of the 18th and 19th centuries.

Who was the first Premier of Nunavut?
After winning a seat in the elections for Nunavut's first Legislative Assembly, lawyer Paul Okalik was selected as the territory's first Premier in March 1999. He officially took office on April 1, 1999, when Nunavut came into being.

Why did Sitting Bull lead his people to Canada?
Determined to occupy Sioux land, the United States launched a campaign in retaliation for Custer's death. Clinging to freedom, Sitting Bull led his people across the border in 1877. However, the tribe received no assistance from the Canadian government. After four years in Canada, hunger forced Sitting Bull to return to the United States and surrender.

Who translated the Bible into Mohawk?

A VERY RELIGIOUS MAN, CHIEF JOSEPH BRANT, Thayendanega, translated several Christian books into Mohawk, including the Gospel of Mark and the Acts of the Apostles. He raised enough money to build the first Anglican Church on the Six Nations Reserve.

Who was The Prophet?
An unlikeable, lazy man, Tecumseh's brother, Tenskwatawa, underwent a great change, having been visited by the Great Spirit in a dream. Convinced that he'd been shown his people's path to salvation, Tenskwatawa urged all First Nations people to return to a traditional way of life.

Which Chief was victorious in Custer's Last Stand?
In 1876, Sitting Bull and his Sioux warriors defeated American war hero Colonel Custer and his men in the Battle of Little Bighorn.

Who killed a grizzly bear?

IN 1866, MEMBERS OF THE BLACKFOOT NATION WERE attacked by a grizzly bear. Their chief, Crowfoot, moved behind the bear and single-handedly killed it with the use of a lance.

Which chief refused to sign a numbered treaty?

Mistahimaskwa, Chief Big Bear, refused to sign Treaty Six because he was convinced that it would lead his people to poverty and a loss of lifestyle. He devoted himself towards establishing an Indian confederacy, before starvation forced him to accept government terms.

Who is the National Chief of the Assembly of First Nations?

In 2001, Matthew Coon Come of the James Bay Cree was elected leader of the assembly. As Grand Chief of the Grand Council of the Crees and Chairman of the Cree Regional Authority, Coon Come first gained national attention for challenging the Quebec government during the 1995 Referendum.

Which Mohawk chief was educated in Scotland?

The son of a Cherokee father and Scottish mother, it is believed that Mohawk Chief John Norton, Teyoninhokarawen, was born in Scotland, where he also received his education. A hero of the War of 1812, Norton was chosen by Joseph Brant as his successor in the Six Nations.

Which chief refused to accept the outcome of the War of 1812?

Sauk Black Hawk was angry with the British for signing the treaty ending the war. In 1832, he fought the unsuccessful Black Hawk War in an attempt to create a confederacy on his nation's traditional territories.

The great Blackfoot warrior and diplomat Chief Crowfoot.

When did we first celebrate Victoria Day?

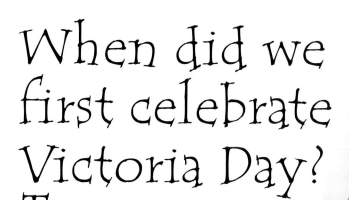

THE HOLIDAY WAS FIRST ESTABLISHED TO honour the birthday of Queen Victoria on May 24, 1845. Originally celebrated in Ontario only, the day became a national holiday shortly after the monarch's death in 1901. Since 1953, Victoria Day has been observed as a celebration of Queen Victoria and Queen Elizabeth II.

It was during Queen Victoria's reign that Canada became a country.

How many sovereigns has Canada had?

Since the 16th century, a total of nine French and 23 British monarchs have reigned over land that is now Canadian territory:

British Sovereigns		French Sovereigns
Henry VII (1497–1509)	Anne (1702–14)	
Henry VIII (1509–47)	George I (1714–27)	
Edward VI (1547–53)	George II (1727–60)	François I (1524–1547)
Mary I (1553–58)	George III (1760–1820)	Henri II (1547–59)
Elizabeth I (1558–1603)	George IV (1820–30)	François II (1559–60)
James I (1603–25)	William IV (1830–37)	Charles IX (1560–74)
Charles I (1625–49)	Victoria (1837–1901)	Henri III (1574–89)
Charles II (1660–85)	Edward VII (1901–10)	Henri IV (1589–1610)
James II (1685–88)	George V (1910–36)	Louis XIII (1610–43)
William III (1689–1702)	Edward VIII (1936)	Louis XIV (1643–1715)
Mary II (1689–94)	George VI (1936–52)	Louis XV (1715–1763)
	Elizabeth II (1952–present)	

Who was the first monarch?

In 1497, King Henry VII became Canada's first monarch when John Cabot claimed the land for England.

Which monarch ruled the longest?

King Louis XIV ruled France and the colony of New France for 72 years. The reign of Queen Victoria lasted 63 years, during which time the Dominion of Canada came into being. The longest a monarch has ruled the country as we know it is Queen Elizabeth II, who celebrated her 50th anniversary on the throne in 2002.

Who represents the Queen in Canada?

The Queen has a total of eleven representatives. The Governor General represents her at the national level. She is represented at the provincial level by ten Lieutenant Governors – one for each province.

Who was the first monarch to visit Canada?

As part of a naval contingent, William IV visited Newfoundland and Nova Scotia in 1786, forty-five years before he was crowned.

When did the Queen first visit Canada?

As Princess Elizabeth, the Queen undertook a cross-country tour of Canada in 1951, the year before she became queen.

Who owned a ranch near Calgary?

As Prince of Wales, the controversial King Edward VIII bought a ranch outside Calgary. He visited his investment three times prior to assuming the throne, and twice after his abdication.

Who was the first reigning monarch to visit?

The first visit to Canada by a reigning monarch was made

by King George VI, who crossed the country in 1939. His daughter, Queen Elizabeth II, has made over two dozen official visits to Canada.

The 1939 Royal Tour in the Canadian west.

Who was the first female Governor General ?

IN JANUARY 28, 1984, JEANNE SAUVÉ BECAME THE FIRST WOMAN TO BE appointed as Governor General of Canada. A former Liberal cabinet minister, she was also the first woman Speaker of the House of Commons.

Saskatchewan-born Jeanne Sauvé was first elected to the House of Commons in 1972.

Which Governor General was a refugee?

Future Governor General Adrienne Clarkson fled Hong Kong as a child in 1942. The previous year, her father, a prominent businessman, lost his property when the Japanese invaded the colony.

What was the King–Byng Affair?

The affair occurred in 1926 when Prime Minister William Lyon Mackenzie King's Liberals lost a motion of no confidence in the House of Commons. Instead of dissolving Parliament as King requested, Governor General Sir Julian Byng called on Arthur Meighen to form the new Government.

How was the affair used to King's advantage?

King portrayed Sir Julian Byng's move as an unacceptable intervention into Canadian politics. After four days in office, Meighen's Conservatives were toppled by King in a motion of no confidence, forcing the new Prime Minister to request that Byng dissolve Parliament. King won the subsequent election.

Which Governor General was a best-selling novelist?

Sir John Buchan, Lord Tweedsmuir, was a prolific author, publishing over 70 books during his lifetime. A commercially successful author, his best-known book is the suspense novel *The Thirty-Nine Steps*, which was published in 1915. Two decades later, Buchan was appointed Canada's fifteenth Governor General.

Who presented the first Governor General's Literary Awards?

Established by the Canadian Authors' Association, the awards were first presented in 1937 by Governor General Sir John Buchan. The winning books, Bertram Brooker's *Think of the Earth* and T B Robertson's *TBR*, were published the previous year.

Which Governor General was son-in-law of the reigning monarch?

Sir John Douglas Sutherland Campbell, Marquess of Lorne, Ninth Duke of Argyll, was husband of Queen Victoria's fourth daughter, Princess Louise Caroline Alberta. He became Governor General in 1878 at the age of 33, the youngest person ever appointed to the position. The duke's brother-in-law, Prince Arthur, third son of Queen Victoria, was Governor General from 1911 until 1916.

Which Governor was recalled?

APPOINTED GOVERNOR OF NEW FRANCE IN 1672, Count Frontenac defied his instructions by greatly expanding the colony's territory. He caused turmoil by placing his dissenters in confinement, selling brandy to the First Nations, and struggling with others over the fur trade. In 1682, he was ordered back to France, but was returned to office seven years later during the height of tensions between the French and the Iroquois Confederacy.

Louis de Baude, Count Frontenac, is considered the greatest Governor of New France.

Who were the Governors of New France?

The Governors of New France were considered the French monarch's representative in the colony. New France had a total of 18 Governors before it fell into British hands. Today's Governor General is considered part of a line that began with Samuel de Champlain, the first Governor of New France.

Where does the Governor General live?

Ottawa's Rideau Hall is the official residence of the Governor General. Built as a private residence in 1838, as Governor General of British North America, Lord Monck became the first public official to live in the house. In 1867, two years after he took up residence, Lord Monck was made the first Governor General of the Dominion of Canada.

When was the first Canadian-born Governor General appointed?

In 1952, Vincent Massey was appointed Governor General. Born into Toronto's prominent Massey family, his father was president of the Massey-Harris Company, and his brother was actor Raymond Massey. Although there is no rule as to place of birth, nearly every Governor General since Massey has been born in Canada.

Which Fathers of Confederation were murdered?

The 1880 murder of George Brown by a man he had never known.

A STRONG BELIEVER IN UNITING THE COLONIES, GEORGE BROWN put aside differences with his political rivals, Sir John A Macdonald and Sir George-Étienne Cartier, to achieve Confederation. The founder of the *Toronto Globe* (now known as *The Globe and Mail*), Brown was killed by a deranged man who had been fired from the newspaper. Thomas D'Arcy McGee was assassinated by Patrick James Whelan, the last Canadian to be publicly hanged on February 11, 1869.

Which Father of Confederation argued against the idea of Provincial Legislatures?
New Brunswick's Robert Duncan Wilmot fought for a strong central government. His opposition to the idea of provincial power led to his initial rejection of the terms of Confederation.

Which Father of Confederation became a very successful Premier?
Sir Oliver Mowat served as Premier of Ontario from 1872 to 1896. He held the office for longer than any other and later served as the province's Lieutenant Governor.

Which Father of Confederation can be blamed for GST?

William Alexander Henry, Nova Scotia's Attorney General, proposed that governments be able to create new senators to override opposition. In 1990, his clause was used to push the Goods and Services Tax Act through the Senate.

Which Fathers were against Confederation?

Not all attendees of the Charlottetown, Quebec, and London conferences were in favour of Confederation. Among those who did not want the union were George H Coles and Edward Palmer from Prince Edward Island.

Whose support for Confederation cost him his office?

Father of Confederation Sir Frederick Bowker Terrington Carter became Prime Minister of Newfoundland in 1865. Four years later he ran for re-election with the promise that he would bring the colony into Confederation. Carter lost the election. It would be another eight decades before Newfoundland would join Canada.

Which Fathers of Confederation became Prime Ministers?

SIR JOHN A MACDONALD WAS MADE THE COUNTRY'S FIRST PRIME MINISTER AT the time of Confederation. Fellow Father of Confederation, Sir Charles Tupper held the office briefly in 1896.

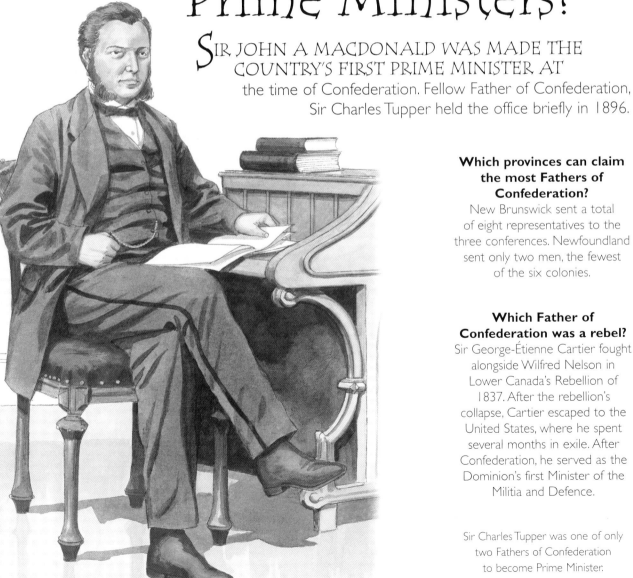

Which provinces can claim the most Fathers of Confederation?

New Brunswick sent a total of eight representatives to the three conferences. Newfoundland sent only two men, the fewest of the six colonies.

Which Father of Confederation was a rebel?

Sir George-Étienne Cartier fought alongside Wilfred Nelson in Lower Canada's Rebellion of 1837. After the rebellion's collapse, Cartier escaped to the United States, where he spent several months in exile. After Confederation, he served as the Dominion's first Minister of the Militia and Defence.

Sir Charles Tupper was one of only two Fathers of Confederation to become Prime Minister.

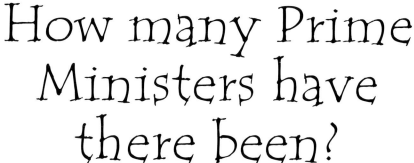

How many Prime Ministers have there been?

SINCE CONFEDERATION CANADA HAS HAD A TOTAL OF 20 PRIME MINISTERS:

1. Sir John A Macdonald (1867–73, 1878–91)
2. Alexander Mackenzie (1873–78)
3. Sir John J C Abbott (1891–92)
4. Sir John Sparrow Thompson (1892–94)
5. Sir Mackenzie Bowell (1894–96)
6. Sir Charles Tupper (1896)
7. Sir Wilfrid Laurier (1896–1911)
8. Sir Robert Laird Borden (1911–20)
9. Arthur Meighen (1920–21, 1926)
10. William Lyon Mackenzie King (1921–26, 1926–30, 1935–48)
11. Richard Bedford Bennett (1930–35)
12. Louis St Laurent (1948–57)
13. John G Diefenbaker (1957–63)
14. Lester B Pearson (1963–68)
15. Pierre Elliott Trudeau (1968–79, 1980–84)
16. Charles Joseph Clark (1979–80)
17. John Napier Turner (1984)
18. Martin Brian Mulroney (1984–93)
19. Avril Kim Campbell (1993)
20. Joseph-Jacques-Jean Chrétien (1993–present)

Which Prime Ministers weren't born in Canada?
Four Prime Ministers were born outside the borders of present-day Canada. Sir John A Macdonald and Alexander Mackenzie were Scottish by birth. Mackenzie Bowell and John Turner were both born in England.

Who declined a knighthood?
The early Prime Ministers were accorded automatic knighthoods for having attained the office. The one exception was Alexander Mackenzie, the second Prime Minister, who turned down the offer of knighthood on three different occasions.

Which Prime Ministers died in office?
The country's first Prime Minister, Sir John A Macdonald, died in 1891, only three months after winning his fourth consecutive majority government. Two and a half years later, Prime Minister Sir John Thompson, one of Macdonald's Conservative successors, suffered the same fate.

Sir John A Macdonald was the first Prime Minister of the Dominion of Canada.

Which Prime Ministers resigned from office?

Nearly half of the country's Prime Ministers have resigned from the position. At the height of the Pacific Scandal, the first Prime Minister, Sir John A Macdonald, became the first to resign. Sir John Abbott and Sir Robert Borden left office due to ill-health. Dissatisfaction in party ranks led Sir Mackenzie Bowell to resign. William Lyon Mackenzie King, Lester B Pearson, Pierre Elliott Trudeau, and Brian Mulroney chose to resign rather than lead their respective governments into further elections.

Which Prime Ministers share the same birthday?

Jean Chrétien was born on January 11, 1934, the 119th anniversary of the birth of Sir John A Macdonald.

24 Sussex Drive in Ottawa is the official residence of the Prime Minister of Canada.

Which Prime Minister served for the longest time?

William Lyon Mackenzie King served three separate terms of office – 1921–1926, 1926–1930, and 1935–1948 – totalling 7,817 days, just less than 22 years. Sir Wilfrid Laurier, who was Prime Minister from July 1896 to October 1911, holds the record for the longest unbroken term of office.

Which Prime Minister "built" ruins?

William Lyon Mackenzie King acquired stones from old buildings being demolished in Ottawa. They were then transported north of the city to Kingsmere, his home in Quebec's Gatineau Hills, where they were used to construct "medieval ruins."

Where does the Prime Minister live?

THE OFFICIAL RESIDENCE OF THE PRIME MINISTER IS 24 SUSSEX DRIVE IN Ottawa. Completed in 1868, the house was originally built by a prosperous mill owner and lumber manufacturer. In 1951, Louis St Laurent became the first Prime Minister to live in the house. Stornoway, also in Ottawa, is the official residence of the leader of the Opposition.

Which Prime Ministers were not "elected"?

Nine Prime Ministers attained the office after the leader of their respective governing parties either died or resigned. Of these, only two, Liberals Louis St Laurent and Pierre Elliott Trudeau, succeeded in winning the next election.

Which Prime Minister sat in the British House of Lords?

As Viscount Bennett, former Prime Minister R B Bennett served in the House of Lords from 1941 until his death. He is the only Prime Minister not buried in Canada.

Canada's leader during the Second World War was William Lyon Mackenzie King.

Who likened living beside the United States to sleeping with an elephant?

Prime Minister Pierre Elliott Trudeau made the comparison in a speech given in Washington. He stated: "Living next to you is in some ways like sleeping with an elephant. No matter how friendly and even-tempered is the beast, if I can call it that, one is effected by every twitch and grunt. It should not therefore be expected that this kind of nation, this Canada, should project itself as a mirror image of the United States."

Which Prime Ministers were lawyers?

The law is the most common occupation for those achieving the office of the Prime Minister. Sir John A Macdonald, Sir John Abbott, Sir John Thompson, Sir Wilfrid Laurier, Arthur Meighan, Louis St Laurent, John Diefenbaker, Pierre Elliott Trudeau, John Turner, Brian Mulroney, and Jean Chrétien were all lawyers.

Who was the first Canadian-born Prime Minister?

Born in what is now Quebec, the country's third Prime Minister, Sir John Abbott, was the first to have been born on Canadian soil. The first to have been born after Canada became a country is Arthur Meighan, who was born in Anderson, Ontario on June 16, 1874.

Which Prime Minister was the grandson of a rebellion leader?

WILLIAM LYON MACKENZIE KING WAS NAMED AFTER his grandfather, William Lyon Mackenzie, the leader of the Upper Canadian Rebellion of 1837.

Which Prime Ministers appear on Canadian currency?

Four politicians appear on Canadian bank notes; they are: Sir Wilfrid Laurier ($5 bill), Sir John A Macdonald ($10 bill), William Lyon Mackenzie King ($50 bill), and Sir Robert Borden ($100 bill). Macdonald and Laurier were first featured on notes issued in 1935, but were replaced by Queen Elizabeth II in 1954. It wasn't until two decades later that Prime Ministers reappeared on Canadian currency.

Who was the first French Canadian Prime Minister?

SIR WILFRID LAURIER BECAME THE FIRST IN 1896. THE ONLY OTHER PRIME MINISTER WHO IS PRIMARILY OF FRENCH ancestry is Jean Chrétien. Louis St Laurent and Pierre Elliott Trudeau were both born to francophone fathers and anglophone mothers.

Sir Wilfrid Laurier campaigning in the general election of 1896.

Which Prime Minister survived an airplane crash?

As a Flying Officer in the Royal Flying Corps during the First World War, Lester B Pearson survived an airplane crash during his first flight. Unfortunately, the future Prime Minister's wartime service ended when he was hit by a London bus during a blackout and was sent home to recuperate.

Which future Prime Minister saved the life of a Prime Minister?

While vacationing in Barbados in 1965, John Turner saved former Prime Minister John Diefenbaker from drowning. At the time, Turner was a rookie Member of Parliament and Diefenbaker was leader of the Opposition.

Which Prime Ministers never married?

William Lyon Mackenzie King and R B Bennett remained bachelors throughout their entire lives. Pierre Elliott Trudeau was married and divorced while Prime Minister.

177

Pierre Trudeau was elected
to succeed Lester B Pearson
as Prime Minister
of Canada at the 1968
Liberal Party convention.

Which Canadian Prime Minister has a message on the moon?

IN 1969, DURING THE FIRST MOON LANDING, COMMANDER NEIL ARMSTRONG deposited a small disk containing messages from 73 world leaders. Pierre Elliott Trudeau, then Prime Minister, composed Canada's contribution: "Man has reached out and touched the moon. Puisse ce haut fait permettre à l'homme de redécouvrir la terre et d'y trouver la paix." ("May that high accomplishment allow man to rediscover the earth and there find peace.")

Which province has produced the most Prime Ministers?
Sir John Abbott, Sir Wilfrid Laurier, Louis St Laurent, Pierre Elliott Trudeau, Brian Mulroney, and Jean Chrétien were all born in what is now Quebec. No Prime Ministers have been born in Prince Edward Island, Saskatchewan, Manitoba, or Newfoundland and Labrador.

Which future Prime Minister first ran for public office at the age of 59?
Although he had long been involved in the Liberal party, Louis St Laurent had never run for office until asked to do so by Prime Minister William Lyon Mackenzie King. In 1942, two months after the request, St Laurent was elected to the House of Commons and was made Minister of Justice. He became Prime Minister when he was 66 years old.

Who was the youngest Prime Minister?
As leader of the Progressive Conservatives, Joe Clark was elected Prime Minister in 1979 when he was 39 years old. Clark took office shortly after his fortieth birthday.

Who was the oldest Prime Minister?
On June 6, 1891, Sir John A Macdonald died in office at the age of 76. He was 52 years old when he first became Prime Minister.

Which Prime Minister was the longest living?
Sir Charles Tupper lived to the age of 94. Other Prime Ministers who lived into their tenth decade were Sir Mackenzie Bowell and Louis St Laurent, who lived to be 93 and 91 years of age respectively. Sir John Thompson had the shortest life, dying in office when he was 50 years old.

Who was the greatest Prime Minister?

Opinions differ greatly as to how well or how poorly each Prime Minister has performed; however, most historians choose either William Lyon Mackenzie King or Sir John A Macdonald. Pierre Elliott Trudeau is often cited as the greatest of recent times.

Who led the greatest federal election victory?

THE ANSWER DEPENDS ON WHETHER ONE MEASURES THE VICTORY IN SEATS OR percentage of popular vote. Brian Mulroney led the Progressive Conservatives to victory in the 1984 federal election with a record number of 211 seats. However, while Mulroney's party achieved 50 percent of the popular vote, Liberal Prime Minister William Lyon Mackenzie King managed 55 percent in the 1940 federal election. In 1958, the Conservatives achieved 208 seats and close to 54 percent of the vote under John Diefenbaker.

Which Prime Minister formed the Union Government?

From 1917 until 1920, Prime Minister Sir Robert Borden's Conservatives were joined by Liberals and independents. The members of the Union government were supportive of Borden's implementation of conscription during the First World War.

Which Canadian became Prime Minister of Great Britain?

Born at Rexton, New Brunswick in 1858, Andrew Bonar Law is the only Prime Minister of Great Britain to have been born outside the British Isles. He lived with an aunt in Scotland from the age of twelve, after his mother's death. In 1900, Law was elected to the British Parliament and, eleven years later, became leader of the Conservative Party. Despite poor health, he served as Prime Minister from October 1922 until May 1923. He died five months later.

Prime Minister Brian Mulroney with American President Ronald Reagan, the two leaders responsible for the Free Trade Agreement.

Who was the first Native Canadian Member of Parliament?

In 1873, Métis Louis Riel became the first Native Canadian to take a seat in the House of Commons. The next Native Canadian to be elected to the Parliament was Progressive Conservative Eugene Rheaume, in 1963.

Who were the youngest and oldest Members of Parliament?

At the age of 20, Liberal Claude-André Lachance became the youngest person to ever sit in the House of Commons when he won a seat in the 1974 general election. Conservative William Anderson Black died while still a Member of Parliament one month before his 87th birthday.

Thomas D'Arcy McGee was the first Canadian politician to lose his life to an assassin.

The funeral of Thomas D'Arcy McGee in Montreal.

Which Member of Parliament was an accomplished poet?

THOMAS D'ARCY McGEE WAS CONSIDERED AN EXCELLENT POET. His talent probably contributed to his skill in giving speeches in the House of Commons. Although he was assassinated less than a year after Confederation, he is remembered as one of the House's best orators.

Who was the youngest person ever to sit in cabinet?

In 1986, days before his 28th birthday, Conservative Member of Parliament Jean Charest was appointed to the Mulroney cabinet as Minister of State for Youth.

Who were the Three Wise Men?

Quebec Liberals Jean Marchand, Gérard Pelletier, and Pierre Elliott Trudeau were dubbed the Three Wise Men after entering federal politics together in 1965.

Who founded *Le Devoir*?

The son of the painter Napoléon Bourassa and grandson of the Rebellion of 1837 leader Louis-Joseph Papineau, Henri Bourassa founded the leading Montreal newspaper in 1910. Bourassa, who served in both provincial and federal governments, was one of the most influential politicians in Canadian history.

Who was the Honorary Officer of the House of Commons?

Stanley Knowles represented the riding of Winnipeg North Centre in the House of Commons for 38 years as a member of the Co-operative Commonwealth Federation and the New Democratic Party. One of the most respected people ever to have sat in the House, he was made Honorary Officer of the House with a place at the Clerk's table after he chose not to run in the 1984 general election.

Who was the longest consecutive serving Member of Parliament?

The longest serving Prime Minister, Sir Wilfrid Laurier, was also the longest consecutive serving Member of Parliament. A member at the time of his death, on February 17, 1919, Laurier had had a seat in the House of Commons for a total of 44 years and 11 months.

Which son of a Premier helped found two political parties?

The son of Ernest Manning, Social Credit Premier of Alberta from 1942 to 1968, Preston Manning founded the Reform Party in 1987. He helped transform the party into the Canadian Reform Conservative Alliance Party thirteen years later.

Who was "The Father of Medicare"?

As PREMIER OF SASKATCHEWAN, A POSITION HE HELD FROM 1944 to 1961, Tommy Douglas struggled against great opposition in creating North America's first Medicare program. Douglas left provincial politics to become the first leader of the New Democratic Party.

A former Baptist minister, Tommy Douglas is best remembered for bringing socialized medicine to Canadians.

Who coined the phrase "corporate welfare bums"?

Former New Democratic Party leader David Lewis achieved his greatest success in the 1972 general election, in which he campaigned against "corporate welfare bums" and the great tax breaks given large corporations in Canada. Winning 31 seats, for the next two years his party held the balance of power in the Liberal minority government of Pierre Elliott Trudeau.

Which Premier was the father of two other Premiers?

Daniel Johnson was elected Union National Premier of Quebec in 1966, a position he held until his sudden death. He was the father of Pierre-Marc Johnson, Parti Québécois Premier of the province for three months in 1985. Another son, Daniel Johnson, was Liberal Premier of Quebec in 1993 and 1994.

Who was Canada's longest serving Premier?

George Murray was Premier of Nova Scotia from 1896 until 1923, a total of over 26 years. Murray's term of office came in the middle of 43 years of consecutive Liberal rule in the province.

Who founded a party based on the ideas of a British economist?

In 1935, future Alberta Premier William Aberhart founded the Social Credit Party based on the theories of economist Clifford H Douglas. That same year, the party won the provincial election and governed Alberta for 35 years and eight months.

Who presided over "les années noires"?

The eighteen years during which Maurice Duplessis was Premier of Quebec are often referred to as "*les années noires*," or "The Dark Years." First elected Premier in 1936, Duplessis is often portrayed as a corrupt and dictatorial leader who had no regard for human rights.

"Bible Bill" Aberhart was a radio evangelist and Premier of Alberta.

Premier René Lévesque was an outspoken advocate for Quebec rights.

Which province has had the most Premiers?

Although it can't count itself amongst the oldest provinces, British Columbia can claim to have had more Premiers than any other. Of the 33 people who have held the office, six never made it to their first anniversary as Premier.

Who was the first woman Premier?

In April 1991, Rita Johnston became Premier of British Columbia after the resignation of her predecessor Bill Vander Zalm. Six months later, her Social Credit government was badly defeated in a provincial election. Johnston lost her seat and retired from politics.

Who was "Wacky"?

W A C Bennett, Premier of British Columbia for two decades, was known as "Wacky" by his detractors. The longest serving of the province's Premiers, Bennett won six provincial elections before being defeated in 1972. Three years later his son, Bill Bennett, was elected Premier.

Which Premier served in the United States Army?

RENÉ LÉVESQUE WORKED AS AN INFORMATION OFFICER FOR THE American army during the Second World War. He later worked as a journalist for Radio Canada International before entering politics in 1960.

Who was the country's first separatist Premier?

Only months after the birth of the Dominion, William Annand's Anti-Confederation Party took 36 of 38 seats in Nova Scotia's first provincial election. Annand proved ineffective in his work for Nova Scotia's withdrawal from Canada.

Isaac Brock was considered the greatest hero in Canadian military history.

Who was victorious at Detroit?

CREDIT FOR THE CAPTURE OF DETROIT, ONE OF THE greatest victories of the War of 1812, rests with Isaac Brock and Tecumseh. The pair cut off American supply routes and began an artillery barrage of the fort. The settlement was surrendered as Brock's soldiers and Tecumseh's warriors prepared for battle.

Who was the greatest Native military leader of the World Wars?

A veteran of the First and Second World Wars, Mohawk Brigadier Magistrate Oliver Milton Martin achieved the highest military rank ever held by a Native Canadian. Martin was also the first Native Canadian to hold a judicial post in Ontario.

Which future Governor General commanded the Canadian troops?

In 1916, Julian Byng took command of the Canadian Army Corps on the Western Front and led Canadian forces to their historic victory at Vimy Ridge. A decade later, he was given the title Viscount Byng of Vimy and became Canada's twelfth Governor General.

Who was known as "Guts and Gaiters"?

The last commander of the Canadian Corps during the First World War, Sir Arthur Currie is generally acknowledged as the country's greatest military leader of the 20th century. His victories, against all odds, at the battles of Passchendaele and Amiens remain two high points in Canadian military history.

Who said, "I will answer your general through the muzzles of my cannon and muskets"?

In 1690, Count Frontenac made the statement – "Je nay point de réponse a faire a votre general que par la bouche de mes canons et à coups de fuzil" – in response to the demand that he surrender Quebec. The general in question, Sir William Phips, failed to take the city.

Who was the first great Canadian soldier?

Born at Montreal in 1661, Pierre Le Moyne d'Iberville is often considered the first great Canadian-born military leader. Among his many accomplishments was the 1697 sinking of two British warships on Hudson's Bay. He was the first Canadian-born soldier to receive France's Croix de Saint-Louis for valour.

An early depiction of The Militia of the Holy Family who were the defenders of Ville Marie (later Montreal).

What was The Militia of the Holy Family?

ESTABLISHED BY PAUL DE MAISONNEUVE, THE FOUNDER OF MONTREAL, the Militia was entrusted with the defence of the settlement against the Iroquois Confederacy.

Who was the man called "Intrepid"?

Winnipeg's William Stephenson worked under the code name as a coordinator of British and American intelligence during the Second World War. Credited with downing more than twenty enemy aircraft, Stephenson was decorated during the First World War. He is thought to have served as the model for "M" in Ian Fleming's *James Bond* novels.

What were Butler's Rangers?

The Rangers was a corps of Loyalists that fought during the American Revolution. Formed and led by John Butler, the son of a British military officer, they launched a series of successful raids from northern New York to Kentucky.

Which general originated the armoured infantry carrier?

Lieutenant General Guy Granville Simonds is often considered the finest general Canada has ever produced. He is credited with the armoured infantry carrier, which was first used during the Second World War.

Who was knighted as a military genius?

Minister of the Militia, Sir Samuel Hughes was credited with many improvements in the Militia and the quick mobilization of the Canadian Expeditionary Force at the beginning of the First World War. Although he was knighted in 1915, the following year Hughes lost his ministry due to a number of patronage scandals.

185

Whose book was used as a political tool?

George Monro Grant transformed Queen's University into one of Canada's leading institutions.

During the summer of 1872, Reverend

George Monro Grant accompanied his parishioner, Sir Sanford Fleming, on a voyage from Halifax to the Pacific Ocean. *Ocean to Ocean*, Grant's record of the journey, was used by the Macdonald government in support of the Pacific railway.

Who led Nova Scotia away from revolution?

Since 1760, evangelist Henry Alline had been travelling throughout Nova Scotia and had become an extremely influential preacher. At the outbreak of the American Revolution, Alline preached that war was sinful and encouraged his followers towards pacifism.

What are the Jesuit Relations?

The Relations are a series of forty annual accounts written by Jesuit priests in New France. Together, the Jesuit Relations provide the most important and accurate record of the history and cultural life of New France between 1632 and 1672. The Superior of the missions in New France, Paul Le Jeune, is credited with launching the series.

Who was "The Poet of the Laurentians"?

Montreal Archdeacon Frederick George Scott was the author of 13 volumes of poetry. He served as a chaplain during the First World War and wrote about his experiences in *The Great War as I Saw It*. One of his children was the poet and lawyer F R Scott.

Who was Alfred Bessette?

Better known as Brother André, Bessette was one of the most popular Canadian religious figures in the 20th century. In 1904, he built a shrine to Saint Joseph on Mount Royal. The present oratory took 31 years to complete and is a Montreal landmark.

Which black preacher lived among the First Nations?

In the late 18th century, John Marrant, a free American black, lived as a missionary among many Native communities. He later founded a religious community in Nova Scotia. His successful biography, *A Narrative of the Lord's Wonderful Dealings with John Marrant, A Black*, was republished sixteen times.

Which surgeon led a Canadian church?

The son of Canadian medical missionaries,

Robert McClure was raised in China. He followed in his parents' footsteps, serving as a surgeon and medical educator in China, Gaza, India, Borneo, Peru, the Caribbean, and Zaire. From 1968 to 1971 he served as the first non-ordained moderator of the United Church of Canada. He continued to fight for those in the Third World into his nineties.

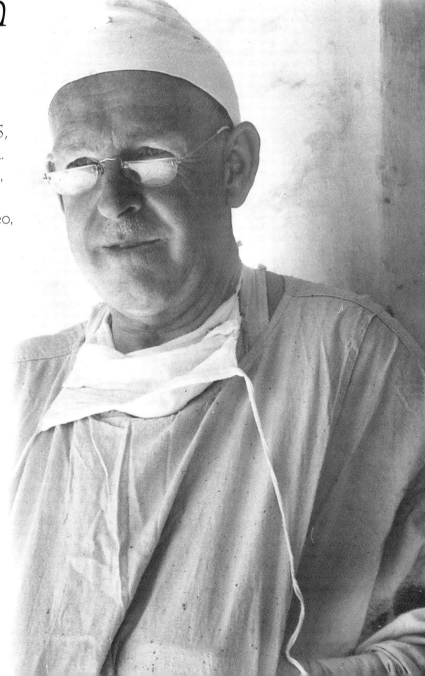

Missionary surgeon Robert McClure's first posting was to China in 1923.

Which spiritual leader is the son of a Governor General?

Jean Vanier, the son of Georges Vanier, is one of the leading advocates of mentally handicapped adults. Renowned for his leadership in spiritual retreats, Vanier is also a best-selling author. Among his books are *Becoming Human* and *Finding Peace*.

Who was Canada's first rabbi?

In 1768, the first congregation, She'arith Israel, more commonly known as the Spanish and Portuguese Synagogue, was founded in Montreal. Ten years later, the congregation engaged Jacob Raphael Cohen, a rabbi from London, England.

Which is Canada's oldest mosque?

Completed in 1938, Edmonton's Al Rashid Mosque is the oldest in North America. James Ailley acted as Imam from the mosque's founding until his death in 1959.

Which poet fought for civil liberties?

ONE OF THE LEADING CANADIAN POETS OF THE 20TH CENTURY, F R SCOTT USED his positions as a professor and lawyer to work for social justice. His work on the Royal Commission on Bilingualism and Biculturalism helped extend French-language rights throughout the country.

F R Scott was a major figure in Canadian law, literature, and politics.

Who drafted the Universal Declaration of Human Rights?
New Brunswick's John Peters Humphrey. A member of the Faculty of Law at McGill University, in 1946 he was appointed Director of the United Nations Division of Human Rights. His draft of the Declaration served as the foundation for the document that was adopted in 1948. Humphrey's contribution to international human rights was not acknowledged until the 1990s when the draft was discovered.

Which journalist and activist helped found Casey House?

Casey House, the world's first hospice devoted to persons with AIDS, was the idea of June Callwood. It is one of over 50 organizations that Callwood has helped found.

Which suffragette was a popular novelist?

In the early 20th century, Nellie McClung was one of the country's leading suffragists and authors. A strong proponent of women's rights, she was instrumental in winning the vote for women. She was elected to the Alberta Legislature in the election of 1921, the first in which women could vote. McClung's 1908 novel, *Sowing Seeds in Danny*, was one of the best-selling Canadian novels of the 20th century.

What was the Toronto Women's Literary Club?

Despite its name, the literary club was actually Canada's first suffrage organization. Established by Dr Emily Stowe in 1877, five years later the club changed its name to the Toronto Women's Suffrage Club.

Reformer and radio host Thérèse Casgrain.

Which Senator lost nine election campaigns?

Despite her failure to be elected to public office, Montreal's Thérèse Casgrain played a very significant role in 20th-century Canada. The daughter of a wealthy financier and Conservative politician, Casgrain devoted herself to dozens of social causes. Pierre Elliott Trudeau appointed Casgrain as an independent Senator in 1970.

Who were "The Famous Five"?

Emily Murphy, Henrietta Muir Edwards, Nellie McClung, Louise McKinney, and Irene Parlby were the Famous Five, a group of prominent women's rights advocates who won the Persons Case in 1929.

Sports

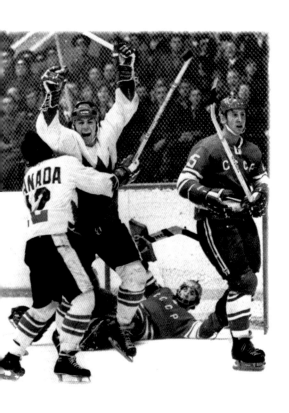

Which historical figure named lacrosse?
The sport was given its name by French missionary Jean de Brébeuf in the 17th century. After witnessing a Native game, he wrote that the sticks reminded him of a bishop's crosier, or staff.

Which popular sport evolved from baggataway?
Lacrosse is derived from baggataway, a game played by several First Nations groups. Games were played by as many as 200 players on fields up to a kilometre in length, and could last as long as three days.

What is double ball?
A traditional game of the Plains Cree, double ball is similar to baggataway. Played primarily by women on a field over one kilometre long, players use curved sticks to pass two joined bags. The first team to throw the double ball across the opposing goal line is declared the winner.

Which international competition celebrates traditional Inuit sports?

Held every two years, the Arctic Winter Games include both traditional Inuit games and more recent northern sports such as hockey. The first games were held in 1970 in Yellowknife.

The Arctic Winter Games have featured teams from Canada, the United States, Greenland, and Russia.

Who plays the high kick?

The high kick is one of the more popular

traditional Inuit games. There are three versions of the sport. Each involves jumping to kick a suspended object and landing in a particular manner. The object, usually a piece of rolled sealskin, is slowly raised. Players are gradually eliminated for failing in the "kick," until only one player, the winner, remains.

Which lake is the setting of Canada's oldest sporting event?

Quidi Vidi Lake in St John's is home to the Newfoundland regatta. Since at least 1826, rowing crews have raced from one end of the lake to the other and back again.

Which sport did General Wolfe's soldiers play?

Documentation indicates that several Scottish officers during the Seven Years' War played golf in Canada.

Which British sport evolved into baseball?

In the 18th and 19th centuries, Canadians played rounders. Very similar to baseball, the sport was played on a diamond-shaped field and featured a batter and pitcher. One of the major differences between the two sports is that in the original rules of rounders, a runner could be eliminated by being hit with a thrown ball.

An Inuit high kicker.

193

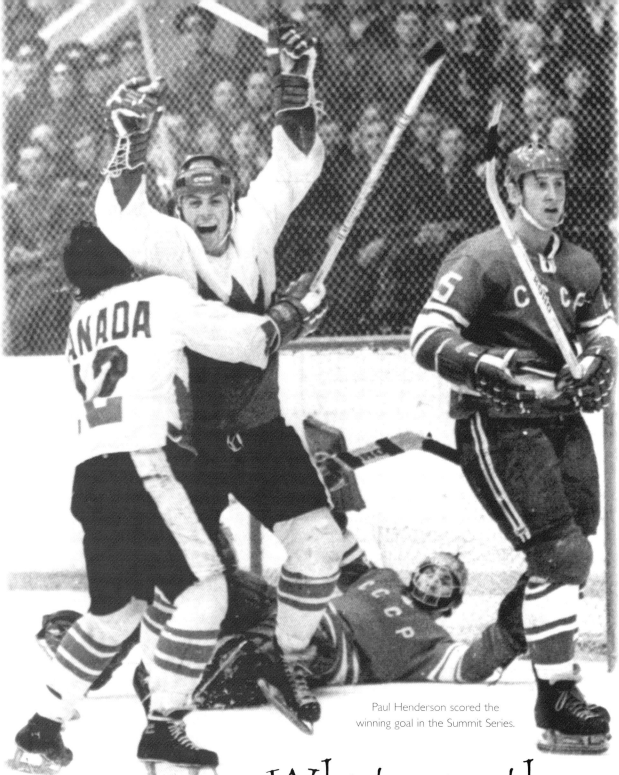

Paul Henderson scored the winning goal in the Summit Series.

What was the World Hockey Association?

Established in 1971, the WHA was a professional hockey league designed to rival the NHL. Although plagued with financial difficulties and troubled franchises, the league attracted dozens of high-profile players, including Bobby Hull, Gordie Howe, and Wayne Gretzky. The WHA merged with the NHL after the 1978–79 season.

What was the Summit Series?

BETTER KNOWN AS THE CANADA/RUSSIA SERIES, THE EIGHT-GAME TOURNAMENT was the first to feature the best Canadian and Soviet hockey players. The series was won in the final minute of the eighth game when Canada's Paul Henderson scored, giving the Canadians six goals to the Soviets' five.

Who was the first player to score 50 goals in 50 games?

1921-2000

Maurice Richard **LE ROCKET**

Maurice Richard won 8 of Montreal's 39 Stanley Cups.

T HE RECORD WAS FIRST SET BY MAURICE RICHARD during the 1944–45 season. Twelve years later he became the first player to achieve 500 goals. The Rocket, as he was known, spent his 18-season career with the Montreal Canadiens, with whom he won eight Stanley Cups.

Where was the first hockey game played?

While Windsor, Nova Scotia claims to be the birthplace of hockey, introducing the game around 1800, the first recorded game took place in Kingston, Ontario on Christmas Day in 1855.

Who was the Chicoutimi Cucumber?

Chicoutimi-born Georges Vezina earned the nickname due to his attitude while tending goal for the Montreal Canadiens. He was said to have been "as cool as a cucumber." The Vezina Trophy is named in his honour.

Who was Stanley?

The Stanley Cup is named after Sir Frederick Arthur Stanley, who served as Canada's Governor General from 1888 until 1893. In the last year of his term, he donated the trophy as an award for Canada's top-ranking amateur club. In 1926, the Stanley Cup was adopted by the National Hockey League as its championship prize.

Which city has been home to the Stanley Cup more than any other?

Hockey's greatest trophy has been won 39 times by teams from Montreal: the Canadiens (24 times), the Wanderers (4 times), the Victorias (4 times), the AAA (3 times), the Maroons (twice), and the Shamrocks (twice).

Which hockey great had his sons as teammates?

Saskatchewan's Gordie Howe, known as Mr Hockey, played eight seasons, from 1973 to 1980, with his sons Mark Howe and Marty Howe as members of the Houston Aeros, the New England Whalers, and the Hartford Whalers.

Who is known as "The Great One"?

Wayne Gretzky is considered by many to be the greatest player of all time. In a 20-season NHL career he set over a dozen records, including most goals scored (894), most assists (1,963), and most points (2,857).

Where is the country's oldest sports club?

Established in 1807, the Montreal Curling Club was the first sports club in Canada and is the oldest curling club in North America.

Which soldiers are said to have invented curling?

Although there is no documentation supporting the claim, some believe that curling was first played by Scottish soldiers stationed in North America during the Seven Years' War.

What was the Richardson Rink?

One of the finest in the history of the game, the Richardson Rink consisted of brothers Ernie and Garnet Richardson, and their cousins Wes and Arnold Richardson.

When was the first Brier?

The Canadian men's championship, the Brier, was first held in 1927 at Toronto's Granite Club. The rink from Nova Scotia under Murray McNeill was awarded the championship.

Curling has been Canada's most-played women's team winter sport since its introduction in the early 19th century.

When was curling introduced as an Olympic sport?

Although curling for men was included at the 1924 Winter Olympic Games, it was then dropped as a medal sport until 1988 when it was reintroduced for both men and women.

Who won the first Olympic medal in women's curling?

CANADIANS JAN BETKER, MARCIA GUDEREIT, AND JOAN McCUSKER, with Sandra Schmirler as skip, were dominant in women's curling during the last decade of the 20th century. In 1998, the team won the first Olympic gold medal for women's curling in Nagano, Japan.

Which province has dominated the Canadian women's championship?
The championship, currently known as the Scott Tournament of Hearts, dates back to 1961. As of 2002, Saskatchewan had won the title 10 times more than any other rink.

Sandra Schmirler was known as "The Queen of Curling."

Which skip won the most Briers?
Between 1959 and 1963, Saskatchewan's Ernie Richardson won four Briers, more than any other skip. Alberta's Randy Ferby also took part in four championship teams, but was skip for only two of them.

Which province has won the Brier the most times?
As of 2002, Manitoba had won the most Briers with 26 victories. The province also holds the record for most consecutive wins, having won the championship five times from 1928 to 1932. New Brunswick, Prince Edward Island, and teams representing the territories have yet to win.

Who was skiing at the age of 100?

AFTER CELEBRATING HIS 100TH BIRTHDAY IN 1975, NORWEGIAN–BORN HERMAN Smith Johannsen was still skiing eight kilometres (five miles) each day. Credited with helping to popularize downhill and cross-country skiing in Canada, he was given the name "Jackrabbit" by his fans. He lived to the age of 111.

How long is the Canadian Ski Marathon?

The marathon runs a 160-kilometre (100-mile) route from Lachute, Quebec to Buckingham, Quebec, overnighting in Montebello. First organized in celebration of Canada's Centennial, the marathon is now an annual event attracting more than 2,000 skiers from around the world.

"Jackrabbit" Johannsen was a ski organizer, coach, instructor, and official.

Who were the first people to ski in Canada?

Although there is no archeological evidence, it is assumed that the Vikings were the first to ski in North America. The Norse people had been using long wooden sticks, the forerunners of what we recognize as skis, for over 3,000 years before they first landed on territory now part of Canada.

Nancy Greene was the most famous Canadian skier of the 1960s.

Who won the first World Cup?

IN 1967, BRITISH COLUMBIA'S NANCY GREENE BECAME the first woman to win the cup. The following year, she was awarded gold and silver medals at the Winter Olympics in Grenoble, France. She won the World Cup a second time in 1969 before retiring from competition. In 1999 Nancy Greene was voted Canada's female athlete of the century.

Who were "The Crazy Canucks"?

In the 1970s, downhill skiers Ken Read, Steve Podborski, Dave Irwin, and David Murray were called the Crazy Canucks for their exciting, high-flying style.

Who was the first Canadian skier to win Olympic gold?

In the 1960 winter games at Squaw Valley, Anne Heggtveit took home a gold medal in the slalom event.

Who won a World Cup?

In 1975, Calgary's Ken Read became the first non-European male with a victory in Val d'Isère, France. That same year, he won the first of five consecutive national championships.

When was the country's first ski competition held?

The first known competition took place in Rossland, British Columbia in 1897.

Who was an Olympic athlete at fourteen?

Kathy Kreiner was the youngest competitor at the 1972 Sapporo Olympics. Four years later, at her second Olympic Games in Innsbruck, Austria, she won the gold medal in the giant slalom.

Which river served as the course of Canada's first ice-skating race?

The country's first recorded ice-skating race took place on the St Lawrence River. In 1854, three army officers raced from Montreal to Quebec City.

Who defended her Olympic title?

Speed skater Catriona Le May Doan won gold in the 500 metres at the 1998 Nagano Olympics. In winning the gold a second time in the 500 metres at the 2002 Salt Lake City, she became the very first Canadian to defend an individual Olympic title.

Who is Canada's greatest Winter Olympian?

THE WINNER OF FOUR OLYMPIC MEDALS, GAÉTAN BOUCHER competed as a speed skater in four Winter Olympics. His best performances came at the 1984 Sarajevo Games where he won two gold medals and a bronze.

Gaétan Boucher is Canada's most successful Winter Olympic athlete.

Who is the "skater with a painter's eye"?

Toller Cranston is considered one of the most creative and artistic of Canada's many figure skating champions. Since retiring from amateur competition, he has devoted much of his time to painting.

Who said "Pain is short-lived, but pride lasts a lifetime"?

World Champion Elvis Stojko made the statement after the 1998 Winter Olympics. Though injured, the figure skater captured a silver medal for his performance.

Who was the first world skating champion?

In 1890, Montreal's Louis Rubinstein was declared champion at the first world figure-skating championships. Held in Russia, the competition was based on compulsory figures and free skating.

Which politician first achieved fame as a figure skater?

In 1962 Otto Jelinek and his sister Marie won the pairs gold medal at the World Figure-Skating Championships in Prague. Ten years later Otto Jelinek was elected to the House of Commons as a Progressive Conservative. He served as Minister of State for Fitness and Amateur Sport in the Mulroney government.

Which figure skating pair received silver and gold medals for the same dance?

Jamie Salé and David Pelletier were awarded silver medals at the 2002 Salt Lake City Olympic Games. However, the couple were later awarded gold medals after a judging scandal was revealed.

Who was "the man with million dollar legs"?

Saint John's Charles Gorman earned the nickname as a world champion speed skater. Despite suffering shrapnel wounds in one leg during the First World War, he managed to set seven world records with his sweeping stride.

Who won every championship?

The daughter of speed skaters, from 1921 until her retirement in 1936 Lela Brooks so dominated speed skating that she held every title available to women.

Who is "The Kid from Caroline"?

Raised in Caroline, Alberta, Kurt Browning is the man behind the nickname. A four-time World Champion, in 1988 Browning became the first to perform a quadruple jump in competition. His car licence plate reads: 1STQUAD.

Olympian Barbara Ann Scott was so popular that a doll was created in her image.

Who was "Canada's Sweetheart"?

BARBARA ANN SCOTT WAS GIVEN THE TITLE IN 1947 AFTER becoming the first North American figure skater to win the World Championship. In 1948, she repeated her success, becoming the first North American to capture a gold medal in the Winter Olympics.

Who won Olympic gold in the bobsled?

In the 1964 Winter Olympics, Vic Emery, John Emery, Peter Kirby, and Doug Anakin surprised their European competitors by winning the gold medal in the sport. At the time, there were no training facilities or bobsled runs in Canada.

Which Winter Olympics was Canada's best?

Canada won more medals at the 2002 Salt Lake City games than any other. The final results were six gold, three silver, and eight bronze.

Which Prime Minister was an Olympic athlete?

As a recipient of a two-year scholarship to England's Oxford University, Lester B Pearson played with the British hockey team at the 1920 Olympics.

Five years after it opened, Calgary's Saddledome housed many of the most popular events at the 1988 Calgary Winter Olympics.

Which Canadians won gold medals at the Calgary Olympic Games?

ALTHOUGH FIGURE SKATERS BRIAN ORSER AND ELIZABETH MANLEY TOOK home silver medals for their performances, no Canadians struck gold in Calgary. The country had previously failed to win a gold medal at the 1976 Montreal summer games.

Which is the only Canadian city to host the Winter Olympics?

Calgary was the host of the XV Winter Olympic Games in 1988. Vancouver, Banff, Montreal, and Quebec have also bid for the right to host the games.

Which was the best Olympics for Canada's men's hockey team?

The Winnipeg Falcons, the Canadian hockey team at the 1920 Winter Olympics, won all five of their games, outscoring their opponents 110 to 3 – an average score of 22 to less than 1.

The 2002 Canadian women's hockey team won the gold medal at the Salt Lake City Winter Olympics.

How many medals have been won by Canada's hockey teams?

THE CANADIAN MEN'S TEAMS HAVE WON A TOTAL OF FOURTEEN MEDALS – EIGHT gold, four silver, and two bronze. The Canadian women's team has won one gold and one silver since women's hockey became a medal sport at the 1998 Nagano games.

Who beat Canada's men's hockey team in 1936?

The team from Great Britain defeated the Canadian team at the games. However, 9 of the 12 victorious players were Canadians who had been born in England, thus eligible for the British team.

Who was the first snowboarder to earn a gold medal?

In 1998, at the Nagano Winter Olympics, Vancouver's Ross Rebagliati became the first person to receive a gold medal in snowboarding. He started participating in the sport in 1987.

Which Canadian biathlete won Olympic gold?

Quebec's Myriam Bédard won the 7.5 and 15-kilometre events at the 1994 Winter Olympics, becoming the first non-European biathlete to take home gold medals.

When was hockey played in the summer?

The 1920 summer games in Antwerp, Belgium featured figure skating and hockey. The International Olympic Committee had hesitated in establishing a winter games, believing it would be too limiting. In fact, the 1924 games in Chamonix, France were recognized as the first Winter Olympic Games only after the fact.

Who were stars in both lacrosse and hockey?
Frederick "Cyclone" Taylor, professional hockey's first star, played lacrosse with the New Westminster Salmonbellies. Edouard "Newsy" Lalonde dominated lacrosse in the early part of the 20th century, while being one of the earliest stars of hockey's Montreal Canadiens.

Who was Minto?
The Canadian Lacrosse Association's junior championship award, the Minto Cup, is named after Sir Gilbert John Murray Kynynmond Elliot, Fourth Earl of Minto, Governor General of Canada from 1898 until 1904. A sports enthusiast, the Governor General and his wife were the founders of the Minto Skating Club in Ottawa.

Which was the greatest team of all time?
The Ottawa Green Gaels are often cited as the greatest team of all time. Between 1963 and 1969 the team played 241 games, losing only 20. They won the Minto Cup seven years in a row.

Who was Mann?
The Mann Cup, the senior championship trophy of the Canadian Lacrosse Association, is named after Sir Donald Mann. A wealthy railway builder and entrepreneur, Mann donated the trophy in 1910.

What was "The Sportsmen's Battery"?
Headed by sports entrepreneur Conn Smyth, the 30th Light Anti-aircraft Battery in the Second World War included every member of the Mimico Mountaineers, the winners of the 1941 Mann Cup.

Who was the "Father of Lacrosse"?

Junior lacrosse team-players challenge one other for the Minto Cup.

Dr George Beers laid down the rules of
modern lacrosse in 1860. His book, *Lacrosse: The National Game of Canada*, was considered the sport's first rule book. In 1867, he established the National Lacrosse Association. A Montreal dental surgeon, Beers founded and edited the *Canada Journal of Dental Science* and was the head of Canada's first dental college.

Which was the first Canadian team to win the Champion's Cup?
In 1999, the Toronto Rock became the first Canadian team to win the National Lacrosse League's championship trophy. The following year, the Rock again won the cup in the final sporting event held in Toronto's famous Maple Leaf Gardens.

The first lacrosse players were the Algonquian tribes of eastern Canada.

Who won Olympic gold?

Lacrosse was an Olympic sport at the 1904 St Louis and 1908 London games. In 1904, the Winnipeg Shamrock Lacrosse Club defeated a local team from St Louis to win the gold medal. In 1908, Canada won the gold by defeating the English team. Although lacrosse was a demonstration sport at the Olympics in 1928, 1932, and 1948, it hasn't regained its official Olympic status.

Where can you visit the Canadian Lacrosse Hall of Fame?

Although lacrosse originated in eastern Canada, the Hall of Fame is located in New Westminster, BC. It was officially opened during centennial year.

Is lacrosse Canada's official national sport?

ALTHOUGH MANY CANADIANS THOUGHT OTHERWISE, CANADA had no official national sport until 1994 when the National Sport Act recognized lacrosse as the country's national summer sport, and hockey as Canada's national winter sport.

Which Canadian teams have played in the National Lacrosse League?

Although the League's origins can be traced back to 1986, it wasn't until the 1997 admission of Hamilton's Ontario Raiders that the League had any Canadian teams. The team was later moved to Toronto, where it was renamed the Toronto Rock. Other Canadian teams are the Ottawa Rebels, the Calgary Roughnecks, the Vancouver Ravens, and the now defunct Montreal Express.

Which Canadian team won the World Series?

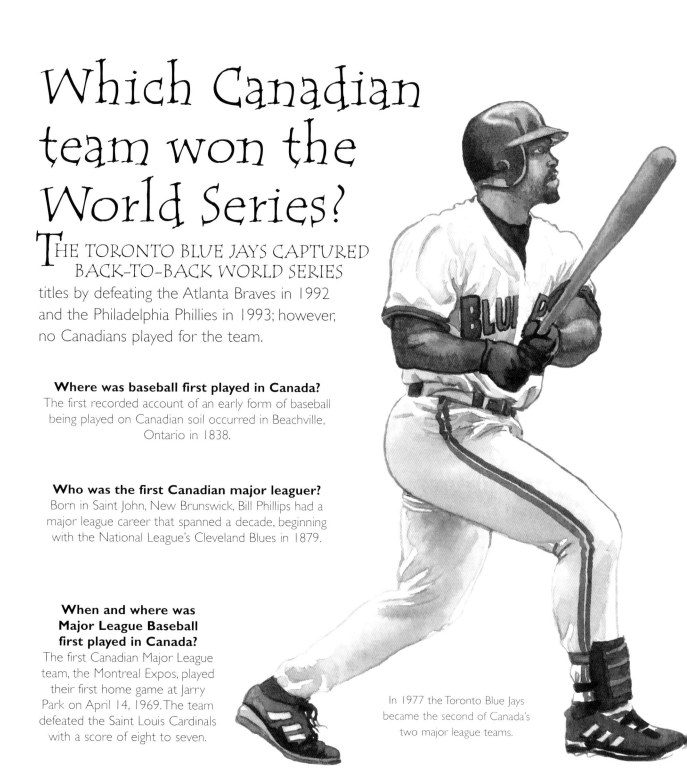

THE TORONTO BLUE JAYS CAPTURED BACK-TO-BACK WORLD SERIES titles by defeating the Atlanta Braves in 1992 and the Philadelphia Phillies in 1993; however, no Canadians played for the team.

Where was baseball first played in Canada?
The first recorded account of an early form of baseball being played on Canadian soil occurred in Beachville, Ontario in 1838.

Who was the first Canadian major leaguer?
Born in Saint John, New Brunswick, Bill Phillips had a major league career that spanned a decade, beginning with the National League's Cleveland Blues in 1879.

When and where was Major League Baseball first played in Canada?
The first Canadian Major League team, the Montreal Expos, played their first home game at Jarry Park on April 14, 1969. The team defeated the Saint Louis Cardinals with a score of eight to seven.

In 1977 the Toronto Blue Jays became the second of Canada's two major league teams.

Where did Jackie Robinson break the "colour barrier"?
Until Jackie Robinson, African-Americans were barred from playing Major League Baseball. In 1945, Robinson was signed by the Brooklyn Dodgers and sent to their Triple-A level International League minor league affiliate, the Montreal Royals. He became the first African-American to play in the minor leagues in the 20th century. In 1947, he played his first major league game.

What was worn by Art Irwin?
Toronto-born shortstop Art "Foxy" Irwin is usually cited as the inventor of the baseball glove. In 1883, he broke two fingers while attempting to catch a ball. He used a stuffed, oversized glove to play future games. Another Canadian, Phil Powers, a catcher with the London Tecumsehs, is sometimes credited with having invented the baseball glove in the 1878.

Which Prime Minister is a member of the Canadian Baseball Hall of Fame?
Lester B Pearson was inducted to the Hall of Fame in 1983. As a young man the future Prime Minister played in the Ontario Intercounty League and later served as an honorary board member of the Montreal Expos. From 1978 to 1986, the Pearson Cup was presented to the winner of an annual exhibition game between the Expos and the Toronto Blue Jays.

Who was the first Canadian to be inducted into the Baseball Hall of Fame?

THE COUNTRY'S GREATEST BASEBALL PLAYER, FERGUSON JENKINS, received the Major League honour in 1991. During a career spanning 19 seasons, Jenkins was one of the finest pitchers in Major League Baseball, receiving the National League Cy Young Award in 1971.

The great pitcher Ferguson Jenkins went on to become Commissioner of the Canadian Baseball League.

Who is the Canadian home run champ?

At the end of the 2002 season British Columbia's Larry Walker had a total of 335 career home runs, more than any other Canadian player.

Which professional league began in 2003?

The Canadian Baseball League began its inaugural season in May 2003 with eight teams: the Calgary Outlaws, Kelowna Heat, London Monarchs, Montreal Royales, Niagara Stars, Saskatoon Legends, Trois-Rivières Saints, and Victoria Capitals. The league's commissioner is Ferguson Jenkins.

Who replaced Babe Ruth?

After the legendary outfielder was traded to the Boston Braves in 1934, the New York Yankees replaced him with Ontario's George Selkirk. During his next nine years on the team, the Yankees won the Pennant five times.

Which team has won the most Grey Cups?

THE RECORD GOES TO EITHER THE HAMILTON TIGER-CATS OR THE

Edmonton Eskimos. The Tiger-Cats were formed through the 1950 merger of the Hamilton Tigers and the Hamilton Flying Wildcats. Together, these teams won the Cup a total of 14 times. The Edmonton Eskimos have won the Cup eleven times, including a record five consecutive championships from 1978 to 1982. On 21 occasions the Grey Cup has been won by teams from Toronto.

The Grey Cup was crafted by Birks Jewellers.

When was the Canadian Football League established?

Although the League didn't begin until 1958, many of its teams are considerably older. The Toronto Argonauts, the Winnipeg Blue Bombers, the Calgary Stampeders, and the Ottawa Rough Riders had all won the Grey Cup before the CFL existed.

Which American city's name is engraved on the Grey Cup?

Baltimore's CFL team, the Stallions, won the cup in 1995, beating the Calgary Stampeders 37 to 20.

Which team holds the record for most touchdowns in a single game?

In 1956, the Montreal Alouettes made twelve touchdowns to defeat the Hamilton Tiger-Cats by a score of 82 to 14. Montreal still holds the record for the greatest number of points scored by a team in a single game.

Who was Grey?

The Grey Cup is named after Sir Albert Henry George Grey, the fourth Earl Grey, who donated the trophy in 1909. The first Grey Cup game featured the University of Toronto against the Parkdale Canoe Club. The University of Toronto won the game by a score of 26 to 6.

What was the "Fog Bowl"?

Held in Toronto, the 1962 Grey Cup game was stopped due to a heavy fog that had rolled in off Lake Ontario. The final 9 minutes and 29 seconds were played the following day. The Winnipeg Blue Bombers beat the Hamilton Tiger-Cats 28 to 27.

Which Prime Minister drank from the Grey Cup?

Pierre Elliott Trudeau drank champagne from the cup on a number of occasions. While Prime Minister he attended seven Grey Cup games, participated in the opening kick-off, and presented the cup to the champions.

Which six cities lost their CFL teams?

The league expanded into the United States for the 1993, 1994, and 1995 seasons. The cities of Baltimore, Birmingham, Las Vegas, Memphis, Sacramento, and San Antonio fielded teams. In 1996, the Baltimore team moved to Canada, becoming the new Montreal Alouettes. All the other American teams folded.

Which team has won the Vanier Cup the most times?

Named after Governor General Georges Vanier, the Vanier Cup is awarded to Canada's national university football champions. The Mustangs from the University of Western Ontario have won the cup six times, two more than their nearest rivals, the Calgary Dinos.

Who is the greatest Canadian receiver?

Most would agree that Montreal-born Terry Evanshen earned the title during his 14-year CFL career. In 198 games as a Stampeder, Alouette, Tiger-Cat, and Argonaut, he caught 600 passes, achieving 80 touchdowns, while fumbling only three times.

What is the oldest CFL team?

The history of the Toronto Argonauts can be traced back to 1873, when members of the city's Argonaut Rowing Club formed a rugby team. The youngest team is the Ottawa Renegade, which entered the league in 2002.

Who is considered the greatest Canadian quarterback?

HAMILTON-BORN RUSS JACKSON IS MOST often cited as the finest quarterback the country has produced. Drafted by the Ottawa Rough Riders in 1958, Jackson broke numerous records during a 12-year career. He won three Grey Cups and was three times voted the league's most outstanding player.

Russ Jackson began playing football professionally at the age of 21.

Which Premier once played in the CFL?

Beginning in 1955, Don Getty spent 10 seasons as a quarterback for the Edmonton Eskimos. He helped the team win two Grey Cup championships in 1955 and 1956. A Quebecer, he was elected as a Progressive Conservative member of the Alberta Legislature in 1967. He became Premier in 1985 after the resignation of Premier Peter Lougheed. Getty himself resigned as Premier in 1992.

Margaret MacBurney
FORWARD

CANADA

EDMONTON
COMMERCIAL
GRADUATES
BASKETBALL
CLUB
WORLD'S
CHAMPIONS

CANADA

J. Percy Page
COACH

CANADA

Mildred
McCormack
FORWARD

Kate Macrae
GUARD

Mae Brown
UTILITY

CAPT
Elsie
GUA

James Naismith considered the Edmonton Grads "the finest team that ever stepped out on a floor."

Which was the greatest basketball team of all time?

THE EDMONTON COMMERCIAL GRADUATES BASKETBALL CLUB, USUALLY REFERRED TO as the Edmonton Grads, is often described as the best team in any sport. Between 1915 and 1940, the Grads won 502 of 522 games. Six decades after the team folded, the Grads' winning record remains unequalled.

Who invented basketball?
Ontario's Dr James Naismith created the game in 1892 while working at a YMCA in Springfield, Massachusetts. At least 10 of the players in the first game were students from Quebec.

Who coached the Grads?
During their 25-year history, the team was coached by only one person, John Percy Page. He was once described by James Naismith as the "greatest coach and the most superb sportsman it has ever been my good fortune to meet."

What stopped the Grads from receiving Olympic medals?
Although the team represented Canada in four Olympic games, winning all 27 of their matches, the Grads weren't awarded medals because they were women. It wasn't until the 1976 Montreal Olympics that women's basketball became an official event.

What is the origin of the sport's name?
The first games were played with a soccer ball using two peach baskets suspended three metres (ten feet) above the floor. The baskets were eventually replaced by iron hoops with suspended cord nets.

Where was the first National Basketball Association game played?
Toronto is considered to be the location of the very first NBA game. Played on November 1, 1946, the New York Knickerbockers defeated the Toronto Huskies 68 to 66. The teams were part of the Basketball Association of America, which evolved into the NBA. The Huskies played only one season with the league. It wasn't until 49 years later that the NBA returned to Canada.

Which Canadian was a member of three championship teams?
Rick Fox was a member of the NBA's Los Angeles Lakers during their three championship seasons in 2000, 2001, and 2002.

Who were the Vancouver Grizzlies?
In 1995, the Grizzlies and the Toronto Raptors became the first Canadian teams in the National Basketball Association since the Toronto Huskies. A lacklustre team with poor attendance, the Grizzlies finished last in their division in five of their six seasons. In 2001, the team was moved from Vancouver to Memphis.

Who was the first Canadian player in the WNBA?
Calgary's Kelly Boucher played for Charlotte Sting in 1998, the year after the Women's National Basketball Association began play. A former member of Canada's Olympic team, she has played professional basketball for teams in the United States, Israel, Germany, Switzerland, Italy, Hungary, and Luxembourg.

Who was W P McGee?
The championship trophy awarded annually in Canadian men's university basketball is named after Rev. William McGee, a teacher and coach at Assumption College. First presented in 1963, the trophy has been won by teams from the University of Victoria on eight different occasions.

Who was the first Canadian to be on a NBA All-Star team?

VICTORIA'S STEVE NASH OF THE DALLAS Mavericks is one of the league's best point guards. A player in the NBA since 1996, he was named to the 2002 All-Star team.

In 2002, Steve Nash (right) became the first basketball player to receive the Lionel Conacher Award as Canada's male athlete of the year.

What was the North American Soccer League?

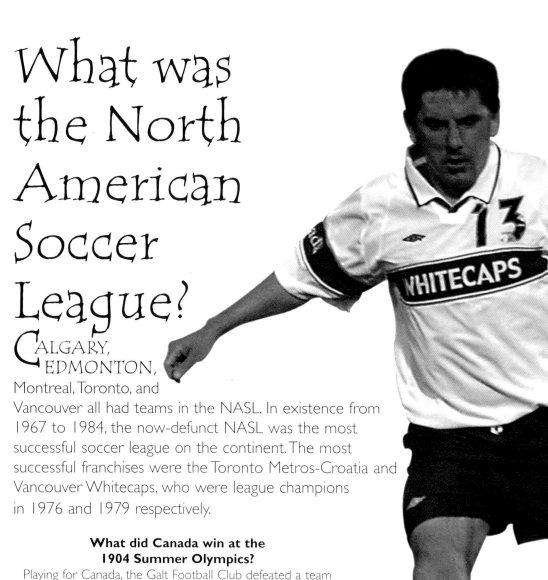

CALGARY, EDMONTON, Montreal, Toronto, and Vancouver all had teams in the NASL. In existence from 1967 to 1984, the now-defunct NASL was the most successful soccer league on the continent. The most successful franchises were the Toronto Metros-Croatia and Vancouver Whitecaps, who were league champions in 1976 and 1979 respectively.

What did Canada win at the 1904 Summer Olympics?
Playing for Canada, the Galt Football Club defeated a team from the United States to win the gold medal. Canada has yet to win another Olympic medal, gold or otherwise, in the sport.

When was the first Canadian soccer game?
Although a variation of the sport had been played in Canada since the early 19th century, the first game as played today took place in 1876 in Toronto.

Is soccer more popular than hockey?
While hockey may be dearest to the heart of the average Canadian, more people participate in soccer. Nearly 700,000 players are registered in Canada, more than any other sport.

Who was known as "Cowboy?"
During the 1950s, Errol Crossan earned the nickname "Cowboy" as the only North American player for several British teams. He played in a total of twelve FA cup games, scoring four goals.

Which goalkeeper won the FA Cup?
From 1931 until 1939, Montreal's James "Joe" Kennaway was a star goalkeeper for the Glasgow Celtic. During his years with the club, Kennaway was awarded two Scottish championship medals and his team won the Scottish FA Cup on three occasions.

The Vancouver Whitecaps continue to play in the United Soccer Leagues' A-League with other Canadian teams from Montreal, Toronto, and Calgary.

Which professional league was "all-Canadian"?

In 1987, the Canadian Soccer League grew out of the ashes of the NASL. The only truly national soccer league, the CSL lasted for only six seasons. Its demise was blamed on poor attendance and the domination of the Vancouver 86ers. Calgary, Victoria, Edmonton, Winnipeg, London, Kitchener, Hamilton, Toronto, North York, Ottawa, Montreal, and Nova Scotia also fielded teams.

How many times has Canada appeared in the World Cup?

In 1986, the men's team reached the finals for the first and only time. They were defeated by France, Hungary, and the Soviet Union. The women's team appeared in 1995 and 1999.

What is the Challenge Cup?

Donated by the English Football Association in 1926, the Challenge Cup is awarded to Canada's champion men's amateur team. Between 1928 and 1960 the New Westminster Royals won the trophy a total of eight times, more than any other team.

Soccer is now played by more Canadian children than any other sport, including hockey.

In which Olympics has Canada participated in soccer?

CANADA HAS SENT A MEN'S TEAM TO ONLY three summer games (1904, 1976, and 1984). Out of a total of eight matches, Canadian teams have won three games, lost four, and had one draw. Canada's record is more impressive when one compares goals for – eighteen – to goals against – nine.

Which city had four different teams in the NASL?

Beginning in 1967, Toronto was home to a succession of four teams: the Falcons, the Metros, the Metros-Croatia, and the Blizzard.

Which Canadian city hosted the summer Olympics?

THE 21ST SUMMER OLYMPIC GAMES WERE HELD IN MONTREAL IN 1976. TORONTO HAS SPENT MILLIONS OF CANADIAN dollars in two failed attempts to become the Games' host city.

Which Canadian was the first to win Olympic gold?
Ontario runner George Orton earned a gold medal in the 2,500-metre steeplechase at the 1900 Paris games. At the same Olympics, he won a bronze for the 400-metre hurdles. Since Canada sent no team to the Paris games, Orton officially competed for the United States.

Which Olympic hero had a damaged heart?
Vancouver's Percy Williams won two gold medals in the 100-metre and 200-metre sprints at the 1928 Amsterdam Olympics. His solo performance has yet to be matched by any other Canadian in international track and field competition. Williams was left with a damaged heart after suffering from rheumatic fever as a child.

Montreal's Olympic Stadium was the centrepiece of the 1976 Summer Olympic Games.

When did Canada boycott the summer Olympics?
Canada was one of 62 countries that boycotted the 1980 Moscow Olympic Games following the Soviet Union's invasion of Afghanistan.

Which Olympic athlete was fired?

A Montreal policeman, Étienne Desmarteau was refused a leave of absence to participate in the 1904 summer Olympics in St Louis. He competed just the same, in the 56-pound weight throwing event, and was promptly fired. On May 14, 1904 Desmarteau became the first Canadian to win an individual gold medal while competing for Canada. Desmarteau returned to Montreal and was immediately rehired. The following year he set two world records in the same event before succumbing to typhoid fever.

Donovan Bailey was the dominant Canadian track and field figure in the 1990s.

Who is the most recent Canadian to be "The World's Fastest Man?"

Donovan Bailey earned the title in the 1990s, despite the fact that he did not compete in track and field until he was in his twenties. He won two gold medals at the 1996 Atlanta Olympic Games.

Who was "The Saskatoon Lily"?

Ethel Catherwood was one of the premier track and field athletes of the early part of the 20th century. She held the world record in the high jump and took home a gold medal in the sport at the 1928 Amsterdam Olympics.

Which Olympic athlete was known as Mister Canada?

Harry Jerome was the world's fastest man. In 1960, he tied a world record by running 100 metres in exactly ten seconds. He also shared the world record for the 100-yard race. Although troubled by injuries, Mister Canada won a bronze medal at the 1964 Olympics, and gold at the 1966 Commonwealth Games.

Which event marred Canada's reputation at the 1988 Olympics?

Canada's Ben Johnson won a gold medal in the 100-metre sprint at the Seoul Olympics, setting a world record in the process. However, two days later Johnson tested positive for steroids and was stripped of the medal.

Famous Names

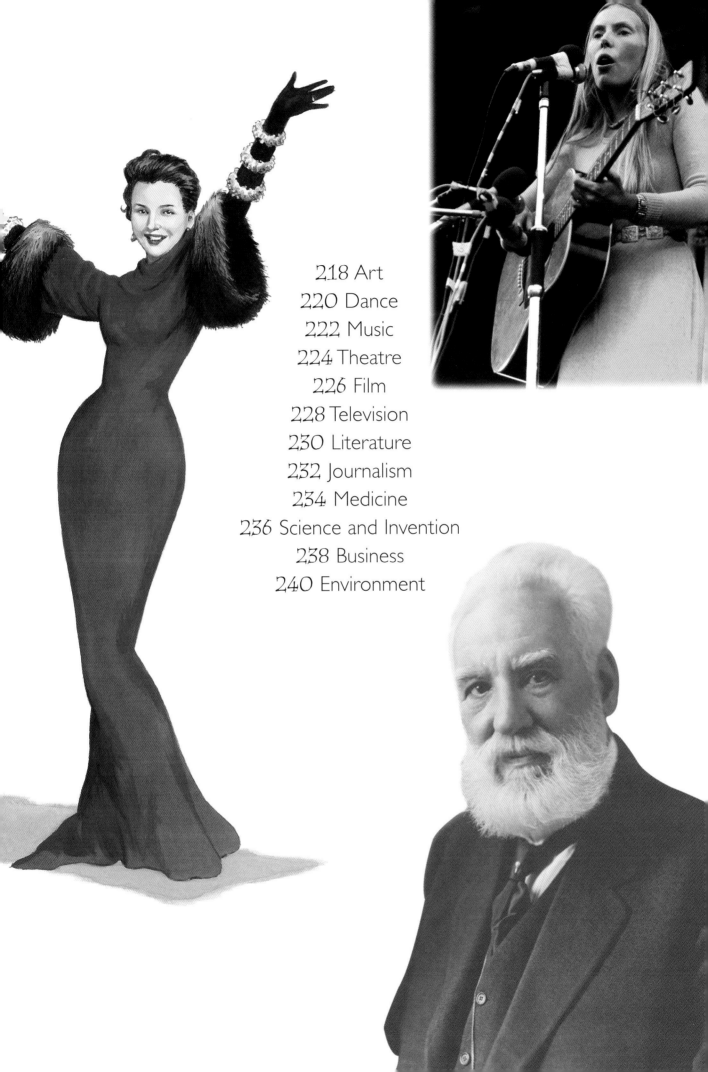

Which artist emulated his grandfather?

British Columbia's Bill Reid was one of Canada's foremost sculptors.

ACCLAIMED SCULPTOR BILL REID WAS WORKING IN RADIO WHEN HE enrolled in a jewellery-making course to follow in the footsteps of his grandfather, Charles Gladstone, a Haida silversmith.

How many people were in the Group of Seven?

The country's most famous association of painters, the Group of Seven, was an association of painters, including original members Franklin Carmichael, Lawren Harris, A Y Jackson, Frank Johnston, Arthur Lismer, J E H MacDonald, and Frederick Varley. A total of ten different painters were at one time or another members of the Group of Seven.

Whose work reflects his Ukrainian heritage?

Born in Alberta to a Ukrainian father, painter William Kurelek's work often depicted the life of Ukrainian immigrants on the Prairies.

Which painter died while canoeing on Canoe Lake?

In 1917, Ontario's Tom Thomson drowned under mysterious circumstances in Algonquin Park's Canoe Lake. Considered by some to be Canada's greatest painter, Thompson is often mistakenly named as a member of the Group of Seven. While he was the friend of several painters in the group, he died three years before the Group of Seven was founded.

Who were known as "The Girls"?

In 1913, Americans Frances Loring and Florence Wyle emigrated to Toronto, where they became known as "The First Women of Canadian Sculpture" or, simply, "The Girls." They lived and worked in an old abandoned church, which also served as a gathering place for Canada's artistic community.

Who worked as a trapper in order to paint?

Swiss-born René Richard trapped and hunted in order to pursue a career in art. He saved enough money to study in Paris, before returning to a life of trapping, hunting, and painting in the remote regions of Canada.

Which artist's eyesight was damaged by his "wanderings"?

Painter Paul Kane wandered through the Canadian west, making hundreds of sketches of landscape, animals, and people of the First Nations. In 1859, he published an account of his travels, *Wanderings of an Artist Among the Indians of North America.* Unfortunately, Kane's eyesight began to fail; likely due to prolonged periods of snowblindness. He was forced to spent his final decade painting in his Toronto studio.

Who was known as "Karsh of Ottawa"?

The famed Ottawa photographer is Yousuf Karsh. During a career that spanned almost seven decades he photographed hundreds of world leaders, entertainers, and writers, including Winston Churchill, Noel Coward, and George Bernard Shaw. In 1987, Karsh sold over 250,000 negatives to the National Archives in Ottawa.

Who painted habitats?

Cornelius Krieghoff is celebrated for his paintings of 19th-century rural Quebec. Born in Amsterdam, he emigrated to the United States, where he joined the army. Krieghoff later deserted and settled in Quebec with his French-Canadian wife. His wife's family served as models for his first paintings.

Who was "the laughing one"?

BRITISH COLUMBIA ARTIST EMILY CARR WAS CALLED KLEE WYCK, MEANING

"the laughing one," by the Nuu-Chah-Nulth people. Her work reflects her interest in the land and First Nations of the Pacific Coast. In later years, Carr became known as a writer. *Klee Wyck,* her first book, was the winner of the Governor General's Award for non-fiction in 1941.

Victoria's Emily Carr received her formal art training in the United States, England, and France.

What is Canada's oldest ballet company?

FOUNDED BY GWENETH LLOYD AND BETTY FARRALLY IN 1939, THE Royal Winnipeg Ballet is the longest continuously operating ballet company in North America. The company began its first Canadian tour in 1945, and spends at least 20 weeks each year on the road.

Who found inspiration in Quebec folklore?
Haitian-born Eddy Toussaint drew on elements of classical ballet, jazz dance, and Quebec folklore. His greatest work was accomplished as the head of the popular Les Ballets Jazz de Montréal.

Who danced with Cirque du Soleil?
The 1994 piece, Satie and Suzanne, was performed by Veronica Tennant and various members of the Cirque. Tennant is better known for having been a leading ballerina with the National Ballet of Canada.

Who is the daughter of Olympic athletes?
Montreal dancer and choreographer Margie Gillis is the eldest daughter of Olympic skiers. Known primarily for her solo performances, one of her only partners was her brother Christopher. Another brother, Jere Gillis, played for several teams in the NHL.

The famous Royal Winnipeg Ballet almost folded in 1954 after a fire destroyed its costumes and sets.

Which famous company began under the name Lock-Danseurs?
In 1980, La La La Human Steps began under the name of its founder Édouard Lock. One of Canada's foremost choreographers, Lock is also a critically acclaimed photographer.

Who created two Canadian ballet companies?
In 1951, choreographer and dancer Celia Franca founded the National Ballet of Canada, the country's most successful ballet company. She also founded the Theatre Ballet of Canada and the National Ballet School.

Which dancer performed with David Bowie?
Montreal's Louise Lecavalier performed with Bowie in 1988 and 1990. Once described as "a flame on legs," she began performing in 1977. In 1981, she joined La La La Human Steps, and was the company's principal dancer for the next 18 years.

Who spent 25 years as a principal ballerina with the National Ballet of Canada?

The National Ballet's Karen Kain and the late Jeremy Blanton.

HAMILTON, ONTARIO'S KAREN KAIN BECAME a principal dancer at the National Ballet of Canada in 1969, a position she held until her final performance with the ballet in 1994. She is now chair of the Dancer Transition Resource Centre, an organization dedicated to assisting dancers after retirement from performance.

Joni Mitchell has recorded many of Canada's most acclaimed albums, including *Blue* and *Court and Spark*.

Which great singer-songwriter wrote a hippie anthem?

"WOODSTOCK," THE ODE TO THE 1969 MUSIC FESTIVAL, WAS WRITTEN BY Joni Mitchell. The Alberta-born musician recorded her first album *Song to a Seagull* in 1968 and is considered one of the greatest singer-songwriters the country has produced. Her most recent album, *Travelogue*, was released in 2002.

Who was "le Canadien"?

Dressed in traditional lumberjack garb, Quebec singer Félix Leclerc was billed as "le Canadien" when performing in France. Credited with spreading French-Canadian folksongs both at home and abroad, Leclerc was also a critically acclaimed poet, playwright, and novelist.

Who is Eileen Regina Edwards?

Born Eileen Regina Edwards in Windsor, country singer Shania Twain was raised in Timmins, Ontario by her mother and Ojibwa stepfather. The future singer adopted the first name Shania from an Ojibwa word meaning, "I'm on my way." Twain recorded her first album in 1993 and had her first commercial success two years later with *The Woman in Me*.

Which pianist overcame tuberculosis?

In addition to suffering a childhood bout of tuberculosis, Montreal's Oscar Peterson has overcome arthritis, a disease he has dealt with since his teenage years. Peterson has gone on to become one of the best jazz pianists of all time, accompanying other legends such as Billie Holiday, Ella Fitzgerald, Dizzy Gillespie, Stan Getz, and Charlie Parker.

Who wrote the national anthem?

The anthem was written by conductor and music director Calixa Lavallée. Although it is known that he composed over 60 works, including several operas and at least one symphony, most of Lavallée's work has been lost. The Congrès National des Canadiens-Français commissioned Lavallée to compose *O Canada* for the 1880 Saint Jean-Baptiste Day celebrations. Although its popularity and use increased over the years, it wasn't until Canada Day in 1980 that the work officially became the national anthem.

Who recorded the best-selling album by a female solo artist?
Jagged Little Pill, the second album by Alanis Morissette, set the record with sales of over 30 million copies. It was also the first album to sell over 2 million copies in Canada, roughly one for every 16 people.

Who wrote another country's national anthem?
Saskatchewan's Bobby Gimby penned "Malaysia Forever," that country's national anthem. In Canada, Gimby is better known for *Ca-na-da*, his celebratory song of the Canadian centennial.

Whose recorded work began and ended with the Goldberg Variations?

THE COUNTRY'S BEST-KNOWN CLASSICAL MUSICIAN, PIANIST AND COMPOSER Glenn Gould first recorded Bach's Goldberg Variations in 1955. A new recording he made of the work was released shortly before his death.

Which member of the Rock and Roll Hall of Fame has a father in the Hockey Hall of Fame?
Neil Young was made a member of the Rock and Roll Hall of Fame in 1995. His father, journalist Scott Young, is known primarily for his hockey writing. He was inducted into the Hockey Hall of Fame in 1988.

Which singer first achieved fame as a poet?
A critically acclaimed poet and novelist, in 1968 Montreal's Leonard Cohen released his first album, *The Songs of Leonard Cohen*. His work has often topped the charts in Canada and several European countries.

The eccentric Glenn Gould was the country's best-known classical musician.

Who played an American President?

The brother of Governor General Vincent Massey, Raymond Massey was acclaimed for his portrayal of Abraham Lincoln. The actor first played the American President in the play, *Abe Lincoln in Illinois*, and reprised the role when it was turned into a motion picture. Massey became so identified with Lincoln that his friend Noel Coward once claimed: "Ray won't be happy until someone shoots him."

Who was Fridolin?

The character was the creation of actor and playwright Gratien Gélinas, considered by many to be the father of modern Quebec theatre. Beginning as a popular radio character in 1937, Fridolin proved so popular that Gélinas continued playing the character for the remainder of his life.

Which playwright was born in the Manitoban wilderness?

Tomson Highway was born on his father's trap-line in the winter of 1951. He achieved national fame 35 years later when his acclaimed play *The Rez Sisters* opened in Toronto.

Where is Balconville?

Balconville by David Fennario, one of the most acclaimed Canadian dramas, is set in Pointe-St-Charles, a working-class area of Montreal. Fennario was born and raised in "The Pointe," and has used the district as the setting of almost all his plays.

What took place on November 14, 1606?

The first piece of Canadian theatre, *Le Théâtre de Neptune en la Nouvelle France*, was performed for Samuel de Champlain in celebration of his return to Port-Royal. The playwright, Marc Lescarbot, spent the winter of 1606–07 at the settlement. The play is considered North America's first non-Native theatrical piece.

Who is Charlie Farquharson?

Don Harron is the creator and actor behind Charlie Farquharson. He first played the character in Spring Thaw, a 1952 satirical review. Harron has also written several books as Farquharson, including *The World and Other Places* and *Olde Charlie Farquharson's Testament*.

Whose plays have been performed in 22 languages?

THE PLAYS OF MONTREAL'S MICHEL TREMBLAY HAVE BEEN PERFORMED around the world in nearly two dozen languages including Yiddish, Haitian Creole, and Hindi. His most widely produced work, *Les Belles-soeurs*, was one of the first to use *joual*, the language of the streets in Quebec.

The prolific and celebrated Michel Tremblay has often been considered the greatest Canadian playwright.

Who was "The Toast of Two Continents"?

Toronto's Beatrice Lillie was the most popular

comedienne of the early 20th century. A close friend of Noel Coward, Winston Churchill, George Bernard Shaw, and Charlie Chaplin, her best-known performance was in *Thoroughly Modern Millie*.

Which stage and screen actor is the great-grandson of a Prime Minister?

Actor Christopher Plummer, famous for his roles in *The Sound of Music*, *Murder by Decree*, and *Delores Claiborne*, is the great-grandson of Prime Minister Sir John Abbott. Coincidentally, Plummer portrayed his great-grandfather's predecessor, Sir John A Macdonald, in the motion picture *Riel*.

Who wrote a musical about Billy Bishop?

John Gray and Eric Peterson were the two creators behind *Billy Bishop Goes to War*, a musical drama about the famous First World War flying ace. In addition to writing the play, the pair were also the original performers. The first production, in 1978, featured Gray as the pianist and narrator with Peterson playing the ace, as well as a number of other characters.

Who played a Prime Minister and his wife?

Linda Griffiths performed as Pierre Elliott Trudeau and his former wife Margaret Sinclair Trudeau in her play *Maggie and Pierre*. Written with Paul Thompson, the play debuted in 1979, the same year Trudeau was defeated by Joe Clark's Progressive Conservatives.

Who produced his first play at the age of 10?

Toronto's Mavor Moore was aged ten when he produced his first play. A playwright since the age of eleven, over 100 of his plays have been performed in Canada. Moore is one of the foremost figures in Canadian theatre. He was the founder of the Charlottetown Festival, first chief producer for CBC television, and a founding governor of the Stratford Festival and the National Theatre School.

Beatrice Lillie was known as "the funniest woman in the world." Here she is seen playing her famous role, Auntie Mame.

Who won Canada's first Oscar?

MARY PICKFORD WON THE 1929 BEST ACTRESS award for *Coquette*, one of the 245 films in which she performed. In addition to her acting skills, Pickford was also an excellent businesswoman. In 1919, she was a co-founder of United Artists and was the first woman in film to earn one million Canadian dollars annually. Coincidentally, Canadians Norma Shearer and Marie Dressler won the next two Academy Awards for Best Actress.

Toronto's Mary Pickford continued to play children's roles well into adulthood.

Who was the most powerful man in Hollywood?

Born in Minsk, Russia, Louis B Mayer was raised in Saint John, New Brunswick, where his father was a junk dealer. Moving to the United States he started a chain of movie theatres. He later founded his own movie production company, merging it with others in 1924 to form Metro-Goldwyn-Mayer.

What was established as a propaganda tool?

Established in 1939, the National Film Board of Canada was originally designed to be used to rally Canadians during the Second World War.

Which brother and sister were Academy Award winners?

A film technician, Montrealer Douglas Shearer won a total of 12 Oscars, including the very first to be awarded in the Sound category. Although he won more than any other Canadian, he never achieved the level of fame earned by his sister, Norma Shearer, who won the Best Actress award for her performance in the 1930 film *The Divorcee*.

Who were the Holland brothers?

In 1894 in New York, two Canadians, the Holland brothers, put on the first paid public exhibition of movies in the world. Two years later in Ottawa, the Hollands gave the first Canadian commercial screening of a film.

Who was King Kong in love with?

Fay Wray played the giant ape's love interest in the original *King Kong*. Born in 1907 in Medicine Hat, Alberta, Wray appeared in dozens of films, including Erich von Stroheim's *The Wedding March* and *The Honeymoon*.

Which Canadian director is considered a master of horror?

The early films of Toronto's David Cronenberg, such as *Shivers*, *Rabid*, and *The Brood*, were among the scariest of the 1970s. The screenwriter and director has continued to make disturbing films, though not always in the horror genre. Among his greatest critical successes are *The Dead Zone*, *The Fly*, *Spider*, and *Crash*.

Who were Neo and Trinity?

Canadians Keanu Reeves and Carrie-Anne Moss played the characters in the popular 1999 film *The Matrix* and its sequels.

Norman Jewison (left) with the American actor, Rod Steiger.

Who directed the highest grossing film of all time?

The 1997 film, *Titanic*, directed by Ontario's James Cameron, is both the most expensive film ever made and the highest grossing film of all time. Among Cameron's other commercial successes are *The Terminator*, *Aliens*, and *Terminator 2*. He also wrote the screenplay to *Rambo*.

What is the greatest Canadian film of all time?

Although everyone has their own favourite, the film cited the most often in critics' polls is *Mon Oncle Antoine*. The movie, directed by Quebec's Claude Jutra, was released in 1971.

Who received the Irving Thalberg Memorial Award?

Renowned director Norman Jewison received the award in 1998. Among his many critically acclaimed films are *In the Heat of the Night*, *Fiddler on the Roof*, *Agnes of God*, *Soldier's Story*, and *Moonstruck*. Named after producer Irving Thalberg, the husband of Canadian actress Norma Shearer, the Academy Award is presented annually to "creative producers whose bodies of work reflect a consistently high quality of motion picture production."

Who were Ernie Coombs and Robert Homme?

ERNIE COOMBS AND ROBERT HOMME WERE MISTER DRESSUP AND THE FRIENDLY GIANT, HOSTS OF THE MOST POPULAR

English-language children's programs in Canada. In 1963, American-born Coombs moved to Canada to work on children's programs for the Canadian Broadcasting Corporation. His show, *Mister Dressup*, ran from 1967 until his retirement in 1996. Homme began playing the Friendly Giant on an American radio show. In 1958, he moved the program to Canadian television, writing and playing in over 3,000 episodes before his retirement in 1985.

Ernie Coombs was known to millions of children as Mister Dressup.

Who was the King of Kensington?
Actor Al Waxman played Larry King in *The King of Kensington*, the country's longest-running situation comedy. The character was just one of over 1,000 television roles the Toronto actor played in his 50-year career.

Which show was subjected to a Parliamentary committee?
The weekly current affairs show *This Hour Has Seven Days* is remembered as much for its creativity as for the controversy it drew. In 1966, it received a Parliamentary committee hearing which lasted several weeks. Although it remains one of the most popular shows of all time, *This Hour Has Seven Days* was cancelled in 1966, 19 months after its debut.

Which Canadians commanded starships?
From 1966 to 1969, Montreal's William Shatner played James T Kirk, captain of *The Enterprise* on *Star Trek*. He later revived the role for a number of Star Trek films. Lorne Greene played Commander Adama of *The Galactica* in the short-lived *Battlestar Galactica* and *Galactica:1980* television series.

How old is the CBC?
The Canadian Radio Broadcasting Commission, the forerunner of the Canadian Broadcasting Corporation, was founded by a 1936 Act of Parliament. Until then, almost all programs broadcast to Canadians were from the United States.

Which critically acclaimed actor is the grandson of a former Premier?
Kiefer Sutherland is the son of actor Donald Sutherland and actress Shirley Douglas. Tommy Douglas, Premier of Saskatchewan from 1944 until 1961, is his grandfather.

Which film beauty played the wife of a monster?

Vancouver's Yvonne De Carlo played Lily, wife of Herman Munster, in television's *The Munsters*. Her exotic looks and talent as a dancer led to a successful movie career, including her finest performance in *The Ten Commandments*.

Which network broadcast out of Melonville?

The SCTV Network, popularly known simply as *SCTV*, was an offshoot of Toronto's Second City troupe. Arguably Canada's greatest comedy program, the show centred on a fictitious television station run by Guy Caballero, played by Joe Flaherty. Other cast members included John Candy, Eugene Levy, Rick Moranis, Andrea Martin, Catherine O'Hara, Martin Short, and Dave Thomas.

Which popular French series became an English hit?

In 1954, a year after its debut in French, *The Plouffe Family* became a hit on the CBC's English network. Known as *Les Plouffes* in French, the series was inspired by novelist Roger Lemelin's novel of the same name.

Who are Matthew Perry's parents?

The *Friends* star is the son of actor John Perry and Ottawa-born Suzanne Perry, former press secretary to Pierre Elliott Trudeau.

Who was known as "our pet"?

Singer Juliette began performing on CBC radio at 15 years of age. From 1954 until 1966, her television program, *The Juliette Show*, aired every Saturday night after *Hockey Night in Canada*.

Mike Myers was one of several Canadians behind *Saturday Night Live*.

Who created Saturday Night Live?

THE POPULAR LATE-NIGHT COMEDY SHOW IS THE BRAINCHILD OF Toronto's Lorne Michaels. Now in its third decade, the show has featured the work of dozens of Canadian actors, musicians, and writers, including Dan Ackroyd, Robin Duke, Phil Hartman, Sean Kelly, Norm Macdonald, Bruce McCulloch, Mark McKinney, Mike Myers, Paul Shaffer, Howard Shore, and Martin Short.

Which comedy duo met at high school?

Johnny Wayne and Frank Shuster, better known as Wayne & Shuster, met in the tenth grade. They began performing on radio during the Second World War and brought their comedy to television in 1954. They continued as a duo until Johnny Wayne's death in 1990.

Who has won the most Governor General's Literary Awards?
The recipient of five Governor General's Literary Awards, Hugh MacLennan won more than any other writer. He received his first award in 1945 for his novel *Two Solitudes*. Two other novels, *The Precipice* and *The Watch that Ends the Night,* also won awards. MacLennan won the award twice for his non-fiction writing with *Cross-Country* and *Thirty and Three*.

Where is Manawaka?
The small town found in much of the writing of Margaret Laurence is modeled on Neepawa, Manitoba, her hometown. Her 1964 book, *The Stone Angel*, which some consider the greatest Canadian novel, was the first to be set in the fictional town.

Which author ran a bookstore?

Munro's books in Victoria was run by Alice Munro and her

former husband. Munro, whose work often appears in *The New Yorker* and *The Atlantic Monthly*, is considered one of the greatest living short story writers. Her collections have earned three Governor General's Awards.

Which award-winning author had her first book published at the age of 20?
Marie-Claire Blais' first novel, *La Belle Bête*, was published in 1959, 20 years after her birth in Quebec City. The novel won the *Prix de la langue française* and was translated into English as *Mad Shadows*. Blais is not only one of Canada's finest authors, she is also one of the most prolific. Among her more than 30 books are the Governor General's Award-winning novels *Les Manuscrits de Pauline Archange*, *Le Sourd dans la ville*, *Soifs*, and *Dans la foudre et la lumière*.

Which author has a typeface named after him?
The honour belongs to Montreal writer Mordecai Richler. The author of *The Apprenticeship of Duddy Kravitz, St Urban's Horseman, Solomon Gursky was Here,* and *Barney's Version*, Richler achieved great critical and commercial success.

Alice Munro received the 1986 Governor General's Award for *The Progress of Love* from Jeanne Sauvé.

Which humorist was a professor of economics?

Stephen Leacock was Professor of Political Economy and Chair of the Department of Economics and Political Science at Montreal's McGill University. Although remembered as a humorist for such books as *Literary Lapses* and *Sunshine Sketches of a Little Town*, it was Leacock's first book, *Elements of Political Science*, that earned him the most money.

Who was Giller?

The Giller Prize is named after Doris Giller, a reporter and book review editor. The prize was first awarded in 1994, the year after her death.

Who was "The People's Poet"?

Prince Edward Island's Milton Acorn earned the title after his collection of poetry, *I've Tasted My Blood*, failed to win the 1968 Governor General's Award for Poetry. Those who felt Acorn had deserved the prize organized the Canadian Poets' Award, popularly known as the People's Poet Award. In 1970, the first Canadian Poets' Award was presented to Acorn in a Toronto tavern.

Which author pretended to be a Japanese American noblewoman?

The daughter of a Chinese mother and British father, Montrealer Winnifred Eaton wrote over a dozen romance novels under the name Onoto Watanna. She passed herself off as a having descended from Japanese aristocracy, appearing in traditional dress in publicity photographs. She later worked on screenplays and screen adaptations in Hollywood. Among her many screen credits are *Shanghai Lady* and *East is West*.

Which novel was inspired by a 19th-century murder?

Anne Hébert's 1970 novel, *Kamouraska*, deals with the murder of an abusive husband. It was partly inspired by the 1839 murder of Achille Taché in the Kamouraska region of Quebec.

Roch Carrier's book, *The Hockey Sweater*, has become one of the best-loved Canadian children's stories.

Who is Canada's National Librarian?

ROCH CARRIER, THE AUTHOR OF "LA GUERRE, YES SIR!" AND *Prayers of a Very Wise Child*, was appointed to the position in 1999. Carrier grew up in Sainte-Justine, Quebec, a town that had no library.

Which writer coined the term "Africadian"?

Poet George Elliott Clarke first used the word as a designation for black Nova Scotians. The recipient of a Governor General's Award for Poetry, Clarke is the editor of *Fire on Water*, a two-volume collection of Africadian writing.

Which award-winning journalist became Governor General?

The country's current Governor General, Adrienne Clarkson, first came to prominence as a journalist and broadcaster. During a career spanning over three decades she worked on a number of television programs, including *Take Thirty*, *Adrienne at Large*, *The Fifth Estate*, *Adrienne Clarkson's Summer Festival*, and *Adrienne Clarkson Presents*.

Who was Maclean?

Maclean's, Canada's weekly news magazine, was named after John Bayne Maclean, who bought the publication in 1905. Founded in 1896, the magazine had a number of names, including *Business*, *The Business Magazine*, *The Busy Man's Magazine*, and *Busy Man's*. In 1911, Maclean gave the magazine his name.

Who is the man behind "Beatlemania"?

Music journalist Sandy Gardiner coined the word "Beatlemania" in a 1963 article in the *Ottawa Journal*. The word was later used as the title of the first Beatles album released in Canada.

Who was Samuel Marchbanks?

ROBERTSON DAVIES WROTE HUMOROUS COLUMNS under the name Samuel Marchbanks while serving as the editor of *The Peterborough Examiner*. The reflections and opinions of the cantankerous Marchbanks were later reprinted in a number of collections, including *The Diary of Samuel Marchbanks*, *The Table Talk of Samuel Marchbanks*, and *Samuel Marchbanks' Almanack*.

Robertson Davies' *Fifth Business* has been described as one of the greatest Canadian novels.

Which is Canada's oldest magazine?

Founded by Edmund Ernest Sheppard in 1887, *Saturday Night* is the country's oldest magazine. The first magazine published in what is now Canada, was *The Nova Scotia Magazine*. Established by Reverend William Cochran in 1789, the periodical ceased publication three years later.

What do *The Intelligencer*, *Le Défricheur*, *The Labour Gazette*, and *Cité libre* have in common?

All were publications that were worked on by future Prime Ministers. Sir Mackenzie Bowell was a printer, editor, and owner of *The Intelligencer*, a newspaper in Belleville, Ontario. Sir Wilfrid Laurier served as editor of *Le Défricheur*. William Lyon Mackenzie King was editor of *The Labour Gazette*. Pierre Elliott Trudeau was the co-founded and director of the magazine *Cité libre*.

In 1971, Barbara Frum became one of the original hosts of *As It Happens*.

Which journalist created the Stratford Festival?

The Shakespearean festival was the brainchild of Stratford-born journalist Tom Patterson. In the years following the Second World War, Patterson collected support for his project, resulting in the establishment of the festival in 1953.

Which newspaper was begun as a tool in the American Revolution?

Montreal's *Gazette*, the oldest continuously published newspaper in Canada, was founded by American Benjamin Franklin in 1775. For eight months of that year, the Americans occupied the city.

Who was the nine-year-old host of *Peter's Program*?

Toronto-born Peter Jennings began his broadcasting career as the host of *Peter's Program*, a half-hour CBC Radio program. He later worked for CBC Television and CTV, before being hired by the American Broadcasting Company.

Who hosted "The Journal"?

ONE OF THE COUNTRY'S BEST-KNOWN JOURNALISTS, BARBARA FRUM began a distinguished career with the CBC as a freelance writer and commentator. She is most often associated as host of radio's *As It Happens* and television's *The Journal*.

Which Prime Minister worked as a newspaper boy?

As a teenager, John Diefenbaker worked as a newspaper boy in Saskatoon. On July 29, 1910, he sold a newspaper to Prime Minister Sir Wilfrid Laurier. The two entered into a lively conversation, ending when Diefenbaker said: "Well, Mr Prime Minister, I can't waste any more time on you. I must get back to work."

Who was the first President of the Canadian Medical Association?

Conservative Sir Charles Tupper is the only Prime Minister who was a physician. He practiced medicine throughout his career and was President of the Canadian Medical Association from 1867 to 1870.

Who was Canada's first Nobel Prize recipient?

The DISCOVERER OF INSULIN, FREDERICK BANTING, received the Nobel Prize for Physiology or Medicine in 1923. A doctor with the University of Toronto, Banting was concerned that his student Charles H Best was not recognized as a co-discoverer and shared his monetary reward with him.

Who was considered the "most influential physician in history"?

The first professor of medicine at Johns Hopkins University, Canada's Sir William Osler earned the title as the author of *The Principles and Practice of Medicine*. First published in 1892, the work was revised many times and was considered an authoritative medical textbook for over three decades. Osler was the first to popularize the importance of a patient's state of mind in achieving a cure and helped create the system of postgraduate training for physicians that is followed to this day.

Credited with the discovery of insulin, Sir Frederick Banting was an accomplished painter and close friend of A Y Jackson.

Which mother and daughter made medical history?

Emily Howard Stowe was inspired to pursue a career in medicine after her husband became ill with tuberculosis. In 1867, she graduated from the New York Medical College for Women, becoming Canada's first female medical doctor. Her daughter, Augusta Stowe Gullen, overcame similar obstacles and, in 1883, was the first woman to receive a complete medical education from a Canadian university.

Who was the first North American nurse?

The daughter of a wealthy French family, Jeanne Mance arrived in New France in 1641. Considered by many as the co-founder – with Paul de Chomedey de Maisonneuve – of Montreal, she worked hard in support of the settlement. In 1645, Mance established the Hôtel-Dieu de Montréal, which she administered until her death. One of the first hospitals in North America, the Hôtel-Dieu is still in operation nearly 360 years later.

Who formed the world's first mobile medical unit?

NORMAN BETHUNE DEVELOPED THE UNIT IN 1938 WHILE SERVING AS Mao Zedong's Army Medical Chief in China. Two years earlier, as a Loyalist surgeon in the Spanish Civil War, Bethune created the first mobile blood-transfusion service.

Which sick children were the first to eat pablum?

Doctors Alan Brown, Theodore Drake, and Fred Tisdall invented the nutritious baby cereal at Toronto's Hospital for Sick Children in 1930. The hospital continues to enjoy royalties generated by the sale of the food.

Who founded the Montreal Neurological Institute?

The leading centre of neurology was established by neurosurgeon Wilder Penfield in 1934. A pioneer in the field of brain surgery, Penfield was also the author of medical textbooks.

Who led the World Health Organization?

Ontario's Brock Chisholm helped draft the operational regulations of the World Health Organization. In 1948, he was elected as its first Director General. Named after Sir Isaac Brock, Chisholm was a tireless worker for the abolition of war.

Montreal surgeon Norman Bethune was a hero in the People's Republic of China.

What was the "Husky"?

DESIGNED BY JOSEPH-ARMAND BOMBARDIER IN 1922, THE "HUSKY" WAS THE FIRST snowmobile. The original design consisted of a sled driven by a propeller. It wasn't until 38 years later that Bombardier created the snowmobile we now recognize as the "Ski-Doo."

Joseph-Armand Bombardier with the first snowmobile.

Who was the first Canadian in space?

As one of seven astronauts aboard the space shuttle *Challenger*, in October 1984 electrical engineer and military officer Marc Garneau became the first Canadian to travel in space. The first Canadian woman to leave the Earth's atmosphere was medical doctor Roberta Bondar, who travelled on board the space shuttle *Discovery* in 1992.

Who was the first Canadian to board the International Space Station?

Electrical and computer engineer Julie Payette visited the station in 1999. A true Renaissance woman, she has earned numerous degrees, holds a commercial pilot's license, speaks five languages, and has sung with the Montreal Symphonic Orchestra Chamber Choir.

Who was Robertson?

P L Robertson invented the Robertson screw and screwdriver in 1908. Although not the most common screw, the Robertson is considered the very best in resisting the tendency for screwdrivers to slip out of the head of the screw.

What was the wirephoto transmitter?

Developed in the years following the First World War, the wirephoto transmitter allowed for the transmitting of pictures without telephone or telegraph wires. The machine was invented for newspaper use by William Stephenson, better known as "Intrepid," and was first used by London's *Daily Mail* in 1924.

Which refugee was awarded a Nobel Prize?

Gerhard Herzberg arrived in Canada as a refugee from Nazi Germany. He was awarded the 1971 Nobel Prize for Chemistry.

Who made helium balloons possible?

We might not be receiving balloon bouquets for birthdays and anniversaries were it not for the work of Ontario's John Cunningham McLennan. In 1915, McLennan developed a method through which helium could be extracted from natural gas. The price of helium soon dropped from up to 6,000 Canadian dollars per cubic foot to 17 cents per cubic foot.

Who made the world's first radio broadcast?

On Christmas Eve, 1906, Reginald Fessenden transmitted music to ships in the Atlantic Ocean, proving that something other than Morse code could be broadcast by wireless means. He was behind more than 500 inventions, including the fathometer, a machine that used sound waves to measure ocean depth.

Which inventor was known as "The Great Farini"?

An accomplished painter, botanist, and explorer, Ontario's William Leonard Hunt was best-known as "The Great Farini," the greatest tightrope walker of his day. At one point in his long career he appeared in New York's Barnum Brothers Circus as The Farini Brothers, playing all three roles himself. In later years, Hunt turned to inventing. Among his many patents were a parachute and folding theatre seats.

Whose invention was "the real McCoy"?

Born in Colchester, Ontario in 1844, Elijah McCoy was the son of former slaves who had fled to Canada. He was educated as an engineer and invented the first device that allowed machines to be lubricated while in operation. Because others were quick to copy his invention, people would often ask for "the real McCoy," an expression that came to mean "the real thing." McCoy's other inventions included the lawn sprinkler and the ironing board.

Was the telephone invented in Brantford, Ontario?

T HE DEBATE OVER THE BIRTHPLACE OF THE telephone is best resolved by the inventor, Alexander Graham Bell. In 1919, he stated: "The telephone was conceived in Brantford in 1874 and born in Boston in 1875."

Inventor Alexander Graham Bell lived in Brantford, Ontario and Baddeck, Nova Scotia.

Who was Mister Sam?

BILLIONAIRE SAMUEL BRONFMAN. BRONFMAN AND HIS BROTHERS

began making whisky in a rural Saskatchewan warehouse. The family grew the modest business into Seagram, the world's largest distillery. Appropriately, his surname is Yiddish for "Whisky Man."

Which New York cosmetics queen was born into poverty?
Elizabeth Arden was born Florence Nightingale Graham to a poor farming couple in Woodbridge, Ontario. She entered into the cosmetics industry in 1909 and within 20 years was making a profit of over nine million Canadian dollars a year.

Who is "the real Prime Minister of Canada"?
The description was once given by Leonard Cohen to Jack McClelland, former publisher of McClelland and Stewart. Established in 1919, Jack McClelland became the head of the company in 1960. Under his direction, the company changed the literary landscape by publishing such writers as Mordecai Richler, Irving Layton, Margaret Laurence, and Margaret Atwood.

Who used beer to build a business empire?
In 1786, John Molson opened Canada's first brewery, selling its output for five Canadian cents a bottle. He invested the profits in a number of ventures, including a steamship line, luxury hotels, a bank, and the Champlain and St Lawrence Railroad, Canada's first railway.

Samuel Bronfman was made a Companion of the Order of Canada by Governor General Roland Michener.

Whose promise was "Satisfaction Guaranteed, or Money Refunded"?
Timothy Eaton, founder of the Eaton's department store, made the promise in 1869 when he opened his first store in Toronto. Over the next few decades Eaton opened stores across the country and developed a lucrative and popular catalogue business.

238

Who founded a television empire?

Former CBC host Moses Znaimer left the corporation in 1972 to found Citytv. He has since moved on as the creative force behind MuchMusic, MusicPlus, MuchMoreMusic, Bravo! and several other ventures.

Which powerful businessman became a powerful politician?

An engineer who developed a lucrative grain elevator business, C D Howe became one of the country's leading business minds. In 1935, he entered federal politics as part of William Lyon Mackenzie King's Liberals. He drew great praise for overseeing Canada's wartime production during the Second World War.

Who saved Expo '86?

Beginning as a used car salesman, billionaire Jimmy Pattison helped salvage the troubled exhibition. As Chairman, he took a project that was behind schedule and in danger of being cancelled, and transformed it into one of the most successful world fairs. He received a token payment of one dollar for his work.

Who is the wealthiest Canadian?

The son of Roy Thomson, a newspaper and television magnate, Kenneth Thomson is considered to be the fourteenth richest person in the world. His business empire includes publishing, oil, and numerous other ventures.

Conrad Black is a businessman and author of *Duplessis*, a biography of the controversial Quebec Premier.

What do William Aitken, Roy Thomson, and Conrad Black have in common?

ALL THREE MEN WERE CANADIAN newspaper tycoons who were given seats in the British House of Lords as, respectively, Lord Beaverbrook, Lord Thomson of Fleet, and Lord Black of Crossharbour.

Grey Owl was the author of *Pilgrims of the Wild, Tales of an Empty Cabin,* and other popular books.

Who was Archibald Belaney?

Belaney is better-known to Canadians as Grey Owl.

A British immigrant, he passed himself off as a Native Canadian, earning a reputation as an author, lecturer, and environmentalist. His true identity remained a secret until shortly after his death.

Who was responsible for the first provincial parks?

Alexander Kirkwood, a clerk of the Crown Lands Department, proposed the first provincial park at Niagara Falls in 1885. Perhaps his greatest accomplishment was in conceiving Algonquin Provincial Park, which he stated would "perpetuate the name of one of the greatest Indian nations that has inhabited the North American continent."

Who released *The Canadian Green Consumer Guide?*

A groundbreaking book, the guide was the work of Pollution Probe, a nation-wide group dedicated to protecting the environment. The organization was founded by a small group of University of Toronto students in 1969.

Who determines Canada's endangered species list?

COSEWIC is the Committee on the Status of Endangered Wildlife in Canada, a committee of experts that assesses and determines which wild species, subspecies, and varieties are in danger of disappearing from Canada.

What event led to the formation of Greenpeace?

In 1971, the Greenpeace Foundation was formed in Vancouver to protest American nuclear tests on Amchitka Island in Alaska. Eleven members of the environmental group sailed a chartered boat, christened *Greenpeace,* into the bomb test range. They were intercepted by the United States Navy.

Which organization defends the environment through the courts?

Since it was established in 1970, the Canadian Environmental Law Association has been using existing laws in an effort to protect the environment.

Which environmentalist created the country's most popular science program?

GENETICIST DAVID SUZUKI WAS THE man behind CBC Radio's *Quirks and Quarks*. A dedicated environmentalist, Suzuki has received dozens of awards and honours for his work.

Scientist and broadcaster David Suzuki.

Who was the founder of *Nature Lore* magazine?
The periodical was founded by 13-year-old Farley Mowat. He used the profits from *Nature Lore* to buy food for geese and ducks that were too ill or frail to migrate south for the winter. A prolific writer, Mowat is the author of dozens of books, including *Never Cry Wolf*, *A Whale for the Killing*, *Sea of Slaughter*, and other works concerned with nature and the environment.

What was the Canadian Coalition on Acid Rain?
The coalition was the first Canadian lobby group in Washington. It was formed in 1981 after the American government disagreed with Canada over the seriousness of acid rain. Ten years later, it was disbanded when the two countries signed the Canada/US Air Quality Agreement, which required the United States to reduce emissions to 40 percent of the 1980 levels by 2010.

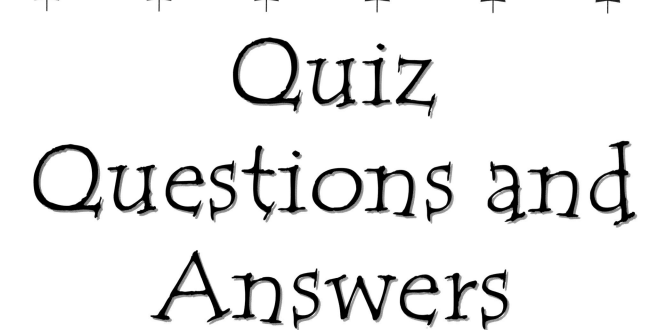

Quiz Questions and Answers

PROVINCES AND TERRITORIES

1. In which year did Canada adopt its own flag?
2. Which province is known in French as La Nouvelle-Écosse?
3. In which future province did the Beothuks live?
4. Who sailed around the world on *The Spray*?
5. Which island was once known as Île St-Jean?
6. How long is the Confederation Bridge?
7. In which province did the Quiet Revolution take place?
8. During which war did Berlin, Ontario change its name?
9. Who wrote *Bonheur d'occasion*?
10. Which Prime Minister held a Saskatchewan riding?
11. What does UFA stand for?
12. Which province was once known as New Caledonia?
13. Which flag features an inukshuk?
14. Which Party did Audrey McLaughlin lead?
15. Which province was created from districts of Athabasca, Assiniboia, and Saskatchewan?

NATURE AND WILDLIFE

1. In which province is "the Canadian Galapagos"?
2. After whom is Canada's longest river named?
3. Where did Martin Frobisher mine fool's gold?
4. What first appeared on the penny in 1920?
5. What kind of plant are the Red Fife and the Marquis?
6. Which dinosaur was named after a new province?
7. What are the Newfoundland, the Nova Scotia duck-trolling retriever, the Tahltan bear dog, and the Canadian Eskimo dog?
8. In which province would one find a shortnose sturgeon?
9. Which bird flies over 35,000 kilometres each year?
10. What did the Huron use as an insect repellent?
11. How many holes are in Percé Rock?

12. Which lake surrounds the Lake on the Mountain?
13. What are known as "hills on hills"?
14. Which park was established to save a herd of bison?
15. Into which oceans does water from Mount Snow Dome flow?

THE FIRST NATIONS

1. What does the word "Inuit" mean?

2. Which provinces are the traditional homes of the Plains Cree?

3. Who made dug-out canoes of red cedar?

4. Which European explorer visited Hochelaga?

5. Which Cree Chief was good at making buffalo pounds?

6. In whose wedding ceremonies did moccasins play an important part?

7. According to the Haida, who coaxed the first people out of a clam shell?

8. Which ceremony was illegal from 1884 to 1951?

9. Who used lacrosse as a means of capturing a fort?

10. Which Iroquois tactics were known to the French as *la petite guerre*?

11. Which figure in Iroquois mythology has a broken nose?

12. Who was "The Heavenly Messenger?"

13. Which sculpture can be seen in Hull and Washington?

14. Who wrote *Green Grass, Running Water*?

15. Who designed a village for the Oujé-Bougoumou Cree?

Quiz answers

PROVINCES AND TERRITORIES

1. 1965
2. Nova Scotia
3. Newfoundland and Labrador
4. Joshua Slocum
5. Prince Edward Island
6. 13 kilometres
7. Quebec
8. The First World War
9. Gabrielle Roy
10. John Diefenbaker
11. United Farmers of Alberta
12. British Columbia
13. Nunavut's
14. The New Democratic Party
15. Alberta

NATURE AND WILDLIFE

1. British Columbia
2. Alexander Mackenzie
3. Baffin Island
4. The maple leaf
5. Wheat
6. The Albertosaurus
7. Canadian dog breeds
8. New Brunswick
9. The Arctic tern
10. Wild mint
11. One
12. Lake Ontario
13. Hoodoos
14. Wood Buffalo National Park
15. The Pacific, Atlantic, and Arctic oceans

THE FIRST NATIONS

1. The people
2. Saskatchewan and Alberta
3. The Haida
4. Jacques Cartier
5. Poundmaker
6. The Cree
7. Raven
8. The Sun Dance
9. Chief Pontiac
10. Guerilla warfare
11. Crooked Face
12. Dekanawida
13. Spirit of Haida Gwaii
14. Thomas King
15. Douglas Cardinal

EXPLORERS AND SETTLERS

1. What was the name Leif Ericson gave to Labrador?

2. What prevented Jacques Cartier from reaching "the Kingdom of the Saguenay?"

3. Which city was founded by Paul de Chomedy de Maisonneuve?

4. What did France sell in 1803?

5. What was the rival of the Hudson's Bay Company?

6. Which Chief brought the Mohawks into the American Revolution?

7. Who is the author of *Roughing It in the Bush*?

8. Which war ended on Christmas Eve in 1814?

9. Who established the Red River Colony?

10. What document proposed the assimilation of French Canadians?

11. Who was the editor of The *Provincial Freeman*?

12. Into which ocean does the Mackenzie River drain?

13. Which explorer was set adrift in James Bay?

14. Who established the first European settlement in Quebec?

15. Which Shawnee Chief fought for the British in the War of 1812?

BUILDING A NATION

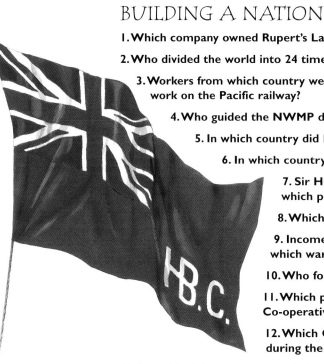

1. Which company owned Rupert's Land?

2. Who divided the world into 24 time zones?

3. Workers from which country were brought in to work on the Pacific railway?

4. Who guided the NWMP during the Long March?

5. In which country did Riel take exile?

6. In which country did Sir John Thompson die?

7. Sir Hugh John Macdonald was Premier of which province?

8. Which city is the " City of Sorrow?"

9. Income tax was introduced to help pay for which war?

10. Who fought beside Canadian troops at Dieppe?

11. Which political party was formed out of the Co-operative Commonwealth Federation?

12. Which Quebec politician was murdered during the October Crisis?

13. In which cities were troops deployed during the October Crisis?

14. The Constitution Proclamation features the signatures of which two Prime Ministers?

15. Which two world leaders met at the " Shamrock Summit?"

WAR AND PEACEKEEPING

1. Which war ended hostilities between France and Great Britain in North America?

2. Which act legalized Catholicism and French civil law?

3. Which European country supported the United States in the War of 1812?

4. Who wrote *Wacousta*?

5. Which federal politician was assassinated in 1868?

6. On which continent was the Boer War fought?

7. In which wars did John McCrae serve?

8. In which city can one visit the Peace Tower?

9. Which war included the "Phony War"?

10. Which Second World War battle caused the closure of the St Lawrence River?

11. In which province was Camp X?

12. Which was "Canada's Fightingest Destroyer?"

13. Which province has its own *Book of Remembrance*?

14. The end of which war is commemorated by the Peace Bridge and Peace Arch?

15. Which famous surgeon served in the Spanish Civil War?

Quiz answers

EXPLORERS AND SETTLERS

1. Markland
2. The Lachine rapids
3. Montreal
4. Louisiana
5. North West Company
6. Joseph Brant
7. Susanna Moodie
8. The War of 1812
9. The Earl of Selkirk
10. The Durham Report
11. Mary Ann Shadd
12. Arctic Ocean
13. Henry Hudson
14. Samuel de Champlain
15. Tecumseh

BUILDING A NATION

1. The Hudson's Bay Company
2. Sir Sanford Fleming
3. China
4. Jerry Potts
5. The United States
6. England
7. Manitoba
8. Halifax
9. The First World War
10. British paratroopers
11. The New Democratic Party
12. Pierre Laporte
13. Ottawa, Montreal, and Quebec City
14. Pierre Elliott Trudeau and Jean Chrétien
15. Brian Mulroney and Ronald Reagan

WAR AND PEACEKEEPING

1. The Seven Years' War
2. The Quebec Act
3. France
4. John Richardson
5. Thomas D'Arcy McGee
6. Africa
7. The Boer War and the First World War
8. Ottawa
9. The Second World War
10. The Battle of the Gulf of St Lawrence
11. Ontario
12. HMCS *Haida*
13. Newfoundland and Labrador
14. The War of 1812
15. Norman Bethune

CANADIAN LEADERS

1. Who succeeded Joseph Brant?
2. Who was queen at the time of Confederation?
3. Who wrote *The Thirty-Nine Steps*?
4. Who founded *The Toronto Globe*, now the *Globe* and *Mail*?
5. Where was Sir John A Macdonald born?
6. Which Prime Minister is not buried in Canada?
7. Who was elected Prime Minister at the age of 39?
8. Who is the son of former Alberta Premier Ernest Manning?
9. Which province elected Canada's first separatist government?
10. Who led the Canadian soldiers at Vimy Ridge?
11. Which poet served as a chaplain during the First World War?
12. Who established Canada's first suffrage organization?
13. Which Prime Ministers ushered in new centuries?
14. Who was Prime Minister during the country's centennial?
15. Which Premier worked for Radio Canada International?

SPORTS

1. How long might a game of baggataway last?
2. Which city once had a hockey team called the Jets?
3. Who was the skip of the Richardson rink?
4. Who was "Jackrabbit?"
5. Which Canadian won four Winter Olympics speedskating medals?
6. Which Canadian figure skaters won silver medals at the Calgary Olympics?
7. Which dental surgeon made the rules for modern lacrosse?
8. Which team won Canada's first Major League Baseball game?
9. Which university won the very first Grey Cup game?
10. For which organization was James Naismith working when he invented basketball?
11. Which Canadian soccer team won an Olympic gold medal?
12. When was Canada's first Olympic gold medal awarded?
13. What was the final score of the final game in the Summit Series?
14. What was the name of the first Canadian team in the National Lacrosse League?
15. Which team sport became a medal event at the 1976 Montreal Olympics?

FAMOUS NAMES

1. Which painter wrote *Klee Wyck?*
2. Who founded La La La Human Steps?
3. In which band was Robbie Robertson a member?
4. Which play was written by John Gray and Eric Peterson?
5. Which Canadian co-founded United Artists?
6. Who is Kiefer Sutherland's father?
7. Who wrote *The Watch that Ends the Night?*
8. Which newspaper did Robertson Davies edit?
9. Who founded the Hôtel-Dieu de Montréal?
10. Who was "Intrepid?"
11. Who built Canada's first railway?
12. Who were "the First Women of Canadian Sculpture?"
13. What was the title of Leonard Cohen's first album?
14. Which humorist taught at McGill University?
15. Who was the Friendly Giant?

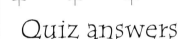

Quiz answers

CANADIAN LEADERS	SPORTS	FAMOUS NAMES
1. John Norton	1. Three days	1. Emily Carr
2. Queen Victoria	2. Winnipeg	2. Édouard Lock
3. Sir John Buchan	3. Ernie Richardson	3. The Band
4. George Brown	4. Herman Smith Johannsen	4. *Billy Bishop Goes to War*
5. Scotland	5. Gaétan Boucher	5. Mary Pickford
6. R B Bennett	6. Brian Orser and Elizabeth Manley	6. Donald Sutherland
7. Joe Clark	7. Dr George Beers	7. Hugh MacLennan
8. Preston Manning	8. The Montreal Expos	8. *The Peterborough Examiner*
9. Nova Scotia	9. The University of Toronto	9. Jeanne Mance
10. Julian Byng	10. The YMCA	10. William Stephenson
11. Frederick George Scott	11. The Galt Football Club	11. John Molson
12. Dr Emily Stowe	12. 1900	12. Frances Loring and Florence Wyle
13. Sir Wilfrid Laurier and Jean Chrétien	13. Canada 6, the Soviet Union 5	13. *The Songs of Leonard Cohen*
14. Lester B Pearson	14. The Ontario Raiders	14. Stephen Leacock
15. René Lévesque	15. Women's basketball	15. Robert Homme

Index

ACKNOWLEDGEMENTS

Illustrations by:
John Butler: 49, 53, 156; James Field: 42, 44, 46, 48, 50, 52, 55, 68–69, 95, 96, 108, 114, 116, 122, 144–145; Mike Lacey: 27, 33, 40–41, 46, 66–67, 74, 77, 82, 84, 92, 97, 101, 102, 104–105, 109, 110–111, 115, 118–119, 120, 123, 124, 143, 148, 151, 154, 167, 173, 174–175, 186, 225; Gilly Marklew: 25, 72–73, 75, 121, 126, 128, 140, 146, 166, 171, 182, 184, 188–189, 196, 205, 206, 215, 231, 234–235, 236; Stephen Sweet: all map and flag illustrations; Mike Taylor: 51, 62–63, 88, 90–91, 98–99, 117, 172; Catherine Ward: 54, 129; Ross Watton: 70–71, 76, 78–79, 106–107, 147, 161, 177. All artists care of SGA Illustration & Design.

Photographs supplied by:
Christian Ascher: © Christian Ascher, Arctic Art Sales 81. Alamy: Brand X Pictures/Alamy, cover flag. Associated Press: © AP / Alastair Grant 136. Bechtel Corporation 21. Bridgeman Art Library: © Stapleton Collection/Bridgeman Art Library 141. Canadian Heritage Gallery: © ID 10171/C-277 National Archives of Canada 17; © ID 21796/C-28544 National Archives of Canada 80; © ID 21758/C-13927 National Archives of Canada 100; © ID 20838/PA-832 National Archives of Canada 127; © ID 21001 & ID 20982/PA-111385 & PA-128080 National Archives of Canada 130-131; © ID 21031/PA129833 National Archives of Canada 132; © ID 21074/PA440705 National Archives of Canada 134; © ID 20808/C-14923 National Archives of Canada 149; © ID 20841/PA-4388 National Archives of Canada 150; ID 21846/PA-2084 National Archives of Canada 153; © ID 20950/PA-145663 National Archives of Canada 155; © ID 20939/PA-132651 National Archives of Canada 157; © ID 202217/PA-170294 National Archives of Canada 158; © ID 21057/PA-139980 National Archives of Canada 163; © ID 21028/PA-111213 National Archives of Canada 178; © ID 21018/PA-36222 National Archives of Canada 181; © ID 21068/PA-115039 National Archives of Canada 183; © ID 20999 232. Mary Evans Picture Library: © Mary Evans Picture Library 103. Fraser Photos: © AP Photo/Kevork Djansezian 203; © Cathie Archbould/Arctic Winter Games International Committee/Fraser Photos 193; © Arctic Winter Games International Committee/Fraser Photos 192; © O. Bierwagen/Ivy Images/Fraser Photos 228; © CBC Still Photo Collection/Fraser Photos 233; © CP Photo 201, 209, 218; © CP Photo/Blaise Edwards 230; © CP Photo/Chuck Mitchell 238; © CP Photo/COA 197; © CP Photo/COA/T 200; © CP Photo/Frank Gunn 239; © CP Photo/Fred Chartrand 170; © CP Photo/Kevin Frayer 211; © CP Photo/La Presse/Remi Lemee 224; © CP Photo/Paul Chiasson 179; © CP Photo/Richard Lam 212; © CP Photo/Toronto Star–Frank Lennon 194; © CP Photo/Winnipeg Free Press/Phil Hossack 220; © Derek Crowe/ Arctic Winter Games International Committee/Fraser Photos 213; © J. DeVisser/Ivy Images/Fraser Photos 59; © Winston Fraser 9, 13, 16t, 22, 23, 30–31, 43, 58, 89, 125, 185, 195, 202, 214; © Peggy Johannsen-Austin/Phil Norton Photos 198; © Keystone Press 199; © courtesy of John Molina/Fraser Photos 210; © H. Mortimer Lamb/BC Archives 219; © Bill Lowry/Ivy Images/Fraser Photos 25, 29, 39, 133; © Megapress 45; © MP/ADC/Keystone Canada 227; © Phil Norton 208; © Southam/The Gazette 207; © Glenn Weiner/Keystone Canada 229; © Larry Wright/Burnaby Now 204. Glenbow Museum: © Glenbow Archives NA-4325-7 169. Richard McGuire: © Richard McGuire 85. NASA 207. National Archives of Canada: © National Archives of Canada /C-014090/Aylette, Charles 83, C-046284/unknown 152, C-067469/unknown 162, C-001590/unknown 168, C-027647/Karsh, Yousuf 176, C-021541/Ellisson & Co. 180, C-083423/Inglis, James 180, C-017335/Moffett Studio 237, C-036786/unknown 240; © National Archives of Canada/ PA-026439/Topley, William James 11; PA-056660/Johnston, Clifford 56; C-094168/Cameron, Duncan 160; © National Archives of Canada/PA-137052/Curtin, Walter 223; PA-185967/Johnston, Alfred Cheney 226; © National Archives of Canada/PA-029555/Winnipeg Photo Company 64; PA-195686/Bell, Ken 221. Natural Resources Canada: © reproduced with the permission of the Minister of Public Works and Government Services Canada 2003 and courtesy of Natural Resources, Geological Survey of Canada, 37, 57. Nova Scotia Museum: © Fisheries Museum of the Atlantic, Lunenburg/F87.163 15; © Nova Scotia Museum of Natural History, Halifax/31641 83. Redferns Music Picture Library: © Ebet Roberts/Redferns 222. Rex Features © Rex Features 135. Strait Crossing Bridge Ltd 19. David Suzuki Foundation: 241. Travel Ink: © Ronald Badkin, cover main photo. United Church of Canada: © United Church of Canada 187. World Ship Society © John T. Hammond 159.